Raymond Chandler's
Philip Marlowe

Raymond Chandler's Philip Marlowe

The Hard-Boiled Detective Transformed

JOHN PAUL ATHANASOURELIS

McFarland & Company, Inc., Publishers
Jefferson, North Carolina, and London

Portions of this work previously appeared as "American Individualism and the Hard-Boiled Detective Hero" in *The McNeese Review*, volume 41 (2003).

LIBRARY OF CONGRESS CATALOGUING-IN-PUBLICATION DATA

Athanasourelis, John Paul, 1952–
  Raymond Chandler's Philip Marlowe : the hard-boiled detective transformed / John Paul Athansourelis.
    p. cm.
  Includes bibliographical references and index.

  ISBN 978-0-7864-4215-7
  softcover : 50# alkaline paper ∞

  1. Chandler, Raymond, 1888–1959 — Criticism and interpretation. 2. Chandler, Raymond, 1888–1959 — Characters — Philip Marlowe. 3. Marlowe, Philip (Fictitious character) 4. Detective and mystery stories, American — History and criticism. I. Title.
  PS3505.H3224Z57 2012
  813'.52 — dc23   2011037371

BRITISH LIBRARY CATALOGUING DATA ARE AVAILABLE

© 2012 John Paul Athansourelis. All rights reserved

No part of this book may be reproduced or transmitted in any form or by any means, electronic or mechanical, including photocopying or recording, or by any information storage and retrieval system, without permission in writing from the publisher.

Front cover image: Dick Powell as Philip Marlowe in *Murder, My Sweet*, 1944; cover design by David K. Landis (Shake It Loose Graphics)

Manufactured in the United States of America

McFarland & Company, Inc., Publishers
  Box 611, Jefferson, North Carolina 28640
     www.mcfarlandpub.com

Table of Contents

Acknowledgments — vii
Preface — 1
Introduction — 3

One. Rugged Individualism in Carroll John Daly and Mickey Spillane — 25
Two. Dashiell Hammett: Individualism in Transition — 54
Three. Marlowe as Negotiator — 70
Four. Marlowe and the Police — 86
Five. Marlowe and the Criminals — 114
Six. Ross Macdonald — 138
Seven. Cinematic Considerations — 161

Conclusion — 178
Chapter Notes — 193
Works Cited — 195
Index — 199

Acknowledgments

Since this book is an outgrowth of my dissertation, I would like to thank my entire dissertation committee at Purdue University — William J. Palmer, Richard Dienst, Robert Paul Lamb, and Marshall Deutelbaum — for its support and guidance. Thanks to Clark Maddux for his invaluable support and contribution to the design of the study.

My colleagues at Bronx Community College helped immeasurably as the book was readied for publication. Thanks to all my family members for moral support and a special thanks to Christine Christopher for keeping me sane.

Preface

I came to the topic of this study quite indirectly, while teaching an introduction to film course at Purdue University. Screening and teaching *The Big Sleep* reminded me of readings of Chandler and Hammett and I recognized the great potential of the genre of detective fiction for my dissertation. This study is a development of that academic work. The focus on American individualism stems from a long sojourn abroad, in Germany, where I experienced a different way of thinking and living. Like so many expatriates, I first gained a clear idea as to what my American identity was.

This study seeks to analyze different strains of individualism as expressed through detective fiction, primarily that of Raymond Chandler. His protagonist, Philip Marlowe, occupies a unique position in the genre: in many ways an ordinary, fallible man, his exceptional skill is not so much the keen analysis of a Sherlock Holmes or the cunning and pugnacity of a Sam Spade, but a knack for communication, connecting the disparate parts of his society. I hope I have been able to make my own lucid connections among the character, author, genre, and readers.

Introduction

The work of Raymond Chandler has, for many readers and critics, come to represent the epitome of the genre of hard-boiled detective fiction. These American detectives of the "tough" school arose as a conscious reaction to the austere, cerebral problem-solvers of the primarily British "whodunit" tradition, and their heroism was posited on the belief that criminal violence could only be answered with violence. Fashioned in the 1920s, the archetypal hard-boiled hero was a fast-talking-and-shooting rogue straddling the worlds of the legal and illegal. As pioneered by Dashiell Hammett and revived by Mickey Spillane, with many hard-boiled writers in between, he was utterly convinced of his private sense of right and wrong and unconcerned with the social repercussions of his acts. Yet Chandler's introverted hero, Philip Marlowe, is distinguished from his predecessors and contemporaries in possessing a more socially conscious code of ethics than that typical of the genre's heroes; this quality of reflection is consistent with democratic consideration of the thoughts, beliefs, and ethics of others.

Until about the mid-1970s, critics tended to interpret Marlowe as a mythic hero aiding those in need from a position outside society, displaying an ethos of superiority that does not ultimately concern itself with problems of everyday life. E. M. Beekman, for example, defines Chandler's protagonist as a romantic hero: "If Marlowe were an archetype he would be a somber knight on a never finished quest, recharging his faith by adversity" (166). George Grella, writing in 1970, sees the genre as an example of romance in the tradition of the mainstream "dominant American novel," driven by the quest motif and linked closely to legend and myth (411–12), whose hero is "too good for the society he inhabits" (418). John G. Cawelti notes the "resemblance to the chivalrous knights of Sir Walter Scott" (151),

Introduction

and the very subtitle of Philip Durham's critical biography, *Down These Mean Streets a Man Must Go: Raymond Chandler's Knight*, underscores a perceived literary-historical underpinning of myth to an otherwise thoroughly modern figure.

More recent critics, concerned, from a fundamentally Marxist position, with the ideology and social positioning of this hero, portray him, in contrast, as "too bad" for society and take him to task for shoring up the bourgeois order. In the context of situating detective fiction within what he calls trivial literature — which functions "to reconcile the upset, bored and anxious individual member of the middle class with the inevitability and permanence of bourgeois society" (29) — Ernest Mandel decries the protagonists of the classic genre, such as Lord Peter Wimsey, Hercule Poirot, and Philo Vance, as "bourgeois dilettantes" (28). While he recognizes significant differences in the hard-boiled genre, the later American detectives nevertheless display "an unmistakable continuity with the private detectives of the traditional sort" (35): cynical on the surface only, they are "at bottom ... sentimentalists" (35). For Mandel, Chandler's efforts in particular have "nothing to do with the social reality of the twenties and thirties" (36).[1]

Mandel echoes Stephen Knight's even more general thesis that "cultural products" provide a "consoling result for the anxieties of those who share in the cultural activity — the audience" (4). Knight's critique insists on an invariable symbiosis of text and audience. Plot, he notes, orders events "in a way that accords with the audience's belief in dominant cultural values" (4).

Taking a somewhat different tack, Bethany Ogden underscores the attitude of the hard-boiled detective as obsessed with corruption and perversity; in his role as narrator, he "describes a world in which he is the sole 'normal' person" (77). She disagrees with the "mythic" view inasmuch as "the antagonistic structure of the hard-boiled story is more in the nature of the fascistic 'us against them' than the romantic 'me against the world'" (84), but the result is pretty much the same since the protagonists are self-centered and dangerous. Joyce Carol Oates echoes Ogden's feminist view, stressing that the genre's "primary truth of the human heart is that men and women, though more frequently women (if they are beautiful), are

Introduction

rotten to the core" (34). Cynthia S. Hamilton sees Marlowe as "an alienated outsider who vindicates that stance by his demonstrable superiority in a society unworthy of his services" (155).

To a large extent, what these critics develop are characterizations of hard-boiled detectives — and Philip Marlowe specifically — that are unremittingly negative and ultimately reductive. The monolithic nature of such criticism serves to bracket and erase authors, genres, and even the vast corpus of texts Mandel considers "trivial." Other critics, however, have discovered means to open this discourse without recourse to the kinds of nonideological structures found in myth-based criticism, i.e., to accept the need for an ideological reading, but to read more carefully.

Giles Gunn confronts this type of ideological criticism in *Thinking Across the American Grain*, in which he poses a pragmatic approach, rooted in the philosophies of William James and John Dewey, to overcome the intellectual dead-end procedure of merely condemning authors on the basis of their supposed politics. Gunn sees pragmatism's value in its ability, on the one hand, to enter into dialogue with postmodern theories that resist totalization and, on the other, to insist on the pervasiveness of the political. For Gunn, James and Dewey recognized that power is hierarchical, but were not convinced that this power is absolute, because the political is in a constant state of flux: "power is never stable and therefore can never be monolithic" (36). Just as Frederick Douglass could exploit capitalist ideology to emancipate himself (32), any individual can find room within the hierarchy for "conflict, contestation, transgression, subversion, and even appropriation" (36). It is within the power of the citizen, therefore, to recognize and exploit the multiplicity of political values where no one camp always speaks the "truth."

In this spirit Gunn criticizes Sacvan Bercovitch's echo of Stephen Knight that "the interlinked system of ideas, symbols, and beliefs comprising ideology and controlling processes of historicization constitutes the chief means 'by which a culture — any culture — seeks to justify and perpetuate itself'" (26). Gunn recognizes a debilitating tendency toward the creation of such absolute values when he detects a "philosophical prejudice built into a position like that of Bercovitch and other ideological critics: that cultural texts are unable to engage in processes of reflection

Introduction

on the values that generate them without at the same time being subsumed by those values" (30), and he faults these critics for glossing over "any sense either that ideologies function in different ways in different circumstances ... or that they are sometimes divided within and against themselves" (31). Illustrating his objections to such monolithic critical stances with examples of Emily Dickinson's poetry, Gunn insists that "even where ideology is omnipresent ... it need not be construed as necessarily omnipotent" (35). A marginalized writer like Douglass, Dickinson carved out her individual position of resistance to a repressive, male-dominated world while writing within that world. I insist that what is true for these writers also applies to the ostensibly "unmarginalized."

Pragmatism, for Gunn, makes no such a priori assumptions; it demands viewing texts as "sites of effective action" (37) and while it resists the temptation to impose a micropolitical agenda onto those actions, it is concerned with the political on the broadest possible level:

> [W]hile pragmatic criticism advocates no particular policies, it does possess a specifiable politics. It is a politics distinguished by the democratic preference for rendering differences conversable so that the conflicts they produce, instead of being destructive of human community, can become potentially creative of it; can broaden and thicken public culture rather than depleting it [Gunn 37].

The genre of detective fiction, like any other, contains a multiplicity of authorial voices speaking, as it were, to one another, and it is important to distinguish them along the lines of the ideologies they represent. As we will see, Philip Marlowe is presented so as to connect members of society who would normally not meet or would be irrevocably antagonistic upon meeting. Chandler exploits him in order to reconcile social differences, interrogating definitions of the legitimate and the illegitimate in American society, and thereby, to borrow Gunn's term, "thickening" public culture. Whether negotiating with a crime boss for information about the whereabouts of a criminal in order to help that criminal (*Farewell, My Lovely*, 1940), or defending his status as a private investigator vis-à-vis a district attorney by claiming that official law enforcement has no greater claim to legitimacy than private action (*The Big Sleep*, 1939), Marlowe incorporates the tensions of an era in which the self-centered, rugged individualist ide-

Introduction

ology of the United States could no longer solve pressing societal problems. In stark contrast to earlier hard-boiled heroes of the wildly individualistic 1920s, Marlowe symbolizes the 30s urge for what Donald E. Westlake calls a need for people to believe in a "commonality rather than isolated individuality" (9).

Gunn draws heavily on the social theory of John Dewey, whose concept of radical democracy was fiercely critical of capitalism, yet, consistent with its roots in 19th-century American progressive thought, resisted elements of Marxism that would restrict the freedom of discourse among all citizens and that resisted any attempts at ideological closure such as found in Mandel's critique of "trivial" literature. As Sean McCann has insightfully noted of Dewey, "[c]itizens would need to discover that true individualism did not mean an antisocial hostility to the common good, but rather the opportunity for self-development that came with participation in 'associated life'" (151).

In Emerson's optimistic spirit, Dewey sought the creation of a society that would maximize democratic discourse and minimize the social depredations of rugged individualism without jettisoning socially meliorative aspects of individualism. Marlowe's every move is similarly motivated by a desire to reach out to the various segments of his environment while simultaneously carefully guarding his sense of individuality, symbolized, on a day-to-day basis, by his private eye status and reclusive lifestyle. In transforming the genre in this direction, Chandler created an excruciatingly fine line for his hero to walk, but the detective succeeds remarkably well at it.

For Ernest Mandel there is no attempt at social interaction; the entire genre suffers from its preoccupation with individual, as opposed to group, security, and the private focus of the private eye stands for a deliberate avoidance of the threat to security from wars, revolutions, and depressions (41–42). Yet, Mandel ignores the fact that any group is composed of individuals and that what he calls private security is the constituent part of public security. Accepting these two realms as complex and possibly paradoxical, but never mutually exclusive, John Dewey focused his energies on the symbiosis of public and private. As Robert B. Westbrook puts it in *John Dewey and American Democracy*,

Introduction

> The good society was, like the good itself, a diverse yet harmonious, growing yet unified whole, a fully participatory democracy in which the powers and capacities of the individuals that comprised it were harmonized by their cooperative activities into a community that permitted the full and free expression of individuality [164].

Chandler's concerns are comparable. The delicate balance between individual initiative and cooperative activities is expressed, on the one hand, by Marlowe's strict ethical code and his stubborn insistence on his individual skills and power, and on the other by his willingness to listen to other perspectives and to act in concert with people he respects.

The Lady in the Lake (1943) contains typical examples of the detective's interactions. Marlowe's initial encounters with clients or police not only serve structurally as exposition, but are intricate negotiations concerning just what the detective is or is not willing to do. He does not, for instance, act out of anger or a desire for revenge, as is the case in novels by earlier hard-boiled writers and Mickey Spillane, but sets his parameters in terms of cooperative work. In negotiating with Derace Kingsley, a potential client in this novel, for example, Marlowe holds firm to his rate of $25 a day plus expenses and "eight cents a mile for my car," demands a $100 retainer, and maintains that he performs "only the fairly honest kinds of work" (which exclude divorce work) (*Later Novels* 7–8). Marlowe speaks in a curt manner in response to the aggressive tone of his potential employer, but once his personal and professional boundaries are accepted (Kingsley even admits that he has enjoyed being "called down" [*Later Novels* 8]), the two men discover they can work together to find the missing woman.

In search of clues to the whereabouts of Mrs. Kingsley, Marlowe is caught breaking into suspected murderer Bill Chess' mountain cabin by Deputy Sheriff Jim Patton, who takes the opportunity to examine Marlowe's detective credentials. Marlowe reciprocates by revealing the name of his employer and his assignment and, one guarded step at a time, the two men proceed to discuss the probabilities of Bill Chess as the murderer. In the spirit of Chandler's ethical law enforcement officials, Patton allows Marlowe to leave without legal repercussions of the break-in, cementing further the cooperative spirit of crime detection. Marlowe, however, insisting tacitly on his individual skills and prerogatives, returns to the cabin

Introduction

and discovers a vital piece of evidence. The alternatives of cooperative and individual investigation have thus been presented in more or less equal measure, but Chandler underscores the need for communal solutions by having Marlowe drive directly to the sheriff's office to share his discovery with his new associate, effectively tipping the scales in the direction of cooperation.

I argue that Chandler's ideology is that of Deweyan radical democracy in contrast to the rugged individualist stances of other hard-boiled writers. Unlike Dashiell Hammett, whose Continental Op, in particular, affirms the acquisitive and vengeful ethos of the American frontier, Chandler fashioned a hero who is conscious of his positive social role and who avoids the extremes of the negative freedom of rugged individualism, the disgusted withdrawal from society, and the ideology of a mythological, larger-than-life "knight" imposing his unreflected moral sense on those around him. What resulted was an attempt, through the figure of Marlowe, to establish a communitarian ethos sorely lacking in the America of the 1930s, '40s, and '50s, the period in which Chandler wrote and in which Dewey focused his intellect on problems of social and political organization. Marlowe's consciousness of the contingent nature of human actions (that communal actions to curb social transgression are always relative to specific cases) echoes the Dewey of *Individualism Old and New*, who urges the reader to think of society not as a monolithic whole upon whose definition we all agree, but to realize that social

> points of contact are not the same for any two persons and hence the questions which the interests and occupations pose are never twice the same.... Harmony with conditions is not a single and monotonous uniformity, but a diversified affair requiring individual attack [*Later Works* V: 120].

Individual subjects and not some transcendent force like the inevitable victory of the working class are always responsible for maintaining the community.

Thus it is vital to interrogate Chandler's texts for a quality too little recognized, that which Paul Skenazy terms his "fiercely democratic sympathies" (1). Not, to be sure, that Marlowe is active in any explicitly political way. He is not given to partisan political utterances and would never be found on a picket line. He does, however, base his activities on an ethos of open discourse and cooperation with all segments of American society.

Introduction

Chandler was the first hard-boiled writer to conceive of a hero whose actions are self-critical and who incorporates faith in human understanding and the possibilities of communication.

A key Marlovian characteristic that fosters cooperation is his lack of perfection and his concomitant consciousness of this lack. He is never endowed with the kind of omniscient and omnipotent powers Dashiell Hammett gave his Continental Op in "The Gutting of Couffignal" and "The Big Knockover," in which he single-handedly subdues entire brigades of criminals. Nor does Chandler allow him the smug and boastful qualities Mickey Spillane gave Mike Hammer. Marlowe is a hero who more than occasionally loses, but whose achievements are all the more significant for those losses. In *The Lady in the Lake,* Marlowe ultimately solves the initial murder, but others are killed in the process, and the reader is made to feel Marlowe's sympathy for even his implacable enemy, corrupt Police Lieutenant Al Degarmo. At the same time, Chandler resists the temptation of portraying these villains as evil geniuses (such as Howard Quincy Travers in Carroll John Daly's 1928 detective novel *The Hidden Hand*) or as ciphers whose only purpose is to pad the body count in Dashiell Hammett's *Red Harvest* (1927).

Although the mystery is solved and a criminal is brought to justice at the end of the novel, Marlowe is betrayed by a friend, Terry Lennox, in *The Long Goodbye* (1953). In both *The Big Sleep* and *The High Window* (1942), sympathetic characters (virtually an anomaly in the pre–Chandler genre) are caught in murderous crossfires: in the former, Harry Jones, out of loyalty to his girlfriend, is poisoned by hit man Lash Canino while Marlowe is helpless to intervene. In the latter the death of George Anson Phillips, a naive and incompetent private eye, elicits Marlowe's sympathy as a victim who succumbs to the complex evils of the city because he doesn't know enough to protect himself from ruthless enemies.

Chandler's particular achievements were to reduce the private eye's dependence on violence, to make clear the detective's link to society even as he strives to keep an analytical distance from it, and to present his code of ethics not as a rugged individualist triumph of the will, but as a vigorous credo of progressive, communitarian values. Chandler managed to portray modern urban American life with all its contradictions — both vital and dangerous, self-centered yet communally conscious. He was not only aware

Introduction

of pervasive civic corruption, but pragmatic enough not to expect that the efforts of his hero could make more than a small difference. He demonstrated these qualities by foregrounding the protagonist's negotiating skills among "legitimate" and "illegitimate" forces in modern urban America (concepts he appreciated in all their complexity), by focusing on the detective's interactions with clients, criminals, and cops. In doing so, Chandler created a particularly modernist fiction of negotiation. His is not the rough justice of the frontier that previous hard-boiled writers had so lustily exploited. In the seven novels Marlowe kills only one man, the aforementioned Canino. The vast majority of murders occur "offstage," and while this technique is doubtless employed to contribute to the needed atmosphere of mystery, it also illustrates the writer's interest in focusing readers' attention on human motivation and the complexity and indeterminacy of motive.[2] Chandler discarded the "black and white hats" of the ruggedly individualistic Western novel, the principal model for American detective fiction. Murder is shown not as an erasure of abstract concepts of good and evil, but as venal, passionate, even accidental, and the system of justice is shown as being far from perfect.

Although he has his share of preconceived, even unenlightened, notions, Marlowe is consistently attuned to the ideas and beliefs of others. The police, for example, are considered in all their complexity; they are not merely foils to his investigative brilliance (as in Conan Doyle), nor corrupt (as in Hammett), nor incompetent (as in Spillane). Chandler learned to present the police as having both positive and negative traits from Hammett, but took the idea much further by presenting, in great detail, what it means to be a "good" or "bad" cop.

Marlowe's adventures are not only a departure from hard-boiled standards, but distinguish themselves from the more cerebral, puzzle-solving deeds of the classical British whodunits. Perhaps because the societies from which they emerged possessed a more rigid class structure, the latter genre assumes a societal stability, an ideal that even the ravages of two world wars could not seriously impair. There is much of this in the works of Agatha Christie. In her first mystery, *The Mysterious Affair at Styles*, set during World War I, the narrator, Hastings, is spending his convalescent leave at the country home of an old friend, John Cavendish. At one point

Introduction

Hastings muses over the passionate loyalty of one of the Cavendish retainers, Dorcas, "a fine specimen ... of the old-fashioned servant that is so fast dying out" (107). In some of Christie's novels the culprit is a foreigner and his expulsion cements social stability. In this case, the man ultimately unmasked as the killer carries the very English name of Inglethorp, yet his appearance, accentuated by a black beard and pince-nez, leads Hastings to consider that the man has "a rather alien note" (6).

The transatlantic differences in the genre are reflected in Chandler's biography. A recent biographer, Tom Hiney, suggests that his subject possessed a "confused nationality" that created problems for the younger Chandler, especially in finding a suitable career (23), but this status was ultimately quite valuable in his writing. Born in Chicago and raised partly in Nebraska, Chandler was brought to England at the age of seven by his Irish-born mother, attended the Dulwich School, and remained in the country until he was 24. This long sojourn gave him insight into a more traditional and more rigidly class-based society. His experience made him not class bound, but class conscious; he had no typically American illusions that the United States was a classless society and was able to incorporate class animosities into his fiction.

On the other hand, he condemned what he felt was an essentially false nature of predominantly British mystery writing, one that often acted as if crime were merely a fictional construct, not a substantial factor in the lives of its victims, perpetrators, and a media audience. In his seminal *Mortal Consequences*, Julian Symons underscores an even broader artificiality of this genre:

> In the British stories, the General Strike of 1926 never took place, trade unions did not exist, and when sympathy was expressed for the poor it was not for the unemployed but for those struggling along on a fixed inherited income. In the American stories, there were no bread lines and no radicals, no Southern demagogues of home-grown fascists. The fairy-tale land of the Golden Age was one in which murder was committed over and over again without anybody getting hurt [104].

Chandler's nagging social conscience, often misinterpreted as jaded morality, drew him away from that which is similar in both genres: the easy, because unreflected, reliance on established formulas.

Introduction

This is not to say that his social conscience placed him squarely on the side of the moralizers. Chandler returned to the United States from France in 1919 after serving in the Canadian Army in World War I. He soon experienced, as did his fellow countrymen, a major increase in crime due, in large part, to the Eighteenth Amendment to the Constitution, which by creating Prohibition placed restrictions on Americans' personal behavior that were unthinkable in ostensibly less democratic Europe. A central theme in his fiction, Chandler commented on the inherent hypocrisy of legislating public morals in "The Simple Art of Murder," an essay written for *Atlantic Monthly* in 1944: his world was one in which "a judge with a cellar full of bootleg liquor can send a man to jail for having a pint in his pocket" (*Later Novels* 991). Marlowe resists such hypocrisy and refuses to see human nature in black-and-white terms.

Soon after the Eighteenth Amendment was passed, the election, in 1920, of Warren G. Harding to the presidency confirmed any doubt the average citizen might have had of corruption in high places: Harding's political cronies, dubbed the Ohio Gang, included Attorney General Harry M. Daugherty, and they established a Georgetown base of operations from which they sold liquor confiscated by the Prohibition Bureau. Prohibition was the product of an active minority that managed to impose its ethical standards — a coercion, as Michael Woodiwiss notes, into a "virtuous and healthy way of life" (1) — that resulted in huge opportunities for bootleggers tacitly supported by the "vices" of ordinary citizens and protected by the very governmental agencies now officially bound to prevent the sale and consumption of alcohol.

Not that Los Angeleno Chandler had very far to look for evidence of the complex symbiosis of intrusive laws, criminals successful in flaunting them, and government officials implicated in exploiting public fears for personal, political and financial gain. One critic of police abuses, Ernest Jerome Hopkins, found that the duties of law enforcement officers in this city in 1931 "were largely the regulating of the average citizen's morals, people's economic views, and what the population might carry in its automobiles" (152). Police in the most notorious open-shop city in the country busied themselves more with cracking the heads of union members and members of minority groups than pursuing the criminals who had suc-

Introduction

ceeded so well in buying protection from law enforcement and civic leaders. Politics in Los Angeles in the 1930s and 1940s was characterized by reformers attacking entrenched, corrupt administrations, only to be, in turn, attacked by successive waves of reform. City and county administrations did little to reduce rum-running, gambling, and prostitution, and both political parties received campaign contributions from mobsters.[3] Despite much reform rhetoric, underworld figures such as Bugsy Siegel were able to conduct business with impunity (until, as in Siegel's case, he was executed by enemy mobsters).

Ostensible civic leaders who condemned, both rhetorically and in terms of actual legal penalties, their fellow citizens' drinking habits while enjoying bootleg liquor and colluding with the criminals that provided it would always be far more culpable for Chandler than the Al Capones and Dutch Schultzes of America.[4] Chandler's hatred of such hypocrisy informed his writing; villains are apt to be those that abuse their power, regardless of which side of the fence of legitimacy they stand, and Marlowe displays a well-seasoned tolerance for ordinary people who indulge in what the elites call vices. The end of Prohibition did not, of course, end either crime or collusion; other "vices" filled the gap when the Eighteenth Amendment was repealed in 1933.

Stephen Knight condemns Chandler for imbuing Marlowe with an isolated, socially and intellectually superior attitude, since "his lonely quality is enough to inspect, judge and dismiss" those he comes in contact with (145), but there is little evidence in the texts to support this claim. Instead, Chandler drew on the contemporary public record in order to portray legitimate and illegitimate forces in Los Angeles. Laird Brunette, the owner of the gambling ship *Paloma* in *Farewell, My Lovely*, for example, is modeled on Tony Cornero, who in 1939 informed on rival gamblers only to have the police shut down his ship, which, since it was moored outside the three-mile limit, operated within the letter, if not the spirit, of the law. Far from dismissing the criminal, Chandler takes pains to place him in the context of law and ethics that he pragmatically recognizes are in flux and that require constant monitoring for their strictures to be viable.

Chandler's lack of faith in received concepts of right and wrong was,

Introduction

of course, hardly unique among writers: Hemingway's disillusionment, as expressed through the character of Frederick Henry in *A Farewell to Arms*, has often been credited as the greatest single influence on the hard-boiled ethos. Chandler's significance, however, was to bring his social conscience to bear in a genre notorious for its oversimplification of the conflict between good and evil. Despite his pioneer labor in creating the first truly three-dimensional hard-boiled detective hero, Dashiell Hammett sidestepped the issue by invoking deterministic concepts of human nature in *Red Harvest* and *The Dain Curse* (1928), in which motives, including those of the protagonist, are presented as "naturally" debased and the ethos of the survival of the fittest is invoked. Chandler, however, transformed the crime genre's fascination with the unbridled power of the individual by forcing his detective to examine and revise actions presented as the ostensible function of the American rugged individualist. Mandel, Knight, and others have criticized Chandler for countering the superhero ethos with defeatist narratives in which his hero withdraws from social responsibility, but Philip Marlowe (and to some extent the earlier "proto–Marlowes" of Chandler's short fiction) does not succumb to the nihilist stance typical of Hammett's Continental Op, who, in *Red Harvest*, becomes "blood simple" and does his utmost to save a city by destroying it. And for all the cunning he displays in playing off adversaries against each other in *The Maltese Falcon* (1929), Sam Spade is a cynic committed to self-preservation and essentially unconcerned with those around him.

By way of contrast, Chandler's heroes are consistently concerned with preserving human life. In "I'll Be Waiting" (1939) Tony Reseck, house detective of the Windermere Hotel, negotiates among Eve Cressy, a young woman waiting for her ex-lover, the lover, Johnny Ralls (just out of the penitentiary), and the gunmen waiting outside the hotel, led by Al, Tony's brother. Al demands that Tony send Eve out, in order to trap Ralls, who owes him money, but Tony decides to help the ex-con escape instead. Ralls is killed, but not before he mortally wounds Al. Tony then resumes his vigil over the sleeping Eve Cressy. This portrayal of negotiation and sacrifice would later be developed in more subtle ways in the creation of Philip Marlowe. But for Chandler, even early on, it was untenable for the hero to forget his own humanity so far as to assume the role of avenger.

Introduction

What Marlowe proves to be in the novels is hinted at in "The Simple Art of Murder." Chandler here criticizes the typical hard-boiled detective as reflecting the kind of general lack of civic concern in communities "where no man can walk down a dark street in safety because law and order are things we talk about but refrain from practicing" (*Later Novels* 991). Chandler's aversion to hypocrisy is underscored by the "we" of this last passage: Marlowe sometimes thinks of himself as an outsider to society, but his conscience is that of a community member and his actions are heightened examples of civic action. Chandler's tenuously held optimism also comes through in the quotation; when civic action takes the place of "talk," a safer community will be created.

Yet for all the strengths of "The Simple Art of Murder" as a précis of what Chandler was trying to achieve in his metamorphosis of the genre, the essay ends with claims made for his hero that Chandler is unable to support: "down these mean streets a man must go who is not himself mean, who is neither tarnished nor afraid" (*Later Novels* 991–2). It is unfortunate that this passage should be so often quoted by critics, for it is seriously misleading. Nothing in the essay or, indeed, in other writings, supports the claim that Marlowe is "untarnished" or unafraid. On the contrary, Chandler succeeded in developing the hard-boiled hero as a flawed individual conscious of all-too-human traits he shares with his antagonists. While Chandler does emphasize the need for his art to have a "quality of redemption," suggesting a purity of motive and action on the part of Marlowe, he also stresses that Marlowe is a "common man" (*Later Novels* 991–92) and that his world is our world, one in which justice must be fought for but cannot always be expected. This is a crucial difference: Marlowe's complexity allows for a greater degree of realism than either the whodunit or the established hard-boiled story inasmuch as he is conscious of his own humanity and grasps the failings of others without becoming overly judgmental.

In his 1970 essay "On Raymond Chandler," Fredric Jameson discerns, somewhat tangentially, qualities of social concern and action in Marlowe. In this far-reaching essay, Jameson defines the British whodunit as a reflection of a society whose stability is rooted in class privilege. American society, on the other hand, is unstable; its members lack a strong sense

Introduction

of permanence or even continuity. Within the "uncharted wilderness" that is our fragmented American life (125), one in which spatial and temporal change have been so radical, Marlowe embodies the kind of fictional construct that "can be superimposed on the society as a whole, whose routine and life pattern serve somehow to tie its separate and isolated parts together" (127). Jameson stresses the "atomistic nature" of American society. In contrast, he posits, Europeans are never alone: "their very solitude is social; their identity is inextricably entangled with that of all the others by a clear system of classes, by a national language, in what Heidegger describes as 'Mitsein,' the being-together-with-others" (131). Marlowe has something of this European sensibility and his profession enables him to exercise that sensibility since it allows him access to all social strata.

Jameson is primarily concerned with the hard-boiled private eye as a connecting link among social classes. He rightly views Marlowe's importance as a negotiator rather than enforcer, but is misleading when he labels him an "involuntary explorer" of modern society (128), suggesting a naturalistic, perhaps fatalistic, philosophy not present in Chandler's fiction. Indeed, in his constant movement from rich clients to gangsters to the police and back again, Marlowe demonstrates a quite conscious effort to understand and to *identify* with members of these groups. His actions are motivated by these concerns more than any traditional mystery solving and thus he explores in voluntary, even self-conscious, ways. Jameson also credits Chandler with anticipating socio-cultural developments not generally observed until after his death: the geographic decentralization and ever-increasing pace of urban life in America beginning in the early 20th century effected and was influenced by a concomitant fragmentation of social classes that "have lost touch with each other because each is isolated in his own geographical compartment" (127).

In this respect Jameson echoes a key tenet of John Dewey's *The Public and Its Problems*, in which the need for societal reform from "below," from the citizenry, is emphasized. For Dewey, citizens must come together on local levels. In Westbrook's formulation, "only in local, face-to-face associations could members of a public participate in dialogues with their fellows, and such dialogues were critical to the formation and organization

Introduction

of the public" (314). Thus the need for connectives was greater than ever before.[5] This Chandler sensed and rendered in the high walls and unsavory bodyguards of the rich and in the broken-down apartments of the indigent on Bunker Hill, social strata not easily brought together. However, Marlowe is no mere go-between, a carrier of messages, but rather seeks social accommodation. A pragmatist, he is even prepared to compromise his own sense of right or wrong with that which can be expected of his allies and adversaries.

Though Marlowe does at times recoil from the seediness of the city, and reacts, for instance, to Carmen Sternwood's sexual overtures in *The Big Sleep* with a Puritan disgust that harks back to the novels of James Fenimore Cooper, he is nevertheless committed to a tangible social task: he *chooses* to live in Los Angeles, thrives on its pace and diversity, and perseveres in a job that forces him to confront the worst the city has to offer. And his "private" status allows him a freedom of movement and action unavailable to the police. His actions go far beyond that which is required of him in order to make his living: it is not, at least initially, part of his job when he befriends Terry Lennox (*The Long Goodbye*), or benignly pursues Moose Malloy (*Farewell, My Lovely*), or decides to seek out George Anson Phillips' murderers (*The High Window*), but done out of interest in fellow, flawed denizens of the big city. That he perseveres even when threatened with danger (or what, for him, is worse: betrayal by someone he trusts, i.e. Terry Lennox) is indicative not so much of his courage as his need to see the job done well. His choice of profession is motivated by a wish to negotiate; his view is consistently social and interactive.

All fictional detectives, regardless of their complexity, are figured members of society and display (often quite indirectly) aspects of their social roles, but critics have shown great skepticism vis-à-vis the social role of this very hero. The present consensus is that the detective's heroic traits reveal ideologically elitist stances or a disposition to fight against or withdraw from society altogether. The violent and vengeful Mike Hammer of Mickey Spillane is often cited as a Fascist extension of qualities already present in the hard-boiled genre. In Spillane's hands the genre devolves into caricature and into spheres of absolute good and evil as, time and

Introduction

again, Hammer assumes the role of police, judge, jury, and executioner of those he pursues. Even within this extreme example, however, there is room for contrastive characterization that suggests, if weakly, more discerning social concern: the relationship between Mike Hammer and police detective Pat Chambers is a continuous dialogue on the legitimacy of authorized versus vigilante justice. That Spillane valorizes the latter has been cause for much critical gnashing of teeth, but he has at least recognized the need for presenting more than one side of the debate, inasmuch as Chambers attempts to rein in Hammer's extreme antisocial and extralegal behavior. Thus even on the level of its least self-reflective narrative hero, we find in the genre a concern for protective, as opposed to punitive, law enforcement.

Chandler takes the issue quite a bit further: he has Marlowe not only debate the police, and other societal representatives, on this point, but debate himself. One example can be found in *The Little Sister* (1949), often cited as containing the most egregious examples of Marlowe's antisocial behavior. Driving to and from Ventura County to quiet jangled nerves, he gives in to the urge to criticize drivers on the road, those driving home to "the blatting of the radio, the whining of their spoiled children, and the gabble of their silly wives" (267). His tirade continues in a restaurant near Thousand Oaks where the food is "[b]ad but quick. Feed 'em and throw 'em out. Lots of business. We can't bother with you sitting over your second cup of coffee, mister. You're using money space" (268). Yet this short chapter is strategically placed as a kind of purgative for the misanthropic thoughts of a man who has, after all, recently witnessed the results of a grisly murder. It is in the nature of his job to confront the negative side of human nature, and Marlowe repeats to himself the phrase "Hold it, you're not human" no less than five times in ritualistic fashion in order to remind himself that he is overreacting. Partially purged, he is able to continue his investigation.

In *The Pursuit of Crime*, Dennis Porter insists that the ideology of the hard-boileds is essentially the same as that of the older British school: he equates the activities of the detective hero with a defense of the bourgeois status quo. Porter's ideological analysis finds adequate support in the British, classical school of Conan Doyle, Christie, and Sayers, whose works

Introduction

are characterized by the cerebral, aloof protagonist, the rigid class system within which he or she operates, and the theme of crime as aberrant behavior which he or she vanquishes. Sherlock Holmes, for instance, can be seen as an eccentric force needed to insure the stability of the status quo as he uncovers crime prodding, as Stephen Knight has indicated, delinquent members of the various classes back to the socially acceptable ethos as defined by the bourgeoisie (90).[6] Porter goes on to assert that the "particular mission" of the detective story "involves the celebration of the repressive state apparatus or at least of that important element of it formed by the police" (121) and that "the point of view adopted is always that of the detective, which is to say, of the police" (125).

Thus at the same time he conflates the role of the police detective with that of the private investigator, Porter posits a single-minded conformity on the detective's part, one that supports the power structure unquestioningly, one, indeed, where "the law itself is accepted as a given" (121), where "the law is never put on trial" (122). This conflation must come as a surprise to anyone familiar with the wary antagonisms that underlie the genre; indeed the police/private eye conflict is one of the least variable generic elements. In Hammett's *The Maltese Falcon*, for example, Sam Spade is first grilled by Police Lieutenant Dundy in his own apartment and, one day later, is assaulted by the policeman when he attempts to protect his client, Brigid O'Shaughnessy. Admittedly, Spade does little to assuage the suspicions of the investigator, who believes that Spade might have murdered his partner, Miles Archer. Nevertheless, it is clear that the role of the private detective is distinct from that of official law enforcement, regardless of how closely related the two might be.

In Chandler the distinction is quite different. In *The Lady in the Lake*, Al Degarmo is portrayed as a cop gone bad, one whose passion for a woman prompts him to break laws and frame innocent people in order to protect her. Marlowe baits this police detective into revealing his guilt (risking a beating or worse at the hands of the infamous Bay City police) yet insists that he's not interested in trapping Degarmo, just concerned that Degarmo will misuse his position further (*Later Novels* 183). This urban, bad cop is contrasted with Jim Patton, the jovial yet capable deputy sheriff of rural Little Fawn Lake. Philip Durham does an injustice both to Chandler and

Introduction

to Patton when he suggests that there is a clear-cut city versus country polarity here: "[t]he corrupt police of the city were contrasted with the sheriff of the mountains — a large, primitive, friendly man who represented the goodness of nature" (95).

Such interpretation might be considered had Chandler not also included Degarmo's superior officer, Captain Webber, in his narrative. Webber shows every sign of being the right kind of law enforcement official. He suspends Degarmo for his extralegal activities and offers Marlowe an explanation of how they occur: police business is a "good deal like politics. It asks for the highest type of men, and there's nothing to attract it to the highest type of men" (*Later Novels* 140). Webber underscores the very real difficulties that hamper proper law enforcement, and through him Chandler expresses his belief that a democratic society can, if only the interest and investment are forthcoming, provide security for its citizens. There is no facile nostalgia for the good old days in Chandler; he recognizes this and other difficulties of law enforcement and can sympathize with efforts to correct them. He is careful in each novel to illustrate the interactions of private investigator and police without confusing their identities.

Porter grants the private eye the *potential* to effect change inasmuch as he embodies the aspirations of the common man to mold his own destiny while at the same time resisting (often corrupt) state institutions. But Porter sees this as an "atavistic," populist individualism, one that recalls the reformist spirit of the muckrakers, but recalls only; ultimately the populist impulse for Porter is one that lacks an anchoring in the present and a vision for the future:

> The radicalism of the hard-boiled tradition ... is a radicalism of nostalgia for a mythical past. If any political program is implied at all, it is one that looks forward to the restoration of a traditional order of things, associated retrospectively with the innocent young Republic and its frontier, a traditional order that was destroyed with the advent of large-scale industrialization [181].

Porter places much emphasis on this historico-mythical status of the genre, and sees the hard-boiled detective as a dead-end figure: "the private eye typically is a hero with nowhere to go and with a mission in which he does not fully believe" (183). He overlooks, however, Marlowe's peripatetic

Introduction

activity in an ever-changing city and implicitly denies that "old" ideas have any validity. We need not jettison established concepts of social progress in order to glean from detective fiction that which is forward looking. In *A Vision of American Law,* Barry R. Schaller tackles problems of justice and authority as expressed in both American legal history and American fiction. He echoes Dewey's call for a new individualism when he defines democratic individualism as one that "envisions individual fulfillment as associated with society's well being" and that "reconciles itself to historical experience and understands the inseparability of private and public liberty" (17).

George Grella, a pioneer critic of the genre, echoes Porter's view of the detective as a figure of impotence. He views the private eye as a champion of introversion, one who "observes a moral wasteland and, with no 'territory' to flee to (unlike Huckleberry Finn) he retreats into himself" (419). For Steven Knight, Chandler has succumbed to the alienating pressures of the modern world, and has chosen to write within a romance tradition in order to present a protagonist who concentrates on maintaining the purity of his own ethos, one who "sees contemporary disorder from the position of a disgusted and disengaged persona, whose own values are defined by his rejection of a social world viewed as a hostile and corrupt unit" (138). It is not just that; in typical hard-boiled style, the hero works alone and thus implicitly insists on the values of rugged American individualism: Knight finds Marlowe self-pitying, constantly threatened, and unwilling to engage with others in any way.

It is the contention of this study, however, that a closer look at Marlowe's actions and interactions will confirm a far more socially concerned attitude on the part of his creator. He is acutely aware of the character and complexity of his world. That which Chandler said in praise of his earlier colleagues in pulp fiction in the introduction to *The Smell of Fear* (a collection of his short fiction), may be said of him: "[t]heir characters lived in a world gone wrong, a world in which, long before the atom bomb, civilization had created the machinery for its own destruction and was learning to use it with all the moronic delight of a gangster trying out his first machine-gun" (9). Chandler's metaphor here neatly links the capability of worldwide destruction with the image of an individual made mad by

Introduction

the general lack of faith in humanity. We may, inversely, read his image as the ideal symbol for that malaise: ignorance and brute force triumphant.

But Chandler does not see the problem as accidental or inevitable, but as a function of corruption: "The law was something to be manipulated for profit and power. The mystery story grew hard and cynical about motive and character, but it was not cynical about the effects it tried to produce nor about its technique for producing them" (9). That corruption could and must be combated; the private eye was, for a time, an appropriate symbolic instrument for fighting it.

Chandler transformed the cynicism of Hammett and other hard-boiled writers into a healthy skepticism, one that is wary of received notions of authority and justice but does not succumb to pessimism or retreat into the self. In Philip Marlowe, Raymond Chandler fashioned a hero who is aware of the fragility of social ties in a highly individualistic society, maintains a sense of moral justice, and refuses to stand aloof from the less-than-perfect world around him. He is socially engaged and active in the city of his choosing and in a profession to his liking. He quite willingly works within a patently hostile environment and is not merely caught between forces of power, but influences events, and is thus a voluntary explorer and a pivotal literary figure.

In order to clearly establish the significance of the hard-boiled genre and Raymond Chandler's position within it, the following two chapters focus on the ideology of American individualism, including its relationship to the myth of the frontier. Chapter one focuses on Carroll John Daly as a representative founder of the genre and Mickey Spillane as an inheritor of that tradition. In chapter two we move to Dashiell Hammett, Chandler's mentor and a writer whose works begin solidly in the rugged individualistic tradition, then gradually display a move toward a more communitarian concept of individualism. Chapter three presents the hard-boiled detective in light of his clear break with rugged individualism and transition into the role of negotiator. Chapters four and five focus on the detective's negotiations with the two primary groups with which he deals, the police and criminals, respectively. Chapter six contrasts Chandler with his most successful protégé, Ross Macdonald, who further developed Chandler's concept of individualism. Chapter seven is a brief examination of selected film

Introduction

adaptations of Chandler's novels, with special focus on individualism as it relates to film censorship and private eye–police relationships. All citations from Chandler's works are taken from the *Library of America* edition, volume I, *Stories and Early Novels*, and volume II, *Later Novels and Other Writings*, unless otherwise indicated.

CHAPTER ONE

Rugged Individualism in Carroll John Daly and Mickey Spillane

It is essential to understand how the detective hero was created in order to clearly trace his further development. His predecessors can be found in the American West. Critics such as John G. Cawelti and Leslie Fiedler see in the detective an urban extension of the frontiersman and the cowboy, asserting his highly personal sense of order and justice within a geographical and temporal sphere where the isolated individual is allowed to invent ethical codes more or less as he goes along. The frontier, of course, predates the cowboy as it moved west from the settlements and cities on the eastern shore. Thus, as early as the colonial period in America, the frontiersman, real or fictional, demonstrates rugged individualism. The hero brings civilization to the wilderness, imposing European values on indigenous peoples. In the novels of James Fenimore Cooper, still set within the borders of what was to become the 13 states, we find Natty Bummpo whose "perverted sense of freedom [is] founded on moral superiority and independence," according to Sam B. Girgus (17). Credit must be given to Cooper, however, for a quite nuanced view of the conflict between the dominant culture and the Other.

In *Gunfighter Nation* Richard Slotkin views Cooper in more subtle fashion: there is less imposition of the protagonist's values and more room for compromise. For Slotkin, Natty Bummpo is "a White man who knows Indians so well that he can almost pass for one" (16). The hero almost literally straddles the frontier, has one foot in each world, and secondary characters, such as Cora Munro in *Last of the Mohicans*, also emphasize the possibility of peace and understanding. But while the frontier hero acts "sometimes as mediator or interpreter between races and cultures," he is nonetheless primarily "civilization's most effective instrument against savagery — a man who knows how to think and fight like an Indian, to turn their own methods against them" (16). "Savagery" is a marker of a people lacking in civilization — seen, of course, from the perspective of the white hierarchy — and is never questioned; neither is the logic that one can utilize violence in order to end violence.

Slotkin continues by examining the similarities of all American popular heroes at great length and posits that the urban detective is what the Western novel's lawman, cowboy, or even gunslinger becomes by the beginning of the 20th century. Or as Robin W. Winks puts it, "Just as Zane Grey and Owen Wister once reflected America's frontier values, so today has the shoot-out at the O. K. Corral moved into the city, the sod hut is replaced by the condominium and the lone hero riding off into the sunset by the lone man who walks the mean streets of our asphalt jungles" (7). The closing of the frontier, shifting demographics, and changes in audience expectations are important factors. Elucidating the ideological background of this transformation, Slotkin examines several social Darwinian thinkers and writers of the late 19th century and highlights the particularly American strain of racism, especially as concerns Indians, that is reconciled with individualism and even progress. Along these lines, he views Frederick Jackson Turner and Theodore Roosevelt as the primary examiners and codifiers of the myth of the frontier. For Slotkin, Roosevelt's West

> is a Darwinian arena in which "races" representing different phases or principals of organization contend for *mastery*.... The lesson Roosevelt draws from his historical fable is that no class or race can stay the march of history, and that those who seek to do so are foes of progress [39].

Slotkin asserts that Roosevelt applies a harsh, survival-of-the-fittest ideology toward indigenous tribes, who are "associated with lower-class Whites who are unable to survive in a society which demands that they work or starve" and who essentially abdicate their rights as individuals (40). Thus rugged individualism proves to be the purview of the elite white male, preferably of northern European stock. All others must recognize this hierarchy, must know their place. Himself a hunter, Roosevelt

One. Rugged Individualism in Daly and Spillane

gives pride of place for true leadership to that circumscribed group: "It is their role as hunters, not their role as farmers, that gives the frontiersmen the power to make history" (49). Regardless of the racial and ethnic identity of the "leader," leadership springs from the individual, not the group.

As the frontier disappears and the dynamics of nation building change with an increasingly urban population, so do the nation's wayward heroes:

> [When] the corruption of civilization replaces wilderness as the scene of drama, and the "urban savage" replaces the Noble Red Man, Hawkeye is transformed from a saintly "man who knows Indians" to a figure whose consciousness is "darkened" by knowledge of criminality [139].

Indeed, eventually this evolution would produce anti-heroes who more than "know" criminality: they partake in it.

Slotkin symbolically renders this development of the Western hero into the urban hero in the pulp-fictive figure of Deadwood Dick, the "original good-badman of the dime-novel world" (143). This character began as a Black Hills outlaw but was transformed into a detective by Edward Wheeler, fighting with and for miners, even unionized miners, for their rights as free Americans against eastern mine owners bent on enslaving the workers in all but name. Slotkin notes a similar development in the historical figures of Buffalo Bill and even Jesse and Frank James, who, as early as 1889, appear fictionally as detectives in New York City (146–49).

> In the hard-boiled detective, the characters and roles of dime-novel outlaw and detective ... are reconciled. The hard-boiled detective is both an agent of law and an outlaw who acts outside the structures of legal authority for the sake of personal definition of justice, which often takes the form of a private quest or revenge [Slotkin 219].

It is this highly personal definition of justice that characterizes the "private" of private eye far more than his status as an entrepreneur dependent on his clientele to earn his living. And the superior historical agent — now the hunter of human game — is able to exercise his prerogative free from the fetters of society. Once the protagonist leaves the rural frontier for an urban society, he is more constrained in his private actions than the frontier hero, but often the difference is quite minimal: in the West authority could be days removed from conflict, but in the city it is immediate: authority is physically closer, but psychologically quite distant, and this is a far more crucial factor.

One writer whose detective hero is indisputably "rugged" is Carroll John Daly, generally acknowledged as the first hard-boiled detective writer, one who subjected the puzzle plot of the classic Anglo-American mystery tale to more explicit violence and heightened the judgmental and executionary aspects of the detective hero. For Slotkin, by the 1920s, when Daly began publishing, his primary detective, Race Williams, reflects the earlier Western ethos, with immigrants taking the place of the now-vanquished Indians, so often the goal of the quest, the object of revenge. The detective

> speaks of himself as living on the "border" between "outlaws" and the police, and his enemies are almost always the racially or ethnically alien bosses of the underworld. Williams is less the tracer of clues than the executor of a vigilante type of justice who operates in the moral and social isolation of the "Indian-hater" and usually solves his case with gunplay [223].

In an article in *Black Mask Magazine* arguing for placing Daly on an equal footing with Hammett as a preeminent hard-boiled stylist, Stephen Mertz comes to a similar conclusion: "Daly took the two-gun American Hero from the wooly plains of the West and transplanted him in New York ... and he gave him the desire and ability to back up his code of individualism, his distrust of authority and his interest in Justice over Legality with a pair of smoking .44's" (2).

Foreshadowing Mickey Spillane's Mike Hammer, Daly's hero prowls the corrupt urban landscape with utter faith in his own superior sense of frontier justice. While at times he cooperates with legitimate law enforcement, Williams generally takes the law into his own hands and constantly reminds the reader of his superior skills vis-à-vis the police and his superior ethical status vis-à-vis "outlaws." His sense of self-worth is anchored by a comic-book imperviousness to danger: "I don't know fear myself— but it must be a terrible thing" (84) is an offhand (and typically self-enamored) comment in *The Hidden Hand* (1928). His invincibility stands out in stark contrast to the vulnerability of his victims and the violence he typically employs against them.

In *The Snarl of the Beast* (1927), the detective-narrator begins by explaining his "tough" philosophy:

One. Rugged Individualism in Daly and Spillane

> I'm just a halfway house between the law and crime; sort of working both ends against the middle. Right and wrong are not written on the statutes for me, nor do I find my code of morals in the essays of long-winded professors. My ethics are my own. I'm not saying they're good and I'm not admitting they're bad, and what's more I'm not interested in the opinions of others on that subject [1–2].

The concept of the "halfway house" is so pervasive in the genre as to be one of the few defining features of all private detectives. The detective must conduct a kind of shuttle diplomacy among all characters, especially police and criminals. Playing both sides against the middle, however, can only make sense if the detective hopes to gain a profit, or some other type of self-aggrandizement, out of the conflict. This feature distinguishes Race Williams, as well as Dashiell Hammett's Continental Op and Mickey Spillane's Mike Hammer, from Raymond Chandler's Philip Marlowe. It is worth noting Williams' insistence on being his one and only judge: to allow others to weigh in on a discussion of his ethics would be to cede the kind of autonomous control so central to his self-definition. The arrogance displayed by Daly's detective is also a hallmark of the "rugged" private eyes. While the circumstance of a corrupt society (most often represented by politicians and police) is a major factor in any private eye's attitudes, the refusal to even discuss professional ethics, let alone disagree about them, is utterly foreign to Chandler's hero.

Daly's extreme focus on the individual is by no means a generic or modern anomaly. Although we are concerned with individualism as an American phenomenon, the concept was inherited from Europeans, Alexis de Toqueville among them, who defined it in negative terms, equating it with egotism because it valorized the individual over the institutions to which that individual belonged. "Egoism is a passionate and exaggerated love of self which leads a man to think of all things in terms of himself and to prefer himself to all" (506). Tocqueville contrasts egoism with individualism, characterizing the latter as "a calm and considered feeling" and therefore superior, but individualism is still the product of "misguided judgment": "individualism at first only dams the spring of public virtues, but in the long run it attacks and destroys all the others too" (506–07).

In *Individualism and Nationalism in American Ideology*, Yehoshua

Arieli traces the centrality of individualism in American history from the colonial period onward, and he maintains that the concept was first given positive connotations in the United States: "the term, which in the Old World was almost synonymous with selfishness, social anarchy, and individual self-assertion, connoted in America self-determination, moral freedom, the rule of liberty, and the dignity of man" (193). This crucial redefinition of the term was the logical extension of the understanding of self by a people who recognized that those old-world institutions were oppressive and that securing the rights of the individual was the most effective means of countering those institutions. Arieli notes E. L. Godkin's "Aristocratic Opinions of Democracy," in which Tocqueville's negative view of individualism is criticized: "It was not the vice and apathy of a society of long standing, but the primordial energy which conquered an empty and wild continent and built a new society, and it reflected the pioneer's survival and the character this mode of life developed" (200).

Behind the growing power of this pioneer ideology in American life was the optimistic belief that the individual, left to his own devices, would "do right," that the faith in the natural rights of man that drove the Enlightenment agenda of the Declaration of Independence could create a just and productive society. Westward expansion allowed the ideology of the autonomous individual to grow; for example, farmers, Jefferson's ideal democratic citizens, established themselves on "new" land that they themselves owned as the frontier moved west and they were, to a large extent, autonomous and self-reliant well into the 19th century. The young nation's appreciation of its unprecedented opportunities for expansion, its sense of Manifest Destiny, was a spur to the initiative of the individual. Independent, however, of a social network such as found in the coastal cities, the man of the frontier, having only himself to fall back on, became the only focus of his world. As Christopher Lasch sees it, "the rugged individualist saw [the world] as an empty wilderness to be shaped in his own image" (10). Of course, viewing it as "empty" already reveals the individualistic bent.

Ralph Waldo Emerson expressed his optimistic belief in the innate goodness of the individual, characterizing, in "Self-Reliance," the integrity of the individual mind as sacred (261), thus strengthening the argument

One. Rugged Individualism in Daly and Spillane

by appealing to a power above that of men. "The creative autonomy of the human spirit and man's unity with ultimate reality set limits on government, social institutions, and prescriptive rights" (Arieli 281–82). God-given powers trump any possible counterargument.

Inheritors of the Emersonian concept of individualism, however, proved both less optimistic about human nature and far less liberal in their political philosophy. For them such beatified individualism served as a justification for the most extreme laissez-faire ideology and Emerson must bear some responsibility in this; where the actions of the individual are *by definition* good and true, he implies, there need be no system of societal checks and balances, no mediation between individual and society. Arieli sees a kind of social blindness in what he calls Emerson's "cosmic optimism," and as a result a "rather devitalized version of his concept of individualism and self reliance were [*sic*] eagerly taken up by contemporaries as apologies for the status quo and became part of the accepted version of American individualism" (285). In this famous essay Emerson does more, however, than merely place the individual in a position superior to that of the collective; he maintains that allegiance to social institutions is *detrimental* to individual growth. An action as simple — indeed as democratic — as voting is for him a sapping of "force" from the individual's "proper life." He dismisses these institutions by pronouncing them dead and deems "great" the man who maintains "the independence of solitude" (263). In so doing he lays the groundwork for the self-aggrandizing and vengeful actions fictionally expressed in the figure of Race Williams.

Emerson's influence has been noted by many critics. In *The Great Tradition* Granville Hicks makes a cogent connection between the depredations of laissez-faire capitalism and industrialization on the one hand and Emersonian individualism on the other in transforming American society:

> [T]he pioneer virtues, when translated into the terms of an industrial economy, were cut-throat competition and ruthless exploitation.... Emerson's teachings ... could be, and they were, so interpreted as to justify the Morgans, Rockefellers, and Carnegies, or they could be restated in terms of the aspirations of the victims rather than the victors. Needless to say, the former interpretation triumphed [30].

Like Arieli, Hicks insists on viewing individualism in pragmatic terms, in terms consistent with historical reality: although he doesn't use the term "individualism," he suggests that an initially valuable and socially defensible concept has been perverted. As a Marxist, he recognizes a benevolent intention, but decries the development as co-opted by a more powerful capitalist ideology.

Thus Race Williams' rugged individualism can be seen as a modern extension of an ideology deeply rooted in American society. If *The Hidden Hand* often reads like a parody of the genre — its plot devices are amateurish and its coincidences stretch the bounds of credibility — it nonetheless reveals the consistent power of the individualistic ethos in its portrayal of the detective hero. This is expressed primarily through suspicion on the part of the detective of any institution that is capable of deadly force and/or of exercising power over him. Williams is contemptuous of the police, whom he portrays as, at best, dumbly loyal, inefficient civil servants and, at worst, dangerous bumblers. Conversely, the detective sees himself, not without considerable pride, as being outside the law as far as the police are concerned: "People — especially the police — don't understand me. And what we don't understand we don't appreciate. The police look upon me as being so close to the criminal that you can't tell the difference" (1–2).

Williams' actions may be motivated by his need to be understood, but for Daly this means an extreme assertion of the self. The detective is, to be sure, a capable professional, but his professional identity is couched in a defensive, even paranoid, assertion that he is on the job and that he's the only individual who can succeed. In a corrupt and violent society, crime has gone unpunished, and since he is eager to fill the void of fighting it left by the corrupt and incompetent, the line between legitimate action and illegitimate force is blurred. Confrontations with criminals become throwbacks to 19th-century progenitors of the detective genre, virtual Wild West showdowns, individual against individual.

Challenged to just such a shootout by one of his enemies in *The Hidden Hand*, Williams attends a crowded horseshoe tournament in Miami. Wedged tightly in the crowd, the detective is ready for immediate action: "My arms were folded across my chest, each hand beneath my coat and up under my armpits. And each hand held a gun" (147). A man with a

One. Rugged Individualism in Daly and Spillane

livid scar emerges from a crowd directly opposite him. Soon their eyes meet and they draw their guns and Williams places two bullets in the victim's skull. As always, Williams, the gunslinger, is the faster, the more skilled in any confrontation. This is an example of only one of several criminals/victims on Williams' hit list dispatched Western-style.

The fact that Williams is never brought to account for the violence he wreaks on others speaks for the essentially aggressive, lawless character of the autonomous individual and the willingness of society to sanction such behavior. Gregory Ford, the agency detective Williams occasionally collaborates with, offhandedly comments on the lack of Williams' accountability, positing that "[t]echnically, I suppose, you'll have to be brought up and admitted to bail. If you're working for the state, you no doubt can fix that. If it's not convenient, ... I could fix it for you. Mere legal detail, you know" (154). For Williams the law and law enforcers are mere detail, lacking interest for the hard-boiled hero, and as such can be safely ignored. While Ford is interested enough in legal repercussions, Williams assumes his exceptional status to the point that the question never arises.

In *The Snarl of the Beast* the role of private eye versus the law is further developed. After a car chase in Central Park, Milly, the sympathetic heroine of the narrative, has just shot and killed a man who threatened her life, and Williams enthusiastically defends her action:

> I must admit that I'm strong for a little loose shooting against loose thinkers. There may be laws of the state or of the government that aren't so good, but the laws of God and man can't be improved upon. Them that live by the gun should die by the gun, is good sound twentieth century gospel [60–61].

It would be more accurate to call this a 19th-century gospel, harking back to the Western, one which equates the individual with God and is superior to laws promulgated by mere men and their institutions.

Later in the novel, ostensibly because they've been tipped off that Williams was "given the works" by his enemies and expect to find him murdered, the police invade his apartment, and this gives Williams the opportunity to criticize the police, one Inspector Coglin in particular: "It was hot stuff to watch him. What a child he was! In his own stupid way he was putting the screws on me" (82). Williams' contempt for the police is inextricably bound to his own inflated sense of self-esteem. He portrays the police as Keystone Kops: "Somewhere off in the night, police and detectives would be getting in the way of each other—firing at their own friends and calling warnings to the prowler on the block." He then almost immediately reasserts his mastery and his autonomy: "I like to play the game alone; where every shadow is an enemy and each bullet I shoot goes in the right direction and reaches the right man" (90). The contrast between the failings of duly constituted authorities and the infallibility of the lone-wolf detective could not be more distinct. It is ironic to note that, for all his braggadocio, Williams is so easily manipulated. Undoubtedly intending to sustain some fragment of suspense throughout *The Hidden Hand*, Daly keeps his protagonist in the dark as to the identity of the eponymous criminal mastermind until the last chapter, when the villain is revealed as Williams' employer, Howard Quincy Travers.

Daly did not grasp the extent to which he made his strikingly unobservant hero the dupe of the client/villain. Comparable to dime-novel Western characters such as Deadwood Dick, Williams is far more the unreflective hired gun ready to kill the patently evil enemies of his clients than a proxy for sheriff or marshal, who could at least be expected to employ a high degree of skepticism in his interactions, if for no other reason than to protect himself. On the contrary, the autonomy Williams is so proud of proves, at least in this novel, to be utterly self-deluding. Williams blindly accepts Travers as a philanthropist who hires the detective to rid Florida of its criminal element, and in doing so he circumvents the legal authorities and becomes a dangerous vigilante, but until Williams kills Travers while protecting a fellow detective, he unwittingly serves the villain in his plan to rid himself of a series of dangerous criminal competitors. Thus Daly achieves a telling, if unintentional, critique of rugged individualism.

In *Gumshoe America: Hard-Boiled Crime Fiction and the Rise of New Deal Liberalism,* Sean McCann notes that in *The Snarl of the Beast,* "Race Williams confronts two linked evils: a gang of vicious criminals headed by the beast of the title and a corrupt, aristocratic family haunted by a tradition of internecine violence." He sees the two groups joined by a common "repudiation of civic responsibility" (126). He also notes the element of irrationality so important in the genre: "Each of them follows tribal passions rather than the dictates of good citizenship" (127). Unquestionably, society in general is characterized as chaotic, even anarchic in Daly's fiction and this, in turn, is based on the apparent lack of order of the Prohibition period. However, McCann ignores the far more telling lack of civic responsibility on the part of the protagonist himself, and it is our task to examine the detective's repudiation of society.

McCann makes the intriguing contrast between two groups who, in the 1920s, were profoundly dissatisfied with modern, industrial American life: the Ku Klux Klan and fictional hard-boiled heroes. Whereas the Klan touted the regenerative power of the racially restrictive community, hard-boiled fiction "seemed more cynical about the law than Klan ideology, less idealistic about citizenship and reform" (76). However, "[b]oth Klan ideologues and the authors of hard-boiled crime fiction wrote as if extralegal action were a natural response to social corruption" (76). Race Williams' unfettered individualism is thus equated with Klan-like vigilantism. Being hard-boiled for McCann is to be cynical as to the prospects of communal harmony and the ability of law enforcement to help achieve it. As a result, unauthorized forces are quick to fill in the void.

Vigilantism is a product of the West, especially its seemingly endless spaces and the inability of duly constituted law enforcement to effectively cover the territory. Vigilantes were not only local citizens fighting the depredations of cattle thieves and others who were perceived as serious threats to the community, but gunslingers paid for their policing activities, not unlike the Pinkertons. McCann traces the spirit of vigilantism in the genre back to Arthur Conan Doyle in *A Study in Scarlet*, in which an American, Joseph Hope, pursues and wreaks revenge upon members of the Mormon Church who have kidnapped, forced into marriage, and killed his fiancée, Lucy Ferrier. "We are plainly meant to feel, as Watson does, both sympathy for Hope's righteous pursuit of justice and revulsion at his all-consuming determination to exact revenge for which he alone will be judge, jury, and executioner" (13). This is, however, getting it backwards: in Doyle the vigilante is not the detective, but the perpetrator. In the classic British detective genre such characters are disturbing aberrations of the otherwise strong, dominant social norm and a clear resolution produces a more or less "happy ending" in which society is again whole. As David

I. Grossvogel puts it, Agatha Christie's readers enjoyed "the comfort of knowing that the disturbance was *contained*, and that at the end of the story the world that they imagined would be continued in its innocence and familiarity" (4). He contrasts the essentially corrupt American society of the hard-boiled writers with Christie's England, where "murder upon the mead was more in the nature of a washable and cathartic stain" (6).

Indeed, Agatha Christie frequently simplifies the situation by making foreigners, those outside acceptable society, the villains. In *Thirteen at Dinner* an upstart American actress who has married an English lord constructs a complex plot to murder her husband and then a fellow American actress who unwittingly aids her. After a third murder she gives herself away when she displays her lack of British education, not realizing that Paris is not just a city in France but a figure in the works of Homer. In *Murder on the Orient Express* it is again an American, a gangster, Rachett, traveling under an assumed name, who proves to be the villain, although in this case it is his murder that Poirot is investigating. All 12 people complicit in the execution of Rachett are found innocent of their act because of the patently deserving character of their victim and the need to restore the proper social balance.

Ross Macdonald recognizes the British social background when he says that "[p]ermeating the thought and language of Conan Doyle's stories is an air of blithe satisfaction with a social system based on privilege" (298). Stephen Knight underscores the class element in such a restoration when he says that "the dynamic meaning of the plot is disorder threatening the normative morality of bourgeois, respectable England" (89) and that "the stories assert that if decent people pulled together, did their duty and fulfilled their moral roles these disorders would not occur" (90). It is generally understood that "decent people" are primarily members of the middle class, the same group from which the perpetrators of crime are taken. As Julian Symons points out, servants might be petty criminals, but not murderers: "It was necessary, in fact, that he should be part of the same social group that contained the other suspects" (102).

Despite the often eccentric, highly individualistic nature of a detective like Holmes or Poirot, the detective tacitly accepts this bourgeois ideology and serves society by helping restore social order. In this sense the British

One. Rugged Individualism in Daly and Spillane

genre is thoroughly optimistic as far as a peaceful future for society is concerned. This style of detective fiction isn't limited to Great Britain. In *The Greene Murder Case* American S. S. Van Dine isolates crime in a New York City townhouse not very different from that which could be found in London, owned and occupied by the rich and eccentric Greene family. Several members of the family are murdered before the perpetrator, the adopted daughter Ada Greene, is captured by the equally eccentric Philo Vance. Not only is Ada's murder spree accounted for by greed for the family fortune and resentment at being treated more as a servant than as a full-fledged family member; she has inherited her murderous ways from a biological father, a notorious German murderer who ended his life in an insane asylum. Social order is restored when the rightful heiress, Sibella, is rescued and comes into her fortune.

The hard-boiled genre is radically different in this respect. The detective is himself the vigilante and neither accepts the unifying societal premise nor his constructive role within it and wreaks bloody, unbridled revenge on his enemies, who are often solid citizens, not social aberrations. It is permeated with a pessimistic attitude toward society. We find Williams in the role of the detective-as-avenger as *The Snarl of the Beast* opens, with him indirectly warning anyone who may take a potshot at him that "[h]e and *his relatives* would come in for a slow ride, with a shovelful of dirt at the end of it" (1, my emphasis). As if it were not enough to defeat any actual threat to his life and triumph over his adversary, the detective feels the need to extend his vengeance in a manner worthy of the Hatfields and McCoys. When vigilante justice has triumphed over a system of laws, rugged individualism has indeed become rabid.

Race Williams is not Daly's only protagonist. The tellingly named Satan Hall appears in *The Mystery of the Smoking Gun* (1933) and his ruggedly individualistic reputation precedes him: Police Captain James T. Harrington, resentful of having Hall forced on his precinct by higher authority, calls him "killer" to his face (2) and "a one-man law" (4), establishing the detective's contempt for authority and readiness for violence at the very beginning of the novel. He is also identified, however, as a cop, categorizing *The Mystery of the Smoking Gun* as a police procedural.

Daly made substantial changes in the 1930s. He invented a new hero whose character veers from the rugged individualism of Race Williams toward the British classicism of Philo Vance. His detective in *Emperor of Evil* is Vivian, "Master of Melody," a successful songwriter who, quite improbably, doubles as "Vee Brown, Killer of Men, assigned to the district attorney's office," an identity known only to his trusty assistant, Dean Cogdon (6). His "assignment" is quite tenuous, yet signals a significant change from the autonomous private eye Williams. He refers to himself as a cop, albeit an "irregular one" (78), but Daly lends him the essential attribute of the independence of Williams.

Also similar to Williams, Brown is "a detective who met violence with violence" and his encounters with his antagonists reflect the earlier detective's Wild West style. He is introduced on the first page along with Mortimer Doran, the district attorney, and Inspector Ramsey as they inspect the body of the victim of the first murder, Mrs. Charles B. Townsend. The characterization of Brown, especially the upper-class language, and the dynamics of the detective/police relationships are reminiscent of Daly's contemporary, S. S. Van Dine, whose Philo Vance habitually worked with District Attorney John F. X. Markham. In *Emperor of Evil* the district attorney is cast in the role of not-terribly-competent superior officer who gives Brown free rein and the inspector constantly questions Brown's abilities and is rabidly jealous of his success. It is clear from the beginning that neither officer of the law can or will be correct in his interpretation of evidence and that Brown will triumph.

The master criminal, Vincent van Houten, Brown's Professor Moriarty, is revealed quite early in the narrative, so there is no real mystery of identity. He is the leader of a vast blackmail ring with power over hundreds of lackeys. Brown's vigilante violence becomes explicit when Cogdon elicits Brown's opinion on the subject of blackmail, asking him "as an individual ... and not as a policeman" what he would do if he were a victim of such a crime. "I would go straight to Mr. Blackmailer and shoot him to death" (8).

After another murder has occurred, tempers flare between Brown and Ramsey, and District Attorney Doran immediately works to keep the peace, using the opportunity to assure Brown that "as long as you don't embarrass the department, Vee, you can work your own way" (84). This is also an

One. Rugged Individualism in Daly and Spillane

opportunity for the rogue detective to criticize the police. Doran is convinced of van Houten's innocence, since "we've checked up van Houten right back to his birth" (85). For Brown this only means that the police are incompetent: "That's the trouble with the police system ... the confusion of respectability with honesty. Van Houten hasn't got a record because the police were too stupid or he was too clever to have anything pinned on him" (85). The implication is that Brown possesses vastly superior intelligence and skills and he promises results in 24 hours. Tempers flare again when Ramsey grabs Condon's arm in anger and Brown knocks it off, insisting that the pair are not to be held accountable to the duly constituted authorities (183).

A radical departure from Daly's Race Williams series is that Vee Brown is capable of making mistakes and able to admit his limits, if only to Cogdon. Victims of the blackmail ring have been murdered as they fail to make payments or if they appear ready to reveal the identity of the blackmailer. The wife of an old college friend of Brown's and Cogden's, Thomas Wilson, is one such victim. Brown pledges her his protection, but is taken unawares when she commits suicide. In a moment unthinkable in a Race Williams novel, Brown admits to his mistake of underestimating his opponent. The tone is much darker in this section of the novel since he knows the victim's family and contemplates a revenge killing to assuage his guilt. Cogdon's voice of reason and Brown's belief that he has already solved the case keep him from executing vigilante justice. The portrayal of this incident seems almost out of place: the ruggedly individualistic attitude is there, but the treatment is three-dimensional, even Chandlerian.

Two-dimensionality soon returns, however. The police, convinced until the end that van Houten cannot be the culprit, serve as foils to the master detective. One last murder is committed, but the victim leaves behind incriminating evidence that leads to a literal showdown between hunter and hunted. Brown's otherworldly skill with firearms, established earlier in the narrative and reminiscent of Race Williams, once again triumphs and the police can't help but recognize the superior lawman in their midst.

A generation later, in the 1940s and 1950s, Mickey Spillane's Mike Hammer established himself as the literary and ethical heir of Race

Williams. A onetime writer of comic books, Spillane outdoes Daly in fashioning a two-dimensional hero unwilling to act within the letter or spirit of the law, insistent on his utter autonomy, addicted to the rough justice of the streets. Spillane himself recognized his debt to Daly. In what he describes as a fan letter to the older writer, he acknowledges that "Race was the model for Mike" and that his own tremendous popularity was made possible by Daly's previous work (3). Max Allan Collins claims in the introduction to volume one of *The Mike Hammer Collection* that Hammer is first and foremost an avenger, a role superior even to that of detective (vii). For Collins the primary value of this approach is reader identification with the detective and his adventures, since "Spillane touched the psyche and libido of the reading public," particularly in the seemingly placid 1950s (ix–x). There is far more at stake, however. Invariably motivated at the start of each novel by the need to pay back violence in kind, with extreme violence and death for the misery inflicted on his friends, Hammer's vigilantism goes far beyond that which most readers could truly accept.

In *I, the Jury* (1947) the revenge motif is immediately established. Summoned by police detective Pat Chambers to a murder scene, Hammer inspects the body of Jack Williams, his companion in war and best friend, tortured and murdered by whomever the private eye now vows to hunt down and kill in like manner. As in all Hammer novels, Chambers is Hammer's foil in a tense relationship, but more importantly serves as the keeper of social norms that Hammer must defy, insisting on reason though always aware that he will get an individualistic and emotional response from Hammer. The policeman invites cooperation while warning Hammer not to work alone, but it is the private eye who insists on his personal right to vengeance: "I want the killer for myself. We'll work together as usual, but in the homestretch I'm going to pull the trigger" (I:6). The detective always insists on ultimate, violent control.

Odette L'Henry Evans greatly exaggerates when she maintains that Spillane's heroes "work side by side with the police force, which they invariably respect and trust" (102). The relationship is at once more one-sided and more complex. Spillane sensed that he needed some give and take between Hammer and the police, but he restricts cooperation to a mini-

One. Rugged Individualism in Daly and Spillane

mum, primarily in the interest of narrative cohesion and development. Evans is closer to the realities of the narrative, however, when she notes that the detective's name is hardly accidental, connoting violence, "related to the tool, relentlessly flattening, driving into the ground" and emphasizes the ruthlessness of Hammer's character (103). This is a more accurate assessment: Hammer is indeed relentless in his pursuit and insistent on isolated action.

Contemptuous, not only of the police but of the entire legal system, which he denigrates as "the tedious process of the law" (I:6), he rails against agreed-upon communal standards, underscoring his personal connection to the victim in order to justify his vendetta: "the law is fine. But this time I'm the law and I'm not going to be cold and impartial" (I:7). Even here the connection to 19th-century theories of individualism is evident. As Arieli stresses, it was Emerson's conviction "that man, grown to full intellectual and moral stature, was a law unto himself, while state compulsion was incompatible with freedom" (283). By taking the murder personally, Hammer assumes just this kind of resistance to "compulsion" to secure his freedom.

This freedom is invariably grounded in violence. In an odd, one-page prologue to *My Gun Is Quick* (1950), for instance, Spillane begins by accusing his reader of enjoying a "vicarious kick" while reading detective fiction and then compares this with the thrill experienced by the sadistically cruel audience of ancient Rome, spicing "their life with action when they sat in the Coliseum and watched wild animals rip a bunch of humans apart" (I:153). He is quick to add that his New York urban jungle is even more vicious than Rome. He considers "looking" for such cruelty as his job (not, curiously, fighting it), and he couches the individual's need for violence in social Darwinist terms: "You have to be quick, and you have to be able, or you become one of the devoured, and if you can kill first, no matter how and no matter who, you can live" (I:153–54). Spillane thus attempts to justify Hammer's subsequent sadistic and cruel actions, but his disclaimer serves more readily to hammer home the self-sufficient, no-man-dare-judge ethos of his hero. Society is unremittingly nasty, brutish, and short: in a violent universe incapable of justice, the individual does best to either sequester himself and observe violence from a comfortable distance or, if involved in violence, make sure that he is more vicious than his opponents. The detective himself is someone who has chosen the latter option and must gather within himself not just the law of the jungle but sole, absolute authority. Sean McCann recognizes this quality in *I, The Jury*, noting that, "[t]he novel's very title celebrates the triumph of personal will over the social apparatus of the law" (202). In more than one novel Spillane foregrounds Hammer's paranoia and the immediate, violent reaction to it, his insistence on working alone, and his contempt for authority.

My Gun Is Quick also provides ample evidence of the bloodlust and sadism so closely bound with autonomy and revenge. In a conversation with his friend, Police Detective Pat Chambers, Hammer touches on one of the advantages his job enjoys over police work: "Sure, you serve justice. You do more good than a million guys working separately, but there's one thing you miss.... The excitement of the chase, Pat. The thrill of running something down and pumping a slug into it" (I:205). Time after time in these novels, Hammer hunts down underworld figures who have threatened or killed some personal connection, someone the detective respects or is in love with. While Chambers futilely plays the voice of reason, Hammer absolves himself of responsibility due to the enormity of the outrage done to him and lashes out in fury, objectifying, in this case in his use of "it," his ostensible victim past any degree of humanity.

Later, echoing his outburst to Chambers, he explains to his lover, Lola Bergan, that the police would like to employ his sadistic vigilante methods against criminals, but they are "tied down by a mess of red tape and have to go through channels" (I:231): institutional restrictions doom the police to ineffectiveness. Much like Race Williams, Hammer revels in his private status, even to the point of assuming that public guardians are envious of his position and power since he can "shoot in self-defense and be cleared in a court of law," so confident is he in his invulnerability (I:231).

Facing Hammer's typical derision of the police in *Kiss Me, Deadly* (1952), Chambers defends the legitimate authorities because they "have the equipment and manpower." As in *My Gun Is Quick*, Hammer counters by underscoring the law of the jungle: "Yeah, sure, but they don't have the attitude.... [Criminals] only respect one thing.... A gun in their bellies

One. Rugged Individualism in Daly and Spillane

that's going off and splashing their guts across the room" (II:370–71). Chambers never tires of making his argument, but he is never successful: the law of the jungle prevails.

Reviled as corrupt protectors of the Mafia, politicians come under the same kind of fire as the police. In this novel Hammer jousts with the FBI as well as the NYPD and, much like in *My Gun Is Quick*, it is only the detective's personal revenge that counts. Asked to cooperate with the former, the detective asserts his self-righteousness, claiming that the brutal injuries he received at the hands of the mob place him in higher authority than president, Congress, or Supreme Court (II:369). Spillane's logic is confusing, to say the least; it places personal suffering above collectively established standards, hardly a foundation for law and law enforcement. Within Spillane's world, however, logic holds. Hammer is only concerned with himself: his words are an expression of his visceral, individualistic credo.

The Big Kill (1951) begins with the revenge motif. In a seedy bar where Hammer is trying to drink without interruption from the other patrons, a man (William Decker, we later discover) suddenly runs out of the bar only to be killed in a drive-by shooting, leaving his year-old son behind. We learn later that Decker was driven to crime by the expenses of his wife's illness and the pressure placed upon him by hardened criminals and he is absolved of guilt just as his death puts him beyond Hammer's wrath.

Having failed to prevent the murder, Hammer declares to Pat Chambers both his intention of avenging the child and his insistence on his right to do so:

> I don't know who the kid is but he's going to grow up knowing that the guy who killed his old man died with a nice hot slug in the middle of his intestines. If it means anything to you, consider that I'm on a case. I have me a legal right to do a lot of things including shooting a goddamn killer if I can sucker him into drawing first so it'll look like self defense [II:186].

There is no explanation, to say nothing of justification, as to where Hammer gets his odd definition of legal rights, but it is clear in the context of the Hammer novels that he occupies the extreme pole of rugged individualism and that he revels in the sadism of enforcing his will on others. The desire to "sucker" the victim is an anomaly in the Hammer novels: usually there is no pretense to even the appearances of self-defense and the image of "drawing first" is a tangible reminder of the code of the West.

Although Hammer's interactions with Chambers are in places friendly, even cooperative, the private eye relishes the opportunity to disrespect the district attorney — here portrayed as an incompetent. Irked that the district attorney orders him around and addresses him simply as "Hammer," he answers, "You can call me *Mister* when you use my name. I don't want any crap from you or your boys and if you think you can make it tough for me just go ahead and try it" (II:234). When Chambers warns him to go easy with the authorities Hammer can only reiterate his plan of revenge:

> I want the guy who made somebody decent revert back to a filthy crime and I want him right between my hands so I can squeeze the juice out of him.
> Where is he, Mike?
> If I knew I wouldn't tell you, friend. I want him for myself [II:237].

There is an echo of Hammer's curious sense of individual rights when Chambers warns him off such action. Hammer's vigilante logic is that "I'm still a citizen and responsible in some small way for what happens in this city.... I have the right to take care of an obligation like removing a lousy orphan-maker" (II:238). Hammer would like us to think of him as an exemplary citizen and a protector of the helpless, but his concept of "removing" only emphasizes his need to work alone and unfettered.

Writing a generation after Daly, Spillane takes up the extreme individualistic vigor of the earlier writer, intensifying the egotism, anger, and paranoia. In his introduction to volume one of *The Mike Hammer Collection*, Collins sees the experience of World War II as a key motivating factor of this revival and asserts that Spillane provided "entertainment that in its violence and carnality reflected a generation's loss of innocence" (I:viii). Charles L. P. Silet also argues convincingly that Spillane reflects the anxieties of servicemen returning from World War II, that the status of women in the workplace, in particular, was seen as a threat to male autonomy, and that his "readership was prepared to accept his simple answers to complex dilemmas of social change" (197–98). The war motif is introduced on the very first page of *I, the Jury* when Hammer identifies the first murder victim as "Jack, the guy who said he'd give his right arm for a friend and did when he stopped a bastard of a Jap from slitting me in two" (I:5). This

One. Rugged Individualism in Daly and Spillane

very male sacrifice against a hated and derided enemy establishes a clear boundary between Us and Them. Thus "simple answers" provide a veneer of old values that allow male readers, the majority of Spillane's readers, to feel superior, in control. In our context, it is no wonder that Hammer is so sensitive about his male identity, and that it is expressed primarily as a desperate insistence on his autonomous position in society.

Vengeance Is Mine (1950) poses perhaps the most extreme example of social aberration that so disturbs Spillane. The plot involves a blackmail ring: fashion models lure out-of-town businessmen into compromising situations that are photographed and the victims are forced to pay or be exposed. Murders are then committed to ensure that the blackmail scheme isn't exposed. The reader follows Hammer's wrong suspicions as to the identity of the killer until the last page when he faces Juno Reeves, the stunning manager of the modeling agency and, as Hammer fantasizes, punning on her first name, "queen of the lesser gods and goddesses" (I:376). Throughout the novel Hammer associates Reeves with Charlotte Manning, the villain who deceived him, the woman he loved and killed in *I, The Jury*, and it's made explicit that he is unable to again kill a woman, regardless of the provocation. Reeves' dress, however, is torn away in the struggle and she proves to be a cleverly disguised man.

Reeves has presented a flawlessly beautiful and sexually provocative front until the very end when, "with eyes blazing a hatred I'll never see again" (I:512) she attempts to kill Hammer, who, of course, is quicker on the trigger. Even after she is dead the detective's disgust is sadistic and self-righteous, expressed as "revulsion" as he "spit on the clay that was Juno" (I:513). This goes beyond the everyday Spillane misogyny: although he would never admit it, his attraction to a person who turns out to be male has shaken his own sense of self. Men and women are threats to that sense of self in surprisingly similar ways. The critical response to Spillane has focused almost exclusively on the detective's sexism: cartoonishly eroticized women are occasionally damsels in distress dependent on the virile male for protection. More often they are femmes fatales who lure the hero into a false sense of security with beauty and sex appeal. There is no question that sex is foregrounded: the figure of Velda, Hammer's voluptuous, yet untouchable, secretary, is evidence enough, but the key point is that

Hammer demands respect and attention from both genders; he insists on controlling their actions and turns dangerous when he doesn't get his way.

Much like in *The Big Kill*, Hammer has generally friendly relations with Pat Chambers and vilifies the district attorney, who strips Hammer of his detective's license and his gun permit. Hammer is understandably angry, but his animosity predates this incident and he has no compunction about deriding the man: "For a D. A. you're a pain in the behind.... If it wasn't for me the papers would have run you in the comic section long ago" (I:354–55). He irrationally stresses not just the man's incompetence, but in his egomania he feels that he is the savior of the man's job. The extreme condescension and animosity toward the D.A. is partly shared by Chambers, and this allows Hammer and Chambers to bond more thoroughly than in other novels. It appears that it is enough to have one figure of authority as the detective's lightning rod. Hammer is "glad to have a friend in the department" (I:353) and although the dialogue is peppered with expressions of one-upmanship and occasional anger, both men regularly meet in bars to discuss the case. Chambers provides valuable information and is even willing to concede that Hammer was correct in calling Chester Wheeler's death murder, not suicide, from the start and provides Hammer with a false alibi.

As in *I, The Jury* the victim is a former soldier, here Wheeler, who has served with Hammer, "comrades-in-arms, happy to be on the right side and giving it all we had," as Hammer puts it. Yet he also emphasizes the surreal isolation of the two men, "two-strong and fighting the war by ourselves." No doubt Spillane meant to focus on camaraderie and self-sacrifice, but the phrasing is significant: now that one is dead, only the survivor is left to finish the war and the implication — "we weren't in any damn jungle. We were right here in New York City where murder wasn't supposed to happen and did all the time" — is that the lone warrior fights against his surroundings, his society (I:365). Although, as a flight instructor, Spillane did not see action in World War II, he highly valued those warrior qualities and imbued Hammer with them. Hammer is a warrior like none other, however. The camaraderie and teamwork of the soldier does not ring true: Hammer has effectively gone AWOL, too often deserting his comrade, Chambers, and any claim to right action.

One. Rugged Individualism in Daly and Spillane

One Lonely Night (1951) stands out in its more explicitly political approach. Published in 1951, the novel's villains are Communists and Spillane spares no invective in portraying them as subhuman. Encountering soapbox orators in Union Square, both speakers and listeners are described as "lump[s] of vomit," "Judas sheep," and "jackal[s]" and Hammer condones the police brutality used on them (II:29). Not only does Hammer infiltrate the "cell" with ease, but is assumed to be an agent of the MVD, Soviet Ministry of Internal Affairs.

In what appears at first to be an unrelated matter, a murder for which a popular politician, Lee Deamer, has been identified as the killer, Pat Chambers not only allows Hammer his usual free hand in the investigation, but enlists his aid since, as he says, "I'm in something that has a personal meaning to me too and I'm afraid of tackling it alone" (II:41). Chambers authorizes Hammer to kidnap Oscar, the psychotic twin brother of Deamer, because acquitting the politician by revealing the true culprit will ruin his career. Hammer discovers that the man Oscar Deamer ostensibly killed was Lee's predecessor in the party hierarchy and his thought is that "Lee ought to be proud of his brother" (II:77). At one cell meeting a general attached to the Soviet Embassy appears with his aides and speaks to the assembled party members as Hammer recognizes "propaganda right off the latest Moscow cable and it turned me inside out. I wanted to feel the butt of an M–1 against my shoulder pointing at those bastards up there on the rostrum and feel the pleasant impact as it spit slugs into their guts" (II:78).

Predictably, Hammer has been playing a lone hand and Chambers tries to bring him to account. Hammer insists once again on his special status. "In your mind every crime belongs to the police, but there are times when an apparent crime is a personal affront and it isn't very satisfying not to take care of it yourself" (II:96). Spillane combines Hammer's loner status with Red Scare ideology and masculinity. When Chambers raises the American principles of toleration and free speech, Hammer counters with the consistent imagery that the nation "is getting soft. They push us all around the block and we let them get away with it" (II:98).

Max Allan Collins notes that Spillane hit a "seeming dry spell from 1952 to 1961" and points to several factors for it: his conversion to the

Jehovah's Witnesses; working in Hollywood, portraying his protagonist, Hammer; and even working in the Clyde Beatty Circus (III:xi–xii). Collins is not far off the mark when he characterizes the chastened Hammer as "weak and uncertain" (III:xiii), but whatever the reason, the first Hammer novel after this hiatus, *The Girl Hunters*, published in 1961, signals a more nuanced treatment of Hammer as a rugged individualist. As the novel opens, Hammer is pulled out of the gutter by two policemen, suffering from the effects of a long-term bender during a period that roughly coincides with the absence of Hammer from bookstores. He's convinced that Velda was killed while working on a dangerous assignment for him seven years earlier and hasn't worked since. Pat Chambers needs Hammer to interrogate a dying man and is otherwise hostile to the private investigator since he was also in love with Hammer's secretary and blames him for her demise. Chambers remains suspicious of Hammer's every move. When a night watchman in Hammer's office building is killed, Chambers guesses, correctly, that Hammer knows more than he's admitting. The dying man questioned by Hammer, Richie Cole, is an undercover FBI agent who tells the PI that Velda is still alive but that he will have to find her soon, before she is killed by enemy agents.

To a large extent, Cole's superior officer, Art Rickerby, replaces Chambers as the duly constituted authority in the novel. The two develop a relationship similar to that which the reader is accustomed: a wary cooperation, punctuated by antagonism brought on by Hammer's antiauthoritarianism. When Hammer asks Rickerby to identify the Dragon, the only enemy name Cole gave him, Rickerby is taken aback, knowing that Hammer shouldn't know anything about a deadly, two-man "execution team" of Communist spies by that name (III:92).

The relationship is based on give-and-take, and Rickerby grants Hammer crucial FBI status that will allow him to legally carry a gun. A similar exchange occurs soon afterward with Chambers: Hammer trades what he learned in Cole's Brooklyn apartment for confirmation that Velda had worked as a spy with Cole during the war. The Hammer-Rickerby duo, however, proves more significant than Hammer-Chambers, and this is underscored by the strong resemblance between the two men. Rickerby tells Hammer, "whatever your motives are, they aren't mine, but they

One. Rugged Individualism in Daly and Spillane

encompass what I want and that's enough for me. Sooner or later you're going to name Richie's killer and that's all I want. In the meantime rather than interfere with your operation, I'll do everything I can to supplement it" (III:116). He thus collapses the difference between duly constituted authority and the lone avenger. The latter dominates, at first. Rickerby is one of Spillane's most intriguing characters by virtue of his inscrutability. Rickerby's avowed interest, stated at his first encounter with Hammer, is personal: to avenge Cole's murder. "I'll go to any extremes to catch the one who did it," he states, and gets Hammer to promise not to kill the Dragon when he finds him (31). Indeed, Rickerby is, if anything, more obsessed with revenge than Hammer. He's "deadly," catlike, someone "who will stop at nothing at all" (III:31).

Rickerby initially revives Hammer's attitude towards jury trials, seen in *My Gun Is Quick*. "A quick kill would be too good, Mike," says Rickerby (III:116), but he upholds the results of the legal system as appropriate punishment: long incarceration that forces the criminal to think about his crime and eventual electrocution are the FBI man's idea of torture.

When all is said and done, Hammer takes back the role of avenger and is determined to go it alone, regardless of the odds. As his friend and ally Hy Gardner puts it, "You're trying to stand off a whole political scheme that comes at you with every force imaginable no matter where you are. Mike, you don't fight these guys alone!" (III:145). But, of course, he does. At the climax of the novel, Hammer finally catches up to the Dragon, who has been one step ahead of him throughout. In its imagery their encounter harks back to Carroll's *Snarl of the Beast*; Hammer pledges to the reader that if the Dragon and the "Commie" forces he represents have succeeded in killing Velda he will carry out vengeance that outdoes anything in all previous novels combined:

> They didn't know how to be *really* violent.... I'd get them, every one, no matter how big or little.... I'd cut them down like so many gapes in ways that would scare the living crap out of them and those next in line for my kill would never know a second's peace until their heads went flying every which way [III:156].

Once Hammer detects the Dragon in the house of an old comrade of Richie Cole, he has to suppress laughing out loud and merely smiles in his sadism and superiority. Since "death is [his] business," he draws on his "animal instinct" to know exactly where the enemy upstairs is. The Dragon is "huge and Indianlike" and equally as inhuman as the private eye in his grin (III:159). He too is catlike and their fight quickly becomes hand to hand, with the Dragon's arms "like great claws" and he a "wild beast" fighting for survival. Hammer proves the successful animal, subduing the Dragon and, honoring his agreement with Rickerby, nailing him to the floor, still alive to face Rickerby's wrath.

The Snake (1964) picks up exactly where *The Girl Hunters* leaves off, as Hammer locates Velda, but immediately is embroiled in an attempt to kill Sue Devon, whom Velda is protecting. Chambers and Rickerby soon appear and Hammer takes the opportunity to assert his independence from the latter, since he has hidden both Sue and Velda, whom Rickerby needs to interview. All clues lead the detective back 30 years to an armored car robbery led by one Sonny Motley. Sue Devon has run away from home, fearing her step father, Sim Torrence, whom she blames for her mother's death many years before. Torrence is a former district attorney, now running for governor, and Hammer rightly surmises that Torrence is the ultimate target, a potential victim of a criminal he successfully prosecuted who now wants revenge.

Having just reconciled with Hammer, Pat Chambers resumes his original position as competitive partner with Hammer. As if to counterbalance Chambers' status, Spillane introduces two new characters, Inspector Grebb, who takes an immediate dislike to Hammer, and District Attorney Charles Force, ambitious and "on the way up" (III:247). When both men press him on the point of not immediately reporting two attacks on his life, Hammer uses the excuse that he's operating in a federal capacity that places him above their jurisdiction, but he fundamentally reiterates his autonomy even beyond the way he always has with Chambers. He threatens Force, telling him, "You'd be surprised what kind of stink I can raise if I want to," then agrees when Force asks him if that's a threat (III:248). Both leave with a tacit understanding that Hammer, though independent, will cooperate inasmuch as he'll keep them posted (III:249). The private eye is absolutely forthright with Chambers, however, and expects Chambers to "get a killer off my back" (III:250). Chambers solidifies his newly regained connection to Hammer, supplying the private

One. Rugged Individualism in Daly and Spillane

eye with research into which released cons prosecuted by Torrence are still at large.

If there is a jarring effect upon reading *The Twisted Thing* after *The Snake*, the order in which they were published, it is likely due to the fact that the former is really *For Whom the Gods Would Destroy*, a manuscript from 1948 that Spillane submitted to his publisher as his later contractual deadline neared (III:xvi). Quite unlike any of the other Hammer novels, the book contains substantial elements of British-style detective fiction. The Christie-like gathering of usual suspects takes place in a country manor, this time in upstate New York, where a rich, brilliant scientist, Rudolph York, has raised a 14-year-old genius son, Ruston, whom Hammer initially rescues from kidnappers. Combining hard-boiled violence with aristocratic family dynamics results in something akin to S. S. Van Dine, notably in his Upper Manhattan–set *The Dragon Murder Case*.

For our purposes, however, power dynamics are very much hard-boiled as Spillane focuses on private eye/cop relationships. Hammer makes his connection to the Yorks when he frees Billy Parks, a rehabilitating ex-con who is the Yorks' chauffeur, from the sadistic clutches of Dilwick, chief of police of Sidon, NY. Hammer defends and protects the much smaller and weaker man. The officer's corruption is documented by York's having offered him a $10,000 reward for the return of his missing son, a bribe this corrupt officer is eager to accept.

Hammer interprets York's bribe as elitist naiveté and gladly accepts the $10,000 as his own retainer. York then awkwardly asks Hammer how good he is at his job, which provides the detective the opportunity to expand on his individualistic philosophy: "I hate the bastards that make society a thing to be laughed at and preyed upon. I hate them so much I can kill without the slightest compunction.... When I kill I make it legal. The courts accuse me of being too quick on the trigger but they can't revoke my license because I do it right" (III:348) This is a return to classic Spillane ideology. Hammer's decisions are based on his personal feelings, which are valued far higher than societal standards. He is also utterly confident in his professionalism and chances for success.

Reminiscent of bad cop Nulty and good cop Randall in Chandler's *Farewell, My Lovely*, Spillane provides an antagonist to Dilwick in Sergeant

Price of the New York State Police. Price admires Hammer and wrests jurisdiction from an incensed Dilwick, explaining to Hammer that "the people of Sidon petitioned the state to assist in all police matters when the town in general and the county in particular was being used as a rendezvous and sporting place by a lot of out-of-state gamblers and crooks," further implicating Dilwick in corruption. Price asks Hammer, "will I be able to expect some cooperation from you?" True to form, Hammer stipulates one condition, that of his ultimate autonomy: if "immediate action" is needed, he'll proceed on his own (III:391). Price agrees, but stipulates that he's making Hammer an exception to the rule since he's familiar with the private eye's work.

Hammer cooperates with Price, pointing out the spot where he left his fingerprints and acceding to a request to provide a fresh set of fingerprint impressions. The fact that prints are requested underscores Price's professionalism and the officer works thoroughly and meticulously. Just as Hammer solves the kidnapping, his employer, York, is murdered and he immediately notifies Price. Price proves to be the physical and intellectual equal of the PI: his handshake is "bone crushing" (III:388) and he is able to poke holes in Hammer's flimsy logic when the latter posits that York's missing lab assistant was murdered by the same hand as York himself.

Hammer once briefly returns to New York City and links up with Pat Chambers, who, he reminds the reader, is "a careful, crafty cop" with "a talent for police work backed up by the finest department in the world" and with whom he shares "mutual respect" (III:450). Together they investigate evidence that Ruston York may not be York's natural son, but a baby who was deliberately switched, prompting his real father, Herron Mallory, to kidnap Ruston 14 years later. Hammer and Chambers then together research Mallory's police record. Hammer returns to Sidon after Chambers offers his continued help even though the case is out of his jurisdiction. Back in Sidon, Price finds himself in the position of refereeing a fight between Hammer and Dilwick, since the latter is determined to arrest the former for all crimes. After the situation has been defused, Hammer shares his New York City information with Price, whom he finds is "a lot like Pat" (III:460).

One. Rugged Individualism in Daly and Spillane

The Mike Hammer novels of the 1960s reflect the ideology of the era. Spillane had, in his first phase, dealt with more than just local crime issues, especially where Red Scare politics played a role, but urban crime was predominant. In this new phase Art Rickerby personifies a CIA–like "higher power" and coincidentally problematizes the revenge motif, proving as vengeful as the private eye. At the same time Rickerby substitutes for Pat Chambers, Hammer's uneasy ally in the first novels, and the result is an incremental improvement in the private eye–police relationship, cooperation that is augmented by the reconciliation between Hammer and Chambers. Especially in *The Twisted Thing*, Spillane draws on good cop–bad cop dynamics established by Chandler.

Ultimately, however, there is little adjustment to Hammer's autonomy. The deals the detective makes with law enforcement are based not on any inherent change in his character, but on the pliability of those public officers. Hammer still has no sense of self-criticism and displays the knee-jerk violent reaction to anyone who challenges his authority. He remains, like Daly's Race Williams, the dispenser of frontier justice, accountable to no one but himself.

CHAPTER TWO

Dashiell Hammett: Individualism in Transition

Carroll John Daly's and Mickey Spillane's protagonists represent the classic rugged individualist as hard-boiled detective. Vicious, self-righteous, and unreflective, they embody extremes of egotism and display barely any sense of cooperation. The work of Dashiell Hammett, however, is far more complex. Although he wrote only five novels, one of which, *The Glass Key*, is not an example of detective fiction, Hammett varied his treatment of individual and society from *Red Harvest* to *The Thin Man*.

Raymond Chandler famously recognized Hammett as the iconic hard-boiled writer in "The Simple Art of Murder"; the key factor for him is Hammett's unflinching realism. In contrast to what Chandler saw as the thoroughly artificial golden age tradition, Hammett

> wrote ... for people with a sharp, aggressive attitude to life. They were not afraid of the seamy side of things; they lived there.... Hammett gave murder back to the kind of people that commit it for reasons, not just to provide a corpse.... He put these people down on paper as they are, and he made them talk and think in the language that they customarily used for these purposes [*Later Novels* 989].

Hammett was the first pulp writer to give depth to his characters, but the realism of his stories wears thin in many places. Plots are sometimes contrived and his detective, though flawed, does not always act within reasonable circumstances. A former Pinkerton detective, one of the rare hard-boiled writers with direct experience in detection, Hammett began writing stories in pulps like *Black Mask*. His protagonist, a nameless agent of the Continental Detective Agency, modeled on Pinkerton, is known simply as the Continental Op. A more fully drawn, realistic figure, one whom Hammett stresses is short, fat, and not inordinately strong, the Op nonetheless shares the brutal infallibility of Race Williams and Hammett underscores this quality by making him face overwhelming odds, no doubt in part to attract and keep the average pulp reader.

In "The Gutting of Couffignal" the Op is initially engaged merely to guard wedding presents in a rich island community. Explosions and gunfire in the night motivate the Op to investigate multiple robberies and killings by which what appears to be a large gang is "gutting" the town. The detective quickly realizes that the entire operation is composed of Russian émigrés living on Couffignal. Their amateurishness — they try to manipulate the detective instead of ignoring or killing him — is their downfall. The Op, typically, is prescient. Most stories end with a wrap-up, in which the detective explains how he solved the case to his boss or some other interested party; in this case, he lists 12 extensive points in his solution. It is in retrospect that we learn that he knew who was guilty almost from the very beginning.

"The Big Knockover" increases the odds against the lone hero tremendously. A criminal mastermind assembles gangsters from all over the country — the Op estimates that "there were a hundred and fifty crooks in the push if there was one" (330) — to rob two banks in downtown San Francisco. Casualties, as the Op tells his boss, the Old Man, run far beyond anything that might have appeared on the front pages of the tabloids: "Sixteen coppers were knocked off, and three times that many wounded. Twelve innocent spectators, bank clerks and the like, were killed and about as many banged around" (331). The military scale of the operation is a stylistic step backwards in terms of verisimilitude, yet something that Hammett would exploit in his first novel.

While the spoils of the robbery are being divided, the mastermind sets factions of crooks against each other, eliminating many of them and leaving all the money to the chosen few. In a key scene the Op invades a gangsters' lair just as one faction is about to eliminate another. He extricates one hoodlum whom he feels is most valuable to him, fighting off "millions of them" as he battles, "blackjack in right hand, gun in left" (353–54), a triumphant hero who relies only on himself.

Hammett laid the groundwork for both the Western setting and the Op's manipulation of others in his story "The Golden Horseshoe," set primarily in hot, sun-drenched Tijuana, replete with barroom brawls and shootouts. Originally hired by a lawyer to find a missing husband, the Op encounters far more. The criminals he has to deal with are superficially united but before long the detective is able to exploit their differences. Knowing that he lacks sufficient evidence to convict them, his tactic is to convince them to flee: "I didn't care where they went or what they did, so long as they scooted. I'd trust to luck and my own head to get a profit out of their scrambling—I was still trying to stir things up" (81).

"Corkscrew" is another strongly Western-flavored story. Hired by land developers to pacify an unruly Arizona area, the Op pretends to be the new deputy sheriff. While he functions effectively as such, enforcing a no-gun ordinance in the town of Corkscrew, his truly effective method of reestablishing order is manipulating a ranch owner and his cowboys to wage war with the forces of another ranch owner and, in the words of one townsman, "encouraging each side to eat up the other and save you the trouble of making any strong play of your own" (257).

Published in 1929, *Red Harvest*, Hammett's first novel, is his most ruggedly individualistic. Carrying over from some of Hammett's short stories published in the pulps, the protagonist-detective, the unnamed Continental Op, acts much like Race Williams and Mike Hammer: he is utterly self-reliant and insists on a personal sense of order and justice. The irony here is that the Op is ostensibly a team member, an employee of the Continental Detective Agency and not a private eye in the classic sense whose activities would be less restricted. Steven Marcus underscores the significance of the Op's employee status as a barrier to corruption; since the Continental forbids its agent "to directly enrich himself through his professional skills, he is saved from at least the characteristic corruption of modern society" (206).

This is, however, to place too much importance on money. Bribery, or more broadly, money, is of no real consequence in the novel, even to the criminal gangs that battle each other. Their conflict is about power and power is defined as brute force. The Op's individualism is expressed in his manipulation of such force and insistence on operating alone to destroy the gangs. The setting of the novel is a Western mining town, which underscores the roots of the genre: the frontier motif, here closer

Two. Dashiell Hammett: Individulism in Transition

to the range war model than that of the gunfighter, is even more pronounced than in Daly or Spillane.

Christopher Metress has argued for considering Dashiell Hammett — in contrast to Chandler, Spillane, and Ross Macdonald — as the hard-boiled writer who succeeded in creating heroes who are more communally oriented and less individualistic. His evidence, however, is less than convincing when he claims that the Continental Op in *Red Harvest* seeks "not self-assertion but loyalty to interests beyond his own" when he accepts a $10,000 retainer explicitly for his detective agency and not for himself (248), thus illustrating selflessness and cooperation. While Metress claims that the Op's actions are "fused momentarily to the reformative desires of a social agency," the only agency the reader can discern is the Continental, a thinly veiled representation of the Pinkerton National Detective Agency Hammett had worked for; thus Metress seems to use a rather literal sense of "agency." This is no social agency at all, merely the loyalty of an employee to his company. Complicating matters further, the historical record provides little evidence of any spirit of social reform in this organization. Founder Alan Pinkerton failed miserably in his efforts to establish an intelligence service during the Civil War, but had great success in the late 19th century in strikebreaking, planting agents provocateurs among union members, a decidedly illiberal model for the Op's agency as viewed by Metress.

The influence of the Pinkerton Agency on hard-boiled fiction is substantial. Christopher T. Raczkowski points out Pinkerton's influence as an author in addition to his role as head of the agency: "Pinkerton was both the author of the first systematic, nation-wide surveillance network in America and the author of seventeen memoirs narrating that surveillance whose popular success did much to inspire a dime detective novel industry that mushroomed in the second half of the century" (632). Specifically, *Red Harvest* draws from Pinkerton a spirit of extralegal vigilantism. Though not always successful, Pinkerton agents functioned essentially as hired guns for mine owners and ranchers, intimidating, even killing, small independent ranchers, cowboys, and (often unionized) miners. The agency was founded in the pre–Civil War period, before most cities had police forces and long before the Federal Bureau of Investigation was created. "Pinkerton's agents had no jurisdictional restrictions, were able to give testimony in court, and were subject only to the agency's supervision" (Raczkowski 633). In essence, the agency was an institution organized to enforce, free of oversight, not the law as publicly established, but the interests of private citizens and corporations. This is no more than efficiently organized vigilantism. As seen in Chapter Two, the type of detective that works for the Continental is in an outlaw tradition that prioritizes private gain or revenge.

In *Red Harvest* bootleggers, gamblers, police, business leaders, lawyers, and the Continental Op himself are involved in mutual alliances, defections, betrayals, all motivated by greed and lust for power. Fomenting warfare among these groups as he "stirred up" rival factions in the short stories, the Op is infected by the local fever, overcome by the naturalistic state that Hammett calls being "blood simple," (104) in which acts of violence are accounted for in terms of primal and violent instincts. In this light it is easy to concur with Slotkin when he links Western fiction with that of Pinkerton: "Daly's stories and Hammett's early work stay within the ideological boundaries of the 'vigilante' Western and the Pinkerton detective tale" (223).

It is against this background that the Op arrives in the corrupt, chaotic mining town of Personville (sardonically dubbed Poisonville by its inhabitants) at the behest of Donald Willsson, publisher of the local newspapers and an incipient reformer. Willsson, however, is murdered before the Op even has a chance to meet him. The dead man's father, Elihu Willsson, fills the void. He is the most powerful man in town and anything but a reformer and has himself precipitated the crisis. In the past he had hired strikebreakers to oppose a strike of the Industrial Workers of the World, commonly known as Wobblies, against his mine. After the strike is broken, however, Elihu Willsson finds his power challenged by the very forces he originally hired. Impressed by the Op's talents, he becomes the Continental's new client and reveals his proprietary privilege by asking the detective to "clean this pig-sty of Poisonville for me" (29), as if the town were literally his property. The Op stresses to his new employer the fact that that he represents the agency, but his loyalty is more complex than Metress implies; he does so in a manner that blurs the boundary between the two: "When I say *me* I mean the Continental." He is at least as much an individual as a team player. In addition, he immediately demands that he's granted "authority to go through with it in [his] own way" (30), placing personal power above that of the organization.

The collective action one might suspect from one agent among many in a detective agency is severely limited in *Red Harvest*. Sent by the main office in San Francisco, Continental operatives Dick Foley and Mickey Linehan appear in Poisonville after the initial bloodletting to assist the Op, but only because the situation is too complex and wide-ranging for one man to handle. The Op assigns them minor tasks and keeps them in the dark as to his intentions. When Linehan reminds the Op of his neglect of duties since he fails to report back to the Old Man, their boss in San Francisco, the Op refuses to back down from his independent course of action:

> It's right enough for the Agency to have rules and regulations, but when you're out on a job you've got to do it the best way you can. And anybody that brings any ethics to Poisonville is going to get them all rusty. A report is no place for the dirty details, anyway, and I don't want you birds to send any writing back to San Francisco without letting me see it first [78].

Leroy Lad Panek recognizes the extent of the Op's autonomy in his dealings with fellow operatives: "The Op consistently treats the other Continental employees as subordinates, ordering them around, and, in fact, usually condescending to them" (150). There is a near-obsessive quality to the Op's need for absolute control and insistence that he alone knows what to do. Robert I. Edenbaum likens the Op's control to that of Hammett as writer: noting the detective's use of the word "experiment" in describing his work in Poisonville, he maintains that "[t]he Op's metaphor makes him the same kind of godlike manipulator the naturalist novelist himself becomes in his experiments with the forces that move human beings to destruction" (110–11). The Op is a manipulator par excellence; there is no one who escapes his assertion of self.

In the introduction to *The Continental Op* collection of short stories, Steven Marcus defines the Op in far too passive a manner. Maintaining that "the Op almost invariably walks into a situation that has already been elaborately fabricated or framed" (xx), Marcus finds the Op deconstructing "the fictional — and therefore false — reality created by the characters, crooks or not, with whom he is involved" (xxi). Marcus appears to read Hammett as he would a postmodern writer conscious of deconstructing the mystery genre. While perpetrators do their best to hide their guilt (and one may call this creating fictions), the crimes the Op investigates are not fictional within the context of the narratives. He doesn't merely expose fabrications, but actively pursues criminals, often using violence as he does so.

As in Daly's fiction, the police are portrayed as foils for the protagonist, but in Hammett's bleak urban landscape the police are more corrupt than incompetent. Chief of Police Noonan is a jovial backslapper who initially compliments the Op's perceptiveness and encourages his speculations (much in the manner of good cops in Chandler) but who is an ally of Lew Yard, a bail bondsman, a fence, and a gang leader. What appears to be a legitimate police murder investigation is soon revealed as a personal vendetta: Noonan is framing Max "Whisper" Thaler for the deed because the gangster is in league with his enemies.

At no point do the police act in an even vaguely ethical manner; vigilante justice in service of the powerful is the rule. Echoing Race Williams' support of Milly's use of deadly force in self defense in *The Snarl of the Beast*, when Elihu Willsson shoots an intruder to death he is vigorously complimented by Noonan: "If everybody did that to their prowlers, it would certainly be fine" (31). Shortly after, claiming to want to give his enemy a chance to surrender, Noonan empowers the Op to negotiate, only to begin shooting while the detective is in the line of fire. Having deduced Noonan's plan, the Op assures Thaler that the Chief has no intention of letting him live long enough to face a jury, and Hammett underscores the pervasiveness of police corruption inasmuch as it is they who help the criminals escape in broad daylight.

Going far beyond his client's instructions, the Op is avowedly out to incite the powers of Personville to eliminate each other, promising to open "Poisonville up from Adam's apple to ankles" (43). His cynicism is underscored by the fact that he spares only his client, Willsson. No real reform is posited, and since the Op is convinced that Willsson will "re-corrupt" the city, no sign of civic improvement is presented. Foreshadowing the kind of paranoid vigilantism and mistrust of democratic institutions

Two. Dashiell Hammett: Individulism in Transition

Mickey Spillane would later exploit and popularize, the Op tells his assistants, "there's no use taking anybody into court.... They own the courts, and, besides, the courts are too slow for us now" (79). He appropriates Willsson's absolute power as absolutely as any 17th-century French monarch.

Even if we provisionally accept Christopher Bentley's view that the Op only feigns taking sides in the gangland war — requesting and receiving, for example, phony alibis from criminals in order to veil his own questionable actions (153) — and that "the Op is as incorruptible as Robespierre" (63), there is still no indication that his actions are in any way meant to serve anyone but himself. Characterizing the Op's actions as "extreme individualism," J. A. Zumoff correctly stresses that "the Op is engaged in a war against the entire world, and trusts nobody but himself" (7). Sean McCann takes a similar position when he says that "even by the undemanding moral terms of vigilante justice, the Op's campaign has degenerated into a pathological search for personal gratification" (80). At best he works out of a blinkered sense of professionalism and company loyalty and, at worst, out of bloodlust worse than that of his enemies. In either case the ethos of rugged individualism accounts for his actions. Thomas Heise underscores the catalytic nature of the detective's sense of self; the Op is the consummate provocateur: "Though by no means idyllic, Hammett's grimy Personville was apparently a relatively peaceful city until the Op makes his entrance. Only when he arrives does the killing begin in earnest" (491). Pinkerton methods are thus wedded to a hyperindividualistic philosophy.

The Continental Op of *Red Harvest* is a quintessential figure of rugged individualism, an unreflective professional, a man of action unconcerned with the legitimacy of his role or the repercussions of his acts. The reader may develop respect for the achievements of the exceptional individual, but the position of that individual is exceptional in self-absorbed, elitist ways.

In *The Dain Curse* (1929) we find a somewhat different set of circumstances, especially regarding the police, although the Continental Op is still always far more capable than the police with whom he deals. In some of the short stories featuring the Op, the detective displays a willingness, even an eagerness, to cooperate with the police. In "The Tenth Clew" the Op works with Detective Sergeant O'Gar of the San Francisco Police Department and states, "He and I had worked on two or three jobs together before, and hit it off excellently" (5). While the two work cooperatively on this case, it is the Op's realization that all the clues they have gathered are red herrings left by the perpetrator to distract their attention. In "The Main Death" the Op works with detectives Hacken and Begg because the police are the first on the scene of a murder and the Continental Agency has been hired to recoup $20,000 that had been in the possession of the murder victim. Here too, although both private and public detectives work cooperatively, it is solely the Op who, trusting his ability to judge character, discovers that there has been no murder, that the victim committed suicide.

But in *The Dain Curse* the previous atmosphere of cooperation is not present, even if we again find O'Gar in the narrative. In the first two sections of the novel, San Francisco police detectives O'Gar and Reddy merely represent, in passing, the forces of officialdom and contribute nothing to the investigation of a jewel robbery that turns out to be fake and a murder that is all too real. The agency having initially been called in by the jeweler's insurance company, the Op dominates the action as more murders are committed in connection with a spiritualist scam. We discover caught in its web Gabrielle Leggett, the daughter of the first victim, who is convinced she has inherited the family curse of the title since all those close to her are killed.

Not until the Op travels to rural Quesada does he interact significantly with local law enforcement officers, both sheriff and marshal, but these men, and indeed the district attorney, are also — compared to Chandler's police — relatively weak foils for the private eye. They provide some additional information to that which the Op has gleaned in San Francisco, but their primary function is to be wrong; they are quick to assume the most superficial and convenient answers to the murders that have occurred.

One motif of this novel that Chandler would later develop in his characterization of Lieutenant Nulty in *Farewell, My Lovely* is that of public officials succumbing to ambition at the cost of productive police work. A San Francisco reporter tells the Op that the sheriff, marshal, and district

Two. Dashiell Hammett: Individulism in Transition

attorney are expending their energies in seeing "which can get his name and picture printed most" and have done nothing by way of the investigation since "[t]hey spend ten hours a day trying to make the front page, ten more trying to keep the others from making it, and they've got to sleep some time" (236). The fact that the police are most active when fighting amongst themselves is also exploited for comic purposes. In the spirit of Sherlock Holmes' humorous denigration of Scotland Yard, the police are incompetents who create far more problems than they solve: Marshal Cotton, for example, is portrayed as a jealous husband trying to frame his wife's lover for murder (240). Throughout, the police are relegated to mere background and the divisions amongst them are so great that only outlandish plot twists allow the crime to be solved at all. It is the Op and the Op alone who triumphs.

In "The Writer as Detective Hero," Ross Macdonald, often cited as Chandler's first and foremost successor in the genre, sees the tough-guy detective as a "classless, restless man of American democracy" (qtd. in Nevins 298–99). Macdonald correctly sees that Sam Spade, for example, "knew the corrupt inner workings of American cities" (299). He credits Spade with having the courage and cunning necessary to survive and succeed in the modern American mean streets. He also recognizes the inheritance of the Western hero since Spade "possesses the virtues and follows the code of the frontier male" (299). But while Macdonald recognizes virtues, he all too conveniently overlooks vices in his analysis. From our perspective, by linking Spade to the Western gunslinger, he admits to the ruggedly individualistic, even antidemocratic, identity of this hero, an identity that links Hammett's hero to that of Daly.

Metress sees this differently, at least in the context of *The Maltese Falcon*. He views Sam Spade's sacrifice of Brigid O'Shaughnessy to the authorities in the novel as an adjustment on the part of a rugged individualist to a "collective code" in the service of a "collective good" (254), emphasizing that Spade hands over to the police the woman he ostensibly loves as an act of self-denial required by those who wish to serve a greater good (255). Metress's evidence, however, is quite thin: Spade's actions are as lacking in communal amelioration as they are bereft of communally oriented negotiation. Spade has been suspicious of O'Shaughnessy and her many aliases from the very beginning and is himself deeply implicated in wrongdoing; the police suspect him of murdering gangster Floyd Thursby and Spade's partner, Miles Archer, and, while he is innocent of these crimes, his chief motivation is self-centered: to save himself from prosecution. William Ruehlmann is right to label Spade as a "counterfeit hero, just as every other primary character is a false front for something else" (74).

Richard Slotkin finds that Hammett's later novels display qualities illustrated far more in Raymond Chandler's novels, based on

> the implication of Hammett's vision of the detective as a moral free agent, an outlaw for the sake of a higher law, a man disillusioned enough to survive in a modern world but still capable of believing in and acting on a traditional concept of honor [228].

Yet, it is in these later novels, *The Maltese Falcon* and *The Thin Man*, that we find moral agency less free, at least in the sense that the protagonist cedes some independence, than in the earlier novels: the protagonist is more willing to cooperate with those around him.

After *The Dain Curse* Hammett jettisoned the agency detective and turned to the independent private eye, Sam Spade. Paradoxically, it is the more explicitly autonomous detective who engages in more cooperative action than the Continental Op ever did, and as part of this transition, the private eye needs to be instructed in how to cooperate. The key is that Hammett incorporates more sympathetic treatment of the police in *The Maltese Falcon* than in previous novels. In this novel Detective Sergeant Tom Polhaus is portrayed as a good cop who tries to keep the peace between his superior officer, Lieutenant Dundy (whom he respects), and Sam Spade (who is his friend) as these detectives question Spade in connection with a murder only hours old. There is, however, no real interaction, or indeed, cooperation, as concerns solving the case. Hammett focuses on Spade's negotiations with Brigid O'Shaughnessy, Caspar Gutman, and Joel Cairo, criminals in search of the fabled falcon, and his constant bargaining with them underscores his own self-centered motivation. Hammett's emphasis is so overwhelmingly on the private eye that the hero struggles solely against broadly conceived, universal forces of evil or indifference, not contingent human forces as represented by the police.

Some scenes, however, anticipate the police/private eye contrasts in

Two. Dashiell Hammett: Individulism in Transition

Chandler. Questioned by Polhaus and Dundy about his activities the night his partner, Miles Archer, died, Spade is caught in a lie when he claims to have notified Archer's widow (305). As the police continue their questioning, now more suspicious than before since they know this to be false (and alone in the knowledge that a second man, Floyd Thursby, has been murdered), Spade's initial reaction is anger: he is unable to reason with men who, the reader must recognize, forego the expected third-degree methods and are using legitimate, even respectful, means in conducting an investigation of a serious crime. Although Spade eventually apologizes, it is Dundy who displays greater fairness, showing sympathy for a possible revenge motive on Spade's part and promising Spade a "square deal" no matter what happens (309).

Later, Polhaus revives his mediation efforts and manages to get Spade to admit that he would have used the same methods as Dundy in running down all possible leads. In doing so he underscores similarities between official and unofficial law enforcement, but Hammett has no fundamental interest in this issue and keeps it in the background. In response he has Spade proudly emphasize the fact that the police have only *tried* to pump him for information, which redounds to Spade's self-assurance and isolation, but not to his willingness to cooperate (389). The first murder of the novel is that of Miles Archer, and it's the police who find the body and notify Spade. Were Spade concerned with solving his partner's murder, it would be logical to cooperate with the police, but he displays little sympathy for Archer and his intention is to cash in on the falcon, and to do this he must deflect police interference. Thus it is Polhaus who has assumed the negotiator role that Philip Marlowe, the private eye, later incorporates, and the ethical core of the novel is occupied not by the private eye, but by a minor character.

And yet the police have briefly forced upon Spade a spirit of cooperation, and this proves to be significant at the end of the novel. Spade notifies the police of Gutman and Cairo's escape and hands O'Shaughnessy over to them for Archer's murder. The focus remains on Spade; he has done all the work. He also recognizes the need to work with the police, if only to protect himself.

The detective in *The Thin Man*, Nick Charles, however, goes Spade one better in terms of cooperative action. Clearly different in tone, with comic elements, and closer to the whodunit tradition of detective fiction than that of the hard-boiled hero, *The Thin Man* displays greater reflection on the part of its hero and a greater willingness to interact with other characters, notably the police. Charles is introduced to the reader as a former detective who has given up the profession in order to manage the business his wife, Nora, has inherited. Visiting New York from San Francisco, the couple encounters members of the Wynant family. Clyde Wynant, the eponymous "thin man," is an inventor for whom Charles once worked and who, at this juncture, has gone missing. Soon after, Julia Wolf, Wynant's secretary, is murdered and Charles is reluctantly drawn into the search for Wynant and into the murder investigation.

In reference to Hammett's work before the publication of *The Maltese Falcon*, Leroy Lad Panek interprets that Hammett believed that "in spite of some inadequacies, the police of the United States and in Britain have developed practical methodologies and do an admirable job of crime detection" (65). In the novels as a whole, Hammett began to incorporate a serious respect for the police in *The Maltese Falcon* and developed it further in *The Thin Man*. In *The Thin Man* one policeman, Flint, is of the Keystone Kops variety. Tasked with tailing Wynant's son, Gilbert, he proves too dense to actually catch him doing anything of interest when he has the chance, roughing Gilbert up in the process. He is a minor character held up to comic scrutiny, but, in contrast, Nick Charles, the detective and first-person narrator, works closely with John Guild, the police officer in charge of the investigation of a murder. The choice of the name Guild itself is indicative of a collective, and although the language he speaks reflects coming up from the ranks, echoing Flint, he is sensitive to Charles' subtleties and, indeed, sensitivity. In the figure of Guild, police are portrayed as competent and ethical, and he and Charles conduct what amounts to a joint investigation.

Appreciating the officially retired detective's skills and precluding any chance that Charles might work against him, Guild urges Charles to help with the case (623). From this point on the two brainstorm about the often bewildering clues and eccentric behavior that come their way. Charles is an acquaintance of the Wynant family and can thus provide insights,

Two. Dashiell Hammett: Individulism in Transition

but this is not of primary value: it is more the intelligence and experience of the seasoned private eye that attract Guild. Guild, in turn, provides the kind of information a police force easily finds, such as the fact that Julia Wolf was an alias and that she had a police record, implicating her in Wynant's disappearance. The policeman suspects Clyde Wynant of Wolf's murder, but Charles is skeptical. Guild asks:

"Don't you think Wynant done it?"
I gave him the same odds I had given [speakeasy proprietor] Studsy: "Twenty-five'll get you fifty he didn't.... I'm not saying Wynant didn't do it. I'm just saying everything doesn't point to him."
"And saying it two to one. What don't point at him?"
"Call it a hunch, if you want," I said, "but—"
"I don't want to call it anything," he said. "I think you're a smart detective. I want to listen to what you got to say" [646].

As the narrative continues and another murder is committed — that of Louis Nunheim, a police informer — Charles and Guild continue their partnership. The police detective confirms that the same gun was used in both murders and Charles informs Guild that he saw the victim's girlfriend at a speakeasy and that she was once known under yet another name, Nancy Kane (684). At this stage in the investigation, there is a rough internal/external division of labor between the detectives, Charles focusing on the Wynant family and Guild handling such evidence as the lack of shell casings at the crime scene (685). The two subsequently compare notes. There is a threat to cooperation when, still later, Charles is told by Herbert Macaulay, Clyde Wynant's lawyer, that Guild suspects the detective of having been in possession of a key piece of evidence and that Guild had asked him if Charles and Julia Wolf were "still playing around together" (693), a suspicion raised by Clyde Wynant's scheming, unstable former wife. The effect is to disturb Charles' cooperative attitude, as he bridles at the insinuation. The very fact that this give-and-take dynamic exists at all, however, is a step forward. The partnership is not broken off; instead, Charles confronts Guild and Guild counters by insisting that he's just doing his job and that Charles has been less than completely forthcoming himself (701–702).

On first reading, these exchanges have the effect of delaying the actual work of detection, which was, perhaps, part of Hammett's intention, part of his playing with the reader's expectations. We may also read in them, however, the writer's concern for cooperative action. Threatened with rupture, the teamwork is only able to continue after each man has aired his grievances. In a scene reminiscent of Agatha Christie, Charles assembles the likely suspects and exposes Macaulay as the killer and Guild and his subordinates come in handy when they take him away.

Charles shows his willingness to cooperate in another way. Where the Continental Op in *Red Harvest* resists any attempts to work with his fellow agency detectives and Spade keeps his distance from the police, Nick has Nora. Although she plays a less conspicuous role in Hammett's novel than she does in the film version of *The Thin Man* (or, for that matter, several sequels), Nora not only takes interest in her husband's work, but assists him as well. At one point when Nick and Guild are discussing the Julia Wolf murder, Guild turns to Nora and says, "I guess this must be pretty dull to you, Mrs. Charles." "Dull? ... I'm sitting on the edge of my chair" (626). Guild seems infatuated with her and fails to appreciate her interest, but her engagement only increases. She brings intelligence, keen powers of observation, and great inventiveness to the investigation.

Late in the novel, when Charles is struggling to solve two murders and is tired of dealing with the frustrating Wynants, Nora suggests, "Why don't we make a list of all the suspects and all the motives and clues, and check them off against—" "You do it. I'm going to bed. What's a clue, Mamma?" Nora avoids defining that which is obvious and gives relevant examples instead:

> "It's like when Gilbert [Wynant] tiptoed over to the phone tonight when I was alone in the living-room, and he thought I was asleep, and told the operator not to put through any in-coming calls until morning."
> "Well, well."
> "And ... it's like Dorothy [Wynant] discovering that she had Aunt Alice's key all the time" [691].

In contrast to the earnestness of the novels featuring the Continental Op, the tone is clearly humorous, as the experienced detective feigns ignorance of the tools of his trade. But Nora has clearly learned from her husband. She has maintained a critical distance from the Wynants that any detective

Two. Dashiell Hammett: Individulism in Transition

needs; her ploy is clever, skillful, and proves valuable; and she acts as her husband's partner in more than just the marital sense.

Dashiell Hammett's Continental Op, Sam Spade, and Nick Charles were models for Philip Marlowe and most of the subsequent hard-boiled detectives. As we have seen, Hammett subtly developed the character of detective, gradually moving the lone-wolf individualist into a position of greater cooperation and, indeed, responsibility. Yet Hammett's protagonists barely engage in the kind of social interactions that Marlowe experiences. In Hammett's novels, notably *The Maltese Falcon*, private eye/police encounters foreshadow Chandler's later efforts, but Hammett's heroes lack any real sign of commitment to social interaction. It would be left to Chandler to establish the hard-boiled detective as a new individualist, and it is by viewing this character in his role of negotiator that we will best discern his transformation.

Chapter Three

Marlowe as Negotiator

The term "private eye" is derived from the watchful ocular symbol of the Pinkerton National Detective Agency and its "We Never Sleep" motto, and indicates, as far as detective fiction is concerned, unofficial (though not necessarily extralegal) investigation. As its homophone "private I" suggests, the figure of the hard-boiled detective is grounded firmly in the individualist ethos of the United States. As Tony Hilfer succinctly puts it, "His real function is to validate the American myth of personal integrity, absolute individualism, and stoic self-control" (7). Armed with such conviction and power, he is, for some, the quintessential urban hero, fighting the good fight against great odds, exemplifying justice amidst the corrupt and the victimized.

A consistent trait of the hard-boiled detective is that he is a loner, and much literary and cultural criticism has focused on his isolation from mainstream society, an isolation that undercuts his viability as a productive member of that society. In contrast to detectives we have seen who use their loner status to avoid social responsibility, flaunt their superiority, or exploit those weaker than themselves, Raymond Chandler's Philip Marlowe is self-critical as well as socially critical. What he sees as his work goes far beyond the often straightforward tasks imposed by his clients; self-employed and without family ties, he exploits the singular nature of his job to negotiate among contesting groups, ever conscious of the fact that simplistic definitions of "good" and "evil" will hamper his efforts. Travelling back and forth from clients to gangsters, from gangsters to police, and back again, he establishes, and allows the reader to consider, the nature of criminal conflict in the modern urban environment. Since the motives of some clients must be questioned, some policemen accept graft, and some gangsters' actions are not always illegal, Marlowe is careful to distinguish actions of individuals in specific situations, reserving judgment until all the facts are in. His commitment to peacekeeping is profound; indeed, the personal danger the detective finds himself in stems primarily from his efforts to reconcile differences among these groups. In this respect Marlowe represents a key change in the composition of the hard-boiled hero.

Richard Slotkin nevertheless holds to the old paradigm and overemphasizes the Western provenance of the hard-boiled detective as exemplified by Marlowe. He posits, intriguingly, for example, that Chandler's detective, like James Fenimore Cooper's Hawkeye, is first and foremost a "rescuer" of the innocent, that both heroes are "engaged in unmasking hidden truth" (94), but he sidesteps contradictory evidence in Marlowe's construction by ignoring that detective's peacemaking efforts, his special brand of shuttle diplomacy. Instead he switches his focus to fictional avatars of rugged American individualism who better follow the paradigm: Dashiell Hammett's Continental Op and Sam Spade, and Mickey Spillane's Mike Hammer. When looking at these figures through cultural, historical, and ideological lenses, their differences become clearer and contrasts emerge. It also becomes clear that the ethos of the detective as that of the rugged American individualist is generally assumed but rarely interrogated.

Many critics have, admittedly, been more concerned with painting large cultural canvases and with delineating the formal continuity of popular genres in American literary history than with establishing the ideological underpinnings of those genres, but their analysis has too often resulted in a glossing over of the subtleties of just those ideologies. Porter, Knight, Slotkin, Cawelti, and others leave the impression that each hero is an interchangeable piece of the fictional puzzle; they have too often "explained" the hard-boiled hero, for example, in terms of what Sam Spade and Mike Hammer do, and have assumed that Philip Marlowe, or even Lew Archer, follow suit. They fail to recognize that the latter two detectives' actions diverge from the ethos of the autonomous individual by reflecting a greater consciousness of their membership in and responsibility towards the community; for example, they question the ethics of official law enforcers and strive to help suspected criminals under the threat of a callous or corrupt judicial system.

In keeping with his view of Chandler as a liberal writer in his ground-breaking *Adventure, Mystery, and Romance*, John G. Cawelti grants Marlowe elements of a social conscience; he underscores the fact that, in comparison with Mickey Spillane's chauvinistic, red-baiting, polarized depiction of right and wrong, "a more liberal writer like Raymond Chandler ascribes the evil to American materialism and greed" (150). However, Cawelti's critique of Chandler as a progressive goes no further; he sees Marlowe as a frustrated and isolated figure. Because the detective is a "marginal man, a loner," he returns, defeated, to his "dusty office in the broken-down office building — an act analogous to the cowboy hero's departure back into the desert — his unsullied isolation and failure maintain the purity of his stance as a man of honor in a false society" (151).

To characterize Marlowe or other detectives as failures, first of all, is to misread detective fiction: hard-boiled detectives are not, admittedly, economic successes by 20th-century capitalist standards, but Philip Marlowe, Sam Spade, and Mike Hammer succeed in what they themselves deem important, whether it be justice, self-assertion, or revenge, respectively. Cawelti's analogy is flawed in other ways, as well. While Marlowe returns to an apartment where no one else lives, he is hardly one to ride off into the sunset. Marlowe has an office in downtown Hollywood; he is no more isolated from the city that surrounds him than is the average businessman. While Marlowe certainly has his moments of introspection, they are also opportunities for reflection; he never sequesters himself in any urban equivalent of the desert; he remains a more or less average citizen attempting to effect change within his own limited world, no more "pure" than most of the clients, cops, and criminals he encounters. A core problem here has been the failure to examine the ramifications of and divergences from the "loner" status: what does it really mean to say that the detective acts alone, that he distances himself from romantic entanglements (or is downright misogynistic), that he accepts any and all assignments but remains aloof from his clients, that he resents the police trying to exert control over his actions, or that he even defines himself as being above the law and ethically superior to those around him?

Marlowe is a construct deeply rooted in the individualist traditions of his genre and nation who yearns to break out of these imposed strictures, and his profession is uniquely suited to embody the often conflicting

Three. Marlowe as Negotiator

demands of the individual and the community. He does isolate himself to some extent, though it is usually to protect himself and to keep others from harm. His judgment is often shown to be superior to that of the police and district attorney, and he does not always cooperate with these duly constituted authorities. He anticipates, however, the socially conscious role Geoffrey H. Hartman sees exemplified in Ross Macdonald's Lew Archer — the private eye as ombudsman, public defender, and social catalyst (221–22).

The crucial difference between him and other contemporary hard-boiled detectives lies in his recognition of personal civic responsibility and his desire, however indirectly formulated, to reach out to his community in the role of negotiator; and as such Marlowe is able to turn his private status to public advantage. He is fully aware of the legal power wielded by and the resources available to the police and of the intelligence and talent some of them bring to their cases, and he does not even reject, out of hand, the less-than-admirable motivations of corrupt officers. He is equally cognizant that an outright, confrontational attitude towards members of the underworld, such as exemplified by Spillane's Mike Hammer, could only result in a dangerous polarization of antagonistic forces and would place him in jeopardy; without negotiation his efforts can never be successful. In sharp distinction to other hard-boiled detectives, his knowledge of his own limitations teaches him to use force judiciously; a primary touchstone of autonomy in the genre is physical force and there is appreciably less violence in Chandler's novels than in those by Daly, Hammett, and others.

In each novel a typical scene is one in which detective and client discuss the limitations of human nature. In *The Long Goodbye* (1953), for example, Roger Wade's publisher, Howard Spencer, tries to hire the detective as a bodyguard and nursemaid for his alcoholic, intermittently violent client, and Marlowe is quick to respond that, aside from the task being beyond his expertise, it would take a magician to prevent any man from indulging in his most cherished vice, and that, indeed, his efforts might exacerbate the situation. He ultimately agrees to locate the by then missing man when Eileen, Wade's wife, impresses upon him the fact that people can't know if they can be of help until they first establish human contact.

Raymond Chandler's Philip Marlowe

Marlowe pragmatically adjusts his stance in accordance with reasonable counterarguments; he is not trapped within rigid professional parameters or egotistic self-consciousness. In addition, Chandler constantly foregrounds the tension between individual and individual, individual and group.

In *American Literature and Social Change*, Michael Spindler grants that while self-interest may have been a productive ideology in the age of Jefferson and Crèvecoeur, Toqueville was right to remain skeptical: in time such an individualistic ideology led "to a disparagement of the social fabric as compared with personal character" (22). Social conditions, he recognized, change over time. For Spindler the concentration of capital in the hands of post–Civil-War industrialists, the creation of cartels, and the reorganization of labor (previously independent merchants, for example, became employees of expanded companies) created a society in which

> [s]elf interest, no longer balanced by self-restraint, became the single, dominating force, and shorn of its humanizing Christian morality, individualism was reduced to a hard egotism that prevailed among both ruling and working classes as civil society became the arena for fierce, egotistical competition [28].

Even if we may be inclined to be more generous than Spindler to the rugged individualists of that era, we find that the nation was conceived not as an interlocking social network, but as an arena in which individuals are given opportunities to prosper.

By the beginning of the 20th century the grave problems of American individualism to which Spindler refers came under renewed scrutiny. For many intellectuals of the Progressive Era, the hopeful idealism of the young nation had degenerated into quite the opposite of what Emerson intended, a polarization of the electorate into camps of the empowered and disempowered threatened to destroy democracy itself. The concentration of wealth and power in the hands of an oligarchic elite in the years after the Civil War created a situation, as described by John Dewey in *Individualism Old and New*, "in which corporateness has gone so far as to detach individuals from their old local ties and allegiances but not far enough to give them a new center and order of life," a prescription for social disaster (*Later Works* V:70–71). Dewey, among others, sought a more positive individualism, one that would foster freedom of action *for* the greater good of the community.

Three. Marlowe as Negotiator

Post–World War I prosperity, however, helped mask the crisis of individuality. In 1922, in *American Individualism,* Herbert Hoover, writing in reaction to the carnage of World War I and certain political ideologies, especially socialism, defends laissez-faire capitalism as the cornerstone of individualism. He contrasts American individualism, a product of a classless society, with that "of the more democratic states of Europe with its careful reservations of castes and classes" (4). He echoes Emerson's optimism that American individualism is "the sole source of progress" (13) and that "[d]emocracy arises out of individualism and prospers through it alone" (48). In addition, the "American pioneer is the epic expression of that individualism, and the pioneer spirit is the response to the challenge of opportunity" (63). His belief, however, was posited on a stunning blindness to the high human costs incurred in national expansion: "Our American individualism ... plowed and sowed two score of great states ... [and] it carried forward every attribute of high civilization over a continent" (64). He fails to acknowledge the depredations of this "pioneering" individualism: "the absorption of the great plains of the West" (65) and the intentional elimination of indigenous peoples. He thus invites the interpretation that individualism, once the progressive ideology of democratic freedoms, has become a convenient public relations euphemism for imperialism. Although Hoover is cognizant of the abuses of extreme individualism, he still invokes the social Darwinist agenda, according to which "rare individuals ... must be free to rise from the mass; they must be given the attraction of premiums to effort" (23).

As if in answer to this seemingly unshakable and optimistic elitism, what is now termed hard-boiled fiction began at just this juncture of American history, injecting a significant dose of its hallmark social pessimism. The hard-boiled detectives are far too aware of the workings of modern urban society — the widespread collusion between politicians and gangsters, for example — to accept any facile social optimism or even the inevitability of democratic progress. They do not, however, necessarily refute the tenets of autonomous individualism. By the late 1940s, the genre's most right-wing exemplar, Mickey Spillane, presents, in the figure of Mike Hammer, the rugged individualist gone sour, succumbing to racial and ethnic hatreds and the political paranoia of the McCarthy era. A dividing line can, however, be drawn between the representatives of rugged individualism who support, even glorify, the exploits of the autonomous individual, and those "new" individuals who (in Dewey's spirit) seek to serve the community in concert with, for example, duly constituted law enforcers.

Chandler deftly contrasts Philip Marlowe and his client, General Guy Sternwood, in *The Big Sleep* with Race Williams and Howard Quincy Travers in Daly's *The Hidden Hand* in terms of old individualism and new. We see quite a bit of the robber baron in Sternwood's character, especially since his wealth is based on one of the classic late 19th-century, cartelized commodities, oil. Ensconced in his monstrous, bombastic mansion — whose front doors "would have let in a troop of Indian elephants" (*Stories* 589) — diligently served by a faithful retainer and so ill as to find relative comfort only in a hothouse, Sternwood is living out his life hobbled by ailments he himself traces to his earlier, self-indulgent lifestyle. He admits that his two daughters have no moral sense whatever because "no Sternwood ever has" (*Stories* 596). The impression he leaves is one of acute self-centeredness humbled by his severe invalid state and the fear of impending death.

Marlowe shows sympathy for the old man, yet refuses to kowtow. He considers Sternwood's predicament carefully, tempering his judgment with his experience as a keen observer of people. Marlowe respects the General, in part because the old man possesses the Marlovian trait of tolerance: no longer physically able to enjoy alcohol or tobacco, he is broad-minded enough not to deny those pleasures to others. After careful deliberation the detective is hired to intercede for Sternwood with Arthur Gwynn Geiger and his supposed blackmail scheme based on the gambling debts of the General's wayward daughter, Carmen. As it is throughout the novel, Marlowe's role vis-à-vis Sternwood is that of an advisor, and he even suggests that swallowing his pride and paying the debts is the best, because less annoying, solution. At no time does Marlowe blindly follow his client's orders, as Race Williams follows those of Travers. Nor do client and detective assume vigilante roles, arrogating to themselves the right to compete with the police.

Marlowe makes no exorbitant claims of his own abilities, as does Race Williams ad nauseam. Upon Sternwood's request, he provides, instead, a

Three. Marlowe as Negotiator

dry biographical account, admitting that he was fired for insubordination from his job as an investigator in the district attorney's office. Inasmuch as Sternwood echoes Marlowe's resistance to authority (he too "test[ed] very high" on insubordination [*Stories* 594]), the two men reflect the Emersonian suspicion of the power of the institution.

This complex process of negotiation and Marlowe's gradual understanding of the General's daughters do more than merely establish fictional exposition. Though he will discover quite a bit more in his investigation, the detective here begins his work on a solid basis of fact and in no way can be duped. In addition, this negotiation can be seen as a confrontation of two distinct types of individualism. In *Individualism Old and New* John Dewey distinguishes the former as freedom *from* restriction, one that "sought to release from legal restriction man's wants and his efforts to satisfy those wants" (*Later Works* V:78). In this respect the robber baron is as rugged an individualist as the Western gunslinger or the hard-boiled detective as represented by Race Williams. In asserting their freedom of action, these individuals arrogate to themselves the authority they deny to social institutions, and are, typically, often virulently, even violently, resistant to anyone who refuses to accept their authority. Marlowe, to the contrary, defines his role as a "new" individual, one, for Dewey, "whose pattern of thought and desire is enduringly marked by consensus with others, and in whom sociability is one with cooperation in all regular human associations" (*Later Works* V:84). Marlowe soon has need to oppose the old individualism of his client, asserting his sense of individualism by presenting reasonable, consensus-building arguments.

Once Geiger has been murdered, Sternwood considers the matter closed, but several murders are linked to the case and Marlowe, taking the initiative, begins to look for Sternwood's friend and ex–son-in-law, the suspiciously missing Rusty Regan. Later in the novel Sternwood chides the detective for looking for Regan, insisting that he had never asked for that particular service. Marlowe counters that the General nonetheless wanted him to find — and hopefully exonerate — Regan and, since Regan is still missing, offers to return his payment for a job done less than well. Sternwood accuses Marlowe of exceeding his authority, and while Marlowe admits this, he nevertheless defends his behavior in terms of professional ethics:

Raymond Chandler's Philip Marlowe

> When you hire a boy in my line of work it isn't like hiring a window-washer and showing him eight windows and saying: "Wash those and you're through." *You* don't know what I have to go through or over or under to do your job for you. I do it my way. I do my best to protect you and I may break a few rules, but I break them in your favor [*Stories* 750].

Marlowe's argument convinces Sternwood that more has to be done and he authorizes the detective to look for Regan and promises him $1,000 if he succeeds. Soon after, Marlowe's hunch that Carmen killed Regan because he repelled her sexual advances proves true, and, wishing to spare a dying man the anguish, he negotiates with Vivian, Carmen's older sister. He has recognized that Carmen's guilt is qualified by the fact that she is mentally unstable, and he poses his solution by means of asking, not telling, Vivian (as would Sam Spade or Mike Hammer) to institutionalize her sister. He adds pressure to his entreaty by setting a deadline of three days for her to act, but the threat remains very vague. That he emphasizes a verbal contract — that Vivian must promise him to sequester Carmen — underscores his conscious role as a negotiator: pressure is exerted but, knowing full well that he himself is now implicated in "family" matters and is thus vulnerable, the pressure remains that of the bargaining table, not thuggish coercion.

Violence and the threat of violence are defining features of the hard-boiled genre: the detective's ability and readiness to use a gun (or fists) and the concomitant courage when on the receiving end of violence while confronting and capturing the criminal contribute immeasurably to his heroic status. The classic whodunit detective story, as conceived by Edgar Allan Poe and developed in Great Britain, by contrast, emphasizes the detective's task of reconstructing events in relative safety instead of apprehending the criminal at risk of life and limb; the goal here, as John G. Cawelti sees it, is to *explain* crime, to reconcile it with a just society. For Cawelti, the American detective, on the other hand, has little if any faith in the social system; he is, indeed, self-absorbed and prone to vigilantism:

> Where the classical detective's role was to use his superior intellect and psychological insight to reveal the hidden guilt that the police seemed unable to discover, the hard-boiled detective metes out the just punishment that the law is too mechanical, unwieldy, or corrupt to achieve [143].

Three. Marlowe as Negotiator

In *Saint with a Gun: The Unlawful American Private Eye*, William Ruehlmann similarly makes a key distinction between these two branches of detective fiction, emphasizing the punitive aspect of the hard-boiled detectives. Expanding on G. K. Chesterton's observation that "when the murderer is caught he is hardly ever hanged," Ruehlmann claims that "the English detective may indeed set [criminals] free ... but the American private eye punishes" (8). Inasmuch as he focuses rather narrowly on the violent exploits of Mickey Spillane's Mike Hammer, he is correct in his interpretation that American hard-boiled detectives take the law into their own hands: Hammer's egregious use of force is utterly foreign to Sherlock Holmes, Lord Peter Wimsey, and Hercule Poirot.

However, Ruehlmann's assertion that "private eye novels are vigilante literature" (9) is a dangerous generalization. Ruehlmann, like Cawelti and Slotkin, traces the American private eye back to the Western hero, who engages in conflicts unfettered by rule of law on the borders of "civilization." He highlights the function of that hero as dispensing frontier justice with a gun or a rope, exercising his rugged individualist ethos with the self-assurance that what he does is always right. Ruehlmann takes this one step further and rejects the idea that the detective is working for "good" by anyone's standard. While Cawelti sees some ameliorative value in the detective's procedure — the punishment is ultimately "just" — for Ruehlmann "the typical tough-guy private eye does not merely interact with social corruption, he collaborates in it" (8). At least as far as Chandler's novels are concerned, Ruehlmann's thesis is faulty; he mistakes Marlowe's willingness to negotiate with criminals for complicity in their acts. In addition, Marlowe's extreme constraint in the use of force (in comparison with other genre heroes) belies the possibility of vigilante, or even vengeful, action. Closer scrutiny reveals that Chandler, a careful student of the detective genre, tempered the violent streak of the self-assured American detective with a dose of British fair play.

Chandler is highly critical of what he considered the artificiality of the classic, puzzle-plot detective story of the golden age of crime fiction. In a letter to Frederic Dannay, for example, he insists that "puzzle merchants, the people who have timetables and ground plans and pay the most meticulous attention to detail, can't write a lick." He takes these writers to task for indulging in "false motivations cooked up for the purpose of mystifying a reader" (*Letters* 284–85). He defends the fiction of Freeman Wills Crofts and R. Austin Freeman since they are "rigidly honest simply because they don't tell lies or conceal material facts," but finds that Agatha Christie "ring[s] in violent reversals of character in order to justify an unexpected motivation" (*Letters* 109). In discussing Dorothy L. Sayers in "The Simple Art of Murder," he faults the author for coming to a "slow realization that her kind of detective story was an arid formula which could not even satisfy its own implications" (*Later Novels* 987). For all his criticism, however, Chandler was not averse to borrowing from the classic detective writers, especially when it was a matter, as Stephen Knight says of Sherlock Holmes, of the hero serving the community (68).

Knight may have been thinking of "The Adventure of the Blue Carbuncle," a story published in *The Strand Magazine* that focuses not on murder, but on the theft of the invaluable eponymous diamond. One man, the plumber John Horner, is incarcerated for being in the wrong place at the wrong time, and Holmes quickly finds the real culprit, James Ryder, an attendant at the hotel from which the gem was stolen, who had framed Horner. He tells Ryder that "there is the making of a very pretty villain in you" (105), but ultimately allows him to escape, and his reasoning is instructive for our consideration of Philip Marlowe's attitude toward criminals. Convinced that the man truly regrets the theft of the gem in question, Holmes explains to Dr. Watson,

> I am not retained by the police to supply their deficiencies. If Horner were in danger it would be another thing, but this fellow will not appear against him, and the case must collapse. I suppose that I am commuting a felony, but it is just possible that I am saving a soul. This fellow will not go wrong again.... Send him to gaol now, and you make him a gaol-bird for life [107].

In "The Boscombe Valley Mystery," Holmes has a similar reason for protecting a man he knows to be guilty, in this case of murder. John Turner killed a man, Charles McCarthy, who had been blackmailing him for 20 years and whose son has been arrested for the murder. Holmes' painstaking investigation establishes the young man's innocence and Turner's guilt, but he does not insist on the guilty man's turning himself over to the police, out of understanding of the blackmail and McCarthy's bad character and because Turner is terminally ill. Instead Holmes devises a kind of delayed confession, telling Turner "I shall jot down the facts. You will sign it, and Watson here can witness it. Then I could produce your confession at the last extremity to save young McCarthy" (66). Similar to his act in "The Adventure of the Blue Carbuncle," Holmes insists on a strict definition of his own role: in this case that does not include being the judge of the guilty man.

At least one American writer patterned his novels on the British model, including the emphasis on intellectual, not physical, force and sympathy for the sometimes heinous murderers: Willard Huntington Wright, who published under the pen name S. S. Van Dine. In a series of mysteries roughly contemporaneous with Hammett's and featuring the detective Philo Vance, Van Dine portrays his detective as an eccentric, a dilettante familiar with the fine arts and Egyptology, a capable translator of the classics, and an instinctive, Holmes-like sleuth, whom W. H. Auden refers to as a "priggish superman" (154). For Julian Symons, he is a "monster of snobbish affectation" (110) and "Wimsey's American cousin" (111). His Watson is his attorney, one S. S. Van Dine, who has retired from practice to assist Vance and to document his cases (thus our narrator). Two other figures serve as assistants: Manhattan District Attorney John F. X. Markham and homicide Detective Sergeant Ernest Heath, who plays a Lestrade-like official foil to Vance. Van Dine's plots generally follow the puzzle pattern of classic British mysteries, typically gathering suspects under one roof for questioning until the murderer is found.

At the end of Van Dine's *The Dragon Murder Case*, it is revealed that Leland, one of the suspects for two murders and the one who initially reported the first murder of a fellow house guest to the police, had suspected his host, Rudolph Stamm, the murderer, all along. This places him in a position similar to James Ryder in "The Adventure of the Blue Carbuncle" inasmuch as he could be accused of a crime, in this case that of withholding evidence. Vance, however, provides a rationale for his silence:

> Naturally, he was torn between his sense of justice and fair play, on the one hand, and his love for Bernice Stamm, on the other.... He wouldn't definitely expose or accuse the brother of the woman he loved. But, as an honorable

man, he couldn't bring himself to countenance what he believed to be deliberate murder [298].

Vance explains this to Markham, who may have considered Leland to have committed a criminal act (especially since a second murder was committed), but Vance's emphasis on Leland's moral dilemma prevents any such consequences. Vance appears in other situations in which he aggrandizes power far out of proportion with his position and in which his treatment of those "assistants," Markham and Heath, reflects a less socially oriented brand of individualism. But in this case, he illustrates a benevolence, a fellow feeling, a loyalty to a moral and societal standard that echoes Holmes' treatment of James Ryder. It is a quality that Chandler understood and applied in his own writing.

Chandler incorporates this Holmesian sense of proportion and sympathy into Marlowe's mediations, avoiding the extremes of Ruehlmann's "vigilantes" without unduly trusting officialdom. We have already seen how he tempers the need to capture the criminal with an appreciation of her disabilities vis-à-vis Carmen in *The Big Sleep*. The many examples of police corruption in the novels, such as that exemplified by Captain Blane in *Farewell, My Lovely* and Moses Maglashan in *The Little Sister*, make it impossible for the socially conscious private eye *not* to take on the role of ombudsman, since no citizen without political influence can expect to be treated fairly in, say, Bay City. Thus Marlowe acts as a buffer, sometimes deflecting physical violence, sometimes engaging his rhetorical skills on behalf of the innocent.

Even when compelled into his negotiator role, Marlowe reveals a level of restraint utterly foreign to Race Williams and the Continental Op. In *Farewell, My Lovely* his investigative work begins only after he is forced to witness both a murder and the incompetent and racially prejudiced police investigation that follows. Moose Malloy, just released from prison, makes Marlowe, a curious bystander, accompany him into Florian's bar at the beginning of the novel. The huge and powerful ex-con is looking for Velma Valento, his former girlfriend, in the place he last saw her, despite Marlowe's attempts to explain to him that the neighborhood has changed and that Florian's is now a black bar. Malloy, proud of his enormous strength, feels free enough to insult the clientele and the bartender with racist lan-

Three. Marlowe as Negotiator

guage, and easily overcomes a bouncer who tries to eject him. Marlowe thus finds himself in the awkward position of identification with the white man he's entered with, realizing that he can hardly succeed in dissociating himself from the monomaniacal Malloy. Malloy illustrates how a gangster can also represent rugged individualism: he seems unruffled by his stint in prison and is quite proud of the fact that his bank robbery was entirely his work, a "solo job" (*Stories* 773).

Malloy continues his search in the manager's office, leaving Marlowe alone with the bartender. Marlowe convinces the bartender not to use the sawed-off shotgun he has hidden under the bar: "This guy is tough ... [and] he's liable to go mean. Drinks do that to him. He's looking for a girl he used to know. This place used to be a white establishment. Get the idea?" (*Stories* 774). The detective has grabbed the man's arm, but, with the bar between them, he has no leverage, no real chance to restrain the worried bartender. He tries instead to make clear to the man how desperate and dangerous Malloy is, while at the same time insisting that he in no way condones what the ex-con is doing. He even explains why accepted social boundaries have been breached, but stresses that mutual prejudices must be momentarily suspended: "You and I are together," he emphasizes. When Malloy kills the manager and escapes, Marlowe must cope as best he can; he grabs the shotgun and a .38 automatic from behind the bar, insuring that no further violence occurs (*Stories* 776).

Even if we grant the fact that Marlowe is, in part, protecting himself, these can hardly be the actions of a character who is, according to Stephen Knight, a "self-seeking individualist" (147). For Knight the attempts to engage in "outward" social mediation in any effective way succumb to the gravitational pull of the detective's self-centeredness. In his interpretation Marlowe merely makes a show of concern for the black microcosm of Florian's bar: "Marlowe never sees [blacks and lower-class people] in autonomous terms as people struggling with their own problems.... The pressures which make negroes seem servile and lower class people seem dirty are nowhere considered" (155). As if in answer to this charge, Chandler has Marlowe return to the black neighborhood for further negotiations.

After Marlowe discusses the case with Lieutenant Nulty, he visits the

Sans Souci Hotel, near the scene of the murder. There he negotiates with the black desk clerk for information regarding the history of Florian's, which, he learns, had been white-owned a few years before. He fails in a gambit to pass himself off as an inspector for the Hotel Protective Department, and, after complimenting the man as someone who can keep a confidence, offers him a drink in exchange for information. The clerk, however, cannot be persuaded quite so easily, and demands information in return. The detective satisfies the clerk's curiosity by informing him that the man who killed Montgomery is a "tough guy out of the jailhouse [who] got sore because it wasn't a white joint" (*Stories* 781).

What follows is more an instance of Marlowe being taught a lesson than a stereotypical private eye conducting a straightforward, information-for-money transaction. The clerk emphasizes the fact that he can't be bought and provides glasses for both men, and when Marlowe asks what Florian's was called six to eight years previously, the wry answer is "Electric signs come kind of high, brother," which confirms Marlowe's guess that the name hasn't changed. When Marlowe asks who ran the bar, the clerk expresses disappointment in him: "I'm a mite surprised at you, brother. The name of that poor sinner was Florian. Mike Florian —" (*Stories* 782).

Marlowe shows signs of resignation and even a lapse in professionalism when he can't locate any Florian in the local telephone book, but his new "teacher" provides him with a city directory, in which he finds the address of Jessie Florian, Mike's widow. The detective ruminates that "I wondered what I had been using for brains all my life" (*Stories* 783); it is important to note that not only does he make simple mistakes, but that he is willing to admit to them and be helped by and appreciative of others. The manner in which he conducts his business is, in turn, appreciated; the clerk returns the whisky bottle and tells the detective, "Your method of approach is soothin' to a man's dignity" (*Stories* 783).

This encounter is by no means crucial in terms of the plot of the novel; it is clear that the experienced detective would have found Jessie Florian by other means. This short scene does, however, demonstrate Marlowe's all-too-human flaws, distancing him from the omniscient and omnipotent representatives of hard-boiled detectives. In opposition to the often arrogant self-assurance of the "rugged" detectives, Marlowe reveals

Three. Marlowe as Negotiator

a high degree of self-realization, a quality which, for John J. Stuhr, is a prerequisite of Deweyan new individualism, inasmuch as "[h]uman beings in our complex world are involved in countless social interdependencies." Individualism is not a matter of "personal self-sufficiency," as in Spillane, but a "process of growth," exemplified in Marlowe by a willingness to learn (93). Marlowe demonstrates a humility rarely found in the genre and his actions belie Stephen Knight's accusations of racism and inner-directedness. Representative of many encounters in Chandler's corpus, these scenes show Marlowe to be, on the one hand, tough enough to oppose the will of rugged individualists, and, on the other, receptive to the help he can get from others and willing to help them in return.

The rugged individualism of the Continental Op and Sam Spade is represented in Chandler not by Marlowe, but by clients such as General Sternwood and criminals such as Moose Malloy. Sternwood incorporates the power and faded authority that wealth can bring, but he also stands for social isolation and impotence: he has no control over his daughters and depends on Marlowe to find his "son," Rusty Regan. Malloy is a more visceral avatar of old individualism, a brawny bully obsessed with a nostalgic view of his preprison life in his search for Velma. Lacking sufficient self-awareness even to realize how powerful he is, he murders Jessie Florian out of a pathetic need for self-assertion.

Marlowe appears in stark contrast to these figures. Knowing well his abilities and his limitations, he struggles to reconnect the loose ends others have left and to arbitrate among warring factions. As the following chapter demonstrates in terms of the detective's relationship with the police, Marlowe is receptive to change and the views of erstwhile opponents, and strives, in the spirit of new individualism, to forge new alliances.

CHAPTER FOUR

Marlowe and the Police

Critical reception of hard-boiled fiction, including that of Raymond Chandler, has tended toward polarization. For Philip Durham, for example, Philip Marlowe is a romantic hero, a modern-day knight tilting against the windmills of corruption and immorality. The detective occupies his time "crusading through the streets of Los Angeles and the surrounding towns looking for ladies to rescue, for the little fellow who needed help, for the wealthy who appeared to be helpless, and for the unscrupulous who deserved a shot of old-fashioned justice" (32).

Quite the opposite of this mythic and heroic view, more recent criticism places Marlowe cynically in league with forces of political oppression or casts him in the role of a resigned, egocentric isolationist. In *The Pursuit of Crime*, for example, Dennis Porter insists on the detective genre's unflinching support for the political status quo. For Porter the genre remains conspicuously silent on salient social features: "The dimension that is missing from formulaic works in the detective genre is, in fact, any recognition that the law itself, with its definitions of crimes and its agencies of law enforcement and punishment, is problematic" (121). Porter is somewhat justified in pointing out that the genre "effectively remained silent about important aspects of crime by narrowly establishing boundaries for its action" (122) inasmuch as Mickey Spillane, for example, rejects due process and provides Mike Hammer with unbounded immunity from the law. Porter overlooks, however, clear instances in the genre of criticism of the law and its enforcement and does not consider the possibility that such limited action can stand for the whole. Although, as he correctly observes, pursuit of crime is emphasized and trial and punishment are usually ignored, there is generally no need to portray the latter; this does not necessarily mean that thorough social critique cannot be contained within the elements that the reader is allowed to see.

Four. Marlowe and the Police

Dashiell Hammett, Chandler's hard-boiled mentor, achieved some degree of social criticism in police/private eye encounters and Chandler himself notably rendered the entire scope of detection, pursuit, and punishment in dense verbal exchanges among private eye, police, criminals, and clients. While, admittedly, Chandler does not have Marlowe discuss judicial precedent with judges or writs with lawyers, he does, quite often, have him debate problems of law and justice with police and district attorneys, with special focus on their uneven enforcement, something well within his ken.

One of Chandler's concerns is for exposing simplistic distinctions between legitimate and illegitimate actions, and he was ahead of his time in exposing the role of class prejudice in condemning criminality. One thread that runs throughout Chandler's novels is the pragmatic insistence that written law cannot be divorced from practiced law, and that faith in a system of justice in a democratic society must be tempered with a healthy dose of skepticism as to the motives of the agents of its enforcement.

Marlowe's legal knowledge is impressive, especially when he must protect himself. He is accused in *The Long Goodbye*, for instance, of being an accessory after the fact to Sylvia Lennox's murder, but he knows that such an accusation will only hold up in court if Terry Lennox is caught and convicted and if he himself is proven to have known about Terry's guilt.

His knowledge is more often utilized to criticize flaws in the system. In *The High Window* Detective Lieutenant Jesse Breeze of the LAPD answers the call when Marlowe finds the murdered body of George Anson Phillips, an incompetent private eye who sought Marlowe's help when his complicity in a forgery scheme went awry. Breeze has a suspect, Del Hench, who lives across the hall from the deceased, and is found with a concealed weapon. Breeze questions Hench's claim that the gun doesn't belong to him and at this juncture Marlowe "puts in [his] nickel's worth" and the two men discuss varying possibilities. After the suspect is taken to police headquarters, Breeze presses Marlowe to account for his own presence, under false identity, in the Bunker Hill flophouse. He seems to accept Marlowe's plausible story, but presses further when the detective refuses to name his client, threatening to throw him "in the can" on grounds that he's "the one who found the body, ... gave a false name to the manager ... and don't give a satisfactory account" of his connection to Phillips (*Stories* 1053). Breeze continues to press Marlowe, emphasizing the fact that the seriousness of a murder investigation takes precedence over the confidentiality of a client-detective relationship. Marlowe counters that such niceties of procedure can only apply when justice itself is fairly and consistently administered:

> Until you guys own your own souls you don't own mine. Until you guys can be trusted every time and always, in all times and conditions, to seek the truth out and find it and let the chips fall where they may — until that time comes, I have the right to listen to my conscience, and protect my client the best way I can [*Stories* 1072].

Breeze and his assistant, Spangler, show up at Marlowe's apartment soon after the second murder, that of Elisha Morningstar, has been discovered. Marlowe puts up with Breeze's inspection of his home (including his .38 automatic) until he gets a phone call instigated by Breeze, who wants a witness who heard a voice at the first crime scene to check Marlowe for voice recognition. The private eye resents this and Breeze counters that "[w]e're not trying to pull anything that's not legitimate. We hope you ain't, either" (*Stories* 1068). For the policeman the fact that the crime is murder expands the boundaries of cop-detective cooperation, and Marlowe later shows that he agrees when he tells his client, Mrs. Murdock, that Breeze gave him 24 hours to reveal her name. Although Marlowe is still chafing at the treatment, he shares a drink with Breeze and Spangler.

Breeze proves to be a relatively good and conscientious professional and his reasoned explanation of why Hench didn't kill Phillips, despite appearances, makes him sound a lot like Marlowe: Hench simply had no motive. Breeze adds, "there are things you know because they are reasonable and have to be so. You don't shoot somebody and then make a lot of racket calling attention to yourself, and all the time you have the gun under your pillow" (*Stories* 1075).

Far from a quietist or reactionary figure, Marlowe is an advocate, a diplomat, and a peacemaker in the mean streets of L.A. He accepts that his environment is corrupt and that political elites are ultimately responsible for that corruption, but he neither supports it, nor hides from it, nor

Four. Marlowe and the Police

becomes as hardened as the criminals, clients, and cops with whom he deals. He actively seeks to improve the system.

It is thus a considerable oversimplification to contend, as does Dennis Porter, that the point of view of the detective story "is always that of the detective, which is to say, of the police" (125). Although he helpfully points toward a crucial ideological binary of the genre, Porter's implied conflation of terms overlooks important police/private eye distinctions. Since he positions himself between equally violent "legitimate" and "illegitimate" camps, Marlowe is often as much in danger at the hands of the police as he is in the clutches of ostensible criminals. A key accomplishment in the creation of Marlowe is the blurring of lines of identity with virtually all with whom he comes in contact. For the police Marlowe is often cast as the "hunted"— seen by them, at least temporarily, as a suspect in crime investigations. On other occasions — such as when he accompanies Lieutenant Randall to Jessie Florian's in *Farewell, My Lovely*— he is treated as a respected, if unofficial, colleague.

Stephen Knight, Dennis Porter, Ernest Mandel, and others approach the genre from a Marxist standpoint, and do so constructively, but flatten the profile of this type of writing in the process, as when Porter makes the blanket assumption that "in order for a novel to be easily comprehensible and to please, a novelist has to go out of his way to avoid confusion and conflict in his reader" (5). A careful reading of Chandler's texts reveals something quite different: an author concerned with portraying a highly complex world, one in which each character has his share of productive and destructive traits, and in which the reader finds herself implicated. Marxist criticism of this genre has failed to assess these complexities, has been all too content to reverse the polarities of good and evil — casting Marlowe, for instance, as the "heavy," instead of analyzing interactions in the texts. Contrary to Mandel's interpretation of the genre, for example, many ideologies are in complex conflict in hard-boiled detective fiction. What has gone unrecognized is a crucial split within the genre that simulates the historical liberalisms so important to Dewey and that is central to Chandler's ideology as figured in Marlowe.

Chandler also reassessed American democratic ideology exemplified by John Dewey in the years before and during his shaping of his heroes —

prototypes for Marlowe — in the pulps. In his extensive socio-political writing, Dewey stresses the distinction between two liberalisms: one based on an older laissez-faire or "rugged" individualism founded on freedom from governmental constraints and a newer liberalism that defines the individual in terms of membership in a democratic society and sees the role of the state in a constructive light.[1]

Beginning with John Locke's claim for the natural rights of the individual to life, liberty, and property in the late 17th century, the earlier ideology was used to combat the forces of arbitrary government. This continued until well into the 19th century, but, as Dewey makes clear in *Liberalism and Social Action*, it degenerated into a confrontational stance against *democratic* society. The older camp championed "individual initiative and effort" and strove "negatively to remove the obstacles that stand in the way of individuals." Dewey's philosophy supports an "organized social action" that recognizes the necessity of cooperation in the democratic community (*Later Works* XI:20–21). For Dewey what is needed in a democracy is "a form of social organization, extending to all the areas and ways of living, in which the powers of individuals shall not be merely released from mechanical external constraint but shall be fed, sustained, and directed" (*Later Works* XI:25). Freedom *for* social action is thus superior to freedom *from* participation.

Dewey takes laissez-faire liberals to task for their lack of historical perspective: "disregard for history ... blinded the eyes of liberals to the fact that their own special interpretations of liberty, individuality and intelligence were themselves historically conditioned, and were relevant only to their own time" (*Later Works* XI:26). While the consciousness given to him by Chandler is not quite the same historical consciousness that Dewey refers to, Marlowe's acute sense of self-reflection and his role define him as a democrat in Dewey's sense of the word. Dewey's concept of democratic culture, in Jeffrey S. Baker's formulation, is one that has "the potential to be self-reflective, self-critical, and self-correcting" (15); these are the very qualities that distinguish Marlowe from other hard-boiled detectives.

Chandler extensively applies Dewey's new individualism by having Marlowe enter into dialogue with the police. He exploits an essentially unexamined premise of the genre: the fact that any crime will bring a pri-

Four. Marlowe and the Police

vate detective into the orbit of law enforcement officers. In Chandler the cases themselves often fade into the background as the private eye and the police problematize law enforcement in ways that must surprise readers looking to discover the culprit before the end of the book and/or expecting rough-and-tumble "Western" thrills. Marlowe's legitimacy as a social actor — one who investigates crime, apprehends criminals, suppresses evidence, etc. — is rigorously questioned by the duly constituted guardians of the law, as he confronts its representatives ranging from uniformed patrolmen on up to district attorneys in each novel. Marlowe neither condescends to nor ignores these officers of the law, even if they are crooked, as is often true in the genre, nor is cowed by them. Not only does police criticism serve to inform Marlowe of his own position; he in turn reveals, or has others reveal, how well the police serve society: law enforcement itself is placed under the microscope as rigorously as any cigar ash of Sherlock Holmes.

Speaking of the portrayal of police in the novel in general, D.A. Miller asserts that the police are consistently kept on the margins of fictional discourse, that "even in the special case of detective fiction, where police detectives often hold center stage, the police never quite emerge from the ghetto in which the novel generally confines them" (3). Positing that the bourgeois novel invokes other, more powerful institutions and sites of power (foremost, the family), Miller overlooks the fruitful possibilities of the hard-boiled novel, as demonstrated by Chandler, to push police and policing (in the broadest possible sense) into the foreground, to interrogate, as one of its primary concerns, the often arbitrary exercise of the power of law enforcement.

Chandler is as conscious as Dewey of the constructed quality of social institutions, and realizes that they are, at best, results of consensus or compromise that may (but may not) properly serve their constituencies. Marlowe, who is also involved in "policing" and indeed may be said to police the police, in this sense stands in for the constructively critical Deweyan citizen. He tutors Nulty in effective procedure in *Farewell, My Lovely* and shares information and collaborates with Randall in the same novel. He cooperates with Bernie Ohls and District Attorney Taggart Wilde in *The Big Sleep*. Marlowe is not averse to playing one role against the other, assuming police identity in order to extract information, such as when he claims to be a member of the Police Identification Bureau in *The Big Sleep*, but is adept at exploiting misunderstandings so as not to break the law. When he first looks up Jessie Florian in *Farewell, My Lovely*, for example, he announces himself as a detective, and Florian, assuming that he's with the police, is too drunk to demand that he specify just what kind. He repeats the ploy later with Florian's neighbor, Mrs. Morrison, who is too eager to indulge in gossip, at first, to question Marlowe's identity. Once they become aware of the ploy, the police tacitly accept the private eye's exploitation of their identity in hopes that his work will simplify their tasks.

In Chandler's work, responsible law enforcement officials are given their day in court. The good cops in *The Lady in the Lake* are characterized by dedication to the job and flexibility in handling people. Although Deputy Sheriff Jim Patton catches Marlowe breaking into a house at Little Fawn Lake, he chooses to overlook the infraction and share information with the detective in hopes of shedding light on a recent murder. Patton's urban counterpart, Captain Webber of the Bay City Police Department, acts in similar fashion. After berating Marlowe for searching the house where another murder has been committed, he accepts Marlowe's explanation that a private eye "wouldn't be likely to pass up the chance" and lets him go free (*Later Novels* 113).

Taken as a whole, the novels examine the detective/police dialogue and present a vast range of police behaviors, with Marlowe acting as the catalyst that brings these behaviors to light. The archetypal encounter is that of the "grilling," in which the private eye, often a suspect himself, is placed in a more or less helpless position before police who often exceed their authority and use force to get what they want. The line of questioning is typically that of establishing what the private eye knows and how much of it is relevant to police investigations; in some cases this is because he obstructs police procedure, but more often it is because, as an outsider, he threatens to interrupt or expose the corrupt machinery of the political hierarchy.

Marlowe, however, functions neither as a neutral questioner nor as the morally or ethically "untarnished" agent that Chandler's 1944 essay,

Four. Marlowe and the Police

"The Simple Art of Murder," suggests; his motives and methods are also flawed and also interrogated. These exchanges serve to illustrate how imperfect his actions can be, indeed, how his all-too-fallible skills lead to exacerbating already painful and deadly situations. The spirit of mutual criticism and self-criticism, in which private and public law enforcers are capable of admitting to their mistakes and accepting less than 100 percent honesty in the interest of a greater good, runs deep in these novels. It also enables them to function as societal barometers, especially inasmuch as the destructively violent nature of American society cries out for rational dialogue.

Marlowe sympathizes with the difficult job policemen have and can fully identify with them. That which Robert B. Westbrook claims for Dewey's sense of individuality can be said for Chandler: "Individuality was the product of an ongoing interaction of the capacities of a human being and an environment made up, in part, of other human beings" (433). The logical step was to give the hard-boiled protagonist those attributes dimly perceived by Hammett in his rendering of Tom Polhaus and Nick Charles and to expand upon them and infuse them with a guarded, yet tangible optimism. This interactive approach makes the task of the detective that much more difficult. Chandler's police can be as antagonistic to his hero as the ostensible criminals. Yet that hero is always forced to extract from these antagonists as much cooperation as possible, and law enforcement officials are as likely as not prepared to share Marlowe's sense of community responsibility. There is little trace in Chandler of the warfare that characterizes Hammett's urban (and even rural Western) jungles. Participants certainly exercise force, but more often collide, test, threaten, debate, and come to tenuous terms with one another.

Chandler's short stories, published in pulp magazines such as *Black Mask*, predate his novels; indeed, characters and plots of the former were "cannibalized" (Chandler's term) and used in those longer narratives. His private eyes go under many names, such as John Dalmas, Pete Anglich, and Ted Malvern, in the stories and all are clear prototypes for Philip Marlowe. Some stories are narrated in the first person, some in the third person, and the language is more transparently hard-boiled: the detective, especially, speaks far more like Race Williams than Philip Marlowe, but the resemblance stops there. There is also a greater degree of violence and murder than in the novels and the protagonists tend to incite warring factions of criminals against each other, not unlike Hammett's Continental Op. In most of the stories the detective-police encounters foreshadow those in the novels but are, for the most part, simpler, due to the length of the form.

The detective's relationship to the police depends on individual policemen and the cops are often corrupt. In "The King in Yellow" the police barely enter the narrative. Club singer Dolores Chiozza, private detective Steve Grayce's client, is being framed for murder and is ready to give herself up to the police, because even if she is not indicted the publicity will ruin her career. But Grayce tells her to speak to her employer, underworld figure Jumbo Walters, since "he'll pick his cops and the ones he picks won't go screaming through the night with reporters sitting in their laps" (*Stories* 453).

In "Blackmailers Don't Shoot" the private eye is named Mallory and is working for an underworld figure named Landrey, protecting movie star Rhonda Farr from blackmail. Mallory's initial encounter with police is characterized by their verbal and physical abuse of him and it is soon established that they are corrupt. One cop, Macdonald, takes Mallory's side when blackmail turns to kidnapping and he acknowledges the limits of his malleability. Four killings later and after Mallory himself has been wounded, the detective encounters Captain of Detectives Cathcart, a "big shabby Irishman with a sweaty face and a loose-lipped grin" (*Stories* 49), who recapitulates the narrative, sympathizes with Mallory's wounds, and assures him that he is not under any suspicion. Mallory is still skeptical, since "[t]here's the D. A. and the coroner. How about them? I'd like to go back as clean as I came away." Cathcart continues to assure Mallory, asserting that "[i]f the D. A. wants to get funny, I can tell him about a few cases his office didn't clean up so good" (*Stories* 51). Thus Mallory is lucky to have fallen into Cathcart's hands: ethical behavior is arbitrary, but at least one police officer cooperates with the private eye and some degree of justice can be attained.

In "Smart-Aleck Kill" police are clean and primarily on the side of the detective, again Mallory, now working studio security for Eclipse Films.

Four. Marlowe and the Police

By the time Mallory meets homicide detectives Weinkassel and Lonergan, one man, an Eclipse director, has been murdered and a cab driver assisting Mallory has been wounded by gunfire and the detective has been in too-close proximity to both. Yet Mallory is treated relatively well. Weinkassel, especially, is patient and understanding in his efforts to learn as much as he can from Mallory. When the inevitable question of the identity of Mallory's client is raised, the standard answer is given: "I was there on business for a client. You can't make me talk about that." After a bit of sparring on this point, Weinkassel relents: "Oke. You can have till the morning. Then you put your papers on the desk, see" (*Stories* 76). Mallory acknowledges the fairness of being granted at least limited time to conduct the investigation freely. There is a hint of the scripted good cop/bad cop style of interrogation but it is undercut when Weinkassel criticizes his partner: "A little less of your crap would go farther, Lonnie" (*Stories* 75). Chandler also gives the police credit for intelligence and having appropriate skills. Focusing on the incident with the cab driver, Weinkassel posits that the attempt was on Mallory's life, which the reader knows to be true. Mallory questions the supposition, primarily on the basis of who was actually shot, but the police detective's logic is far stronger: "The car was outside while you was still inside. The hack driver was outside. If the guy with the gun had wanted him, he didn't have to wait for you to come out" (*Stories* 75). Chandler here foreshadows the more complex interactions among official guardians of the law.

In "Trouble Is My Business" Chandler eschews the formula found in most of the short stories and constructs a narrative much more like he would in the novels. Hired to prevent a young woman, Harriet Huntress, who's "got her hooks into a rich man's pup" (*Stories* 515), from siphoning money off of the rich man, John Dalmas quickly finds himself in the crossfire of a far more complicated and deadly game. Three people, including the "pup," Gerald Jeeter, are killed and Dalmas comes close to being murdered himself before he solves the case. After the second killing, of a mentally unstable thug, police detectives Finlayson and Sebold visit Dalmas in his apartment since he was at the scene of the crime and they've been tipped off that Dalmas was the shooter. They search his apartment and check his pistol to see if it's been recently used. These two officers establish a good cop/bad cop style of interrogation that Chandler will expand upon in his novels.

Their dialogue exudes a wry toughness: "We're a couple of swell guys not to get funny with," remarks Finlayson (*Stories* 540). They check Dalmas' private investigator credentials and when the PI refuses to give them information he conceals as a professional courtesy to his client, Sebold, the bad cop begins to threaten him: "Smart guy.... I like 'em that way—with my blackjack" (*Stories* 541). Such a boldface threat is actually more egregious than in other short stories or novels and elicits a tired sigh from good cop Finlayson. As the interrogation intensifies Dalmas loses his patience and replies, "Maybe you better skip the gang-buster stuff and tell me what's stuck in your nose. I get along with cops—except when they act as if the law is only for citizens" (*Stories* 542). Although the narration claims that the detective's words have no effect, Finlayson makes sure to get back to facts that Dalmas can either confirm or deny, reining in Sebold's irrational outbursts; he even excuses his colleague's behavior, explaining to Dalmas that the man's wife left him recently.

Chandler's first novel, *The Big Sleep*, tentatively explores the area of police/private eye antagonism and cooperation that would soon become a major thematic focus. Bernie Ohls, the chief investigator for the district attorney of Los Angeles County, is introduced as an old acquaintance of Marlowe's, one friendly enough to have recommended the private eye to General Sternwood in the matter of Geiger's blackmail scheme. Reminiscent of Polhaus/Spade exchanges, the two men demonstrate mutual respect; Ohls is deferential while questioning Marlowe about the identity of Sternwood's now-dead chauffeur, Owen Taylor: "I don't want to crowd you, Marlowe. Just tell me, did the job have anything to do with him?" (*Stories* 624). Marlowe answers in the negative. The police discover what could be the mark of a sap on the side of Taylor's head and Ohls asks, "Sure you can't help me on this?" Marlowe does not respond, but thinks, "I liked him putting it that way. It let me say no without actually lying" (*Stories* 634). As they discuss Taylor's past, Marlowe—concerned about General Sternwood's fragile health—asks Ohls to leave the old man out of the investigation, and the reader soon discovers that Ohls has complied with this request; they agree on cooperating for the same humanitarian reason.

Four. Marlowe and the Police

Ohls next appears when he responds to Marlowe's call, from Geiger's house, to pick up his prisoner, Carol Lundgren, who has just killed Joe Brody. He, Lundgren, and Marlowe proceed to the house of District Attorney Taggart Wilde, who, as interconnected murders in his jurisdiction increase, must referee among the law enforcement agencies involved. What follows is a many-sided debate on professional ethics as two of the participants are brought to task for their actions. Marlowe is introduced to Cronjager, an LAPD detective who has just begun to investigate Brody's murder. Ohls deliberately baits Cronjager, claiming that "Marlowe put the arm on [Lundgren] for you" and has "played it kind of close to the vest." Police/private eye antagonisms in later novels are foreshadowed in Cronjager's acerbic retort: "I love private dicks that play murder close to the vest" (*Stories* 669).

Ohls appears to take pleasure in needling the less-than-arduous or efficient police detective. When Cronjager faults Ohls for being "coy" about Marlowe's involvement, Ohls lays into him, criticizing police in general: "I spend most of my time telling them where to put their feet so they won't break an ankle" (*Stories* 669). Cronjager counters that he still possesses enough native intelligence to implicate Marlowe in Brody's death: "So all you did was not report a murder that happened last night and then spend today foxing around so that this kid of Geiger's [Lundgren] could commit a second murder this evening." Chandler initially presents Cronjager as the bad cop, but immediately complicates matters, since Cronjager's logic is quite sound and his judgment fair. He continues: "If Geiger's death had been reported last night, the books could never have been moved from the store to Brody's apartment. The kid wouldn't have been led to Brody and wouldn't have killed him" (*Stories* 670). Thus Cronjager's failure is a direct result of Marlowe's failure to report a crime.

Marlowe feels, however, that protecting his client is his primary responsibility and that he could not have anticipated subsequent events. Yet, sensitive to the accusation, he responds by accusing the police of consistent rash action, of "shoot[ing] down some scared petty larceny crook running away up an alley with a stolen spare" (*Stories* 670). The fact that the police are often guilty of haste and overreaction, however, does not absolve him of a degree of guilt or even complicity; he cannot claim that police procedure guided his own actions. The disjunction of the two examples underscores the fact that Marlowe is in the wrong and it is well within Chandler's conception of the character that he is prone to such mistakes. The flaws in the system are thus laid out and the suggestion of cooperative action is indirectly made. The system itself is analyzed in great detail, even within this confined space, whereas in the work of most of Chandler's predecessors and contemporaries, a two-dimensional relationship between private eye and police is stressed.

In Chandler's novels his flawed hero is generally superior in intellect to law enforcement officers. For the private eye to be proven more astute than the police is something the hard-boiled detective writers inherited from Conan Doyle and the British detective writers of the golden age. Sherlock Holmes, for example, was not above condemning Scotland Yard's Peter Jones as an "absolute imbecile in his profession" (36) in "The Red-Headed League" and in this story as well as others he clearly proves himself to be by far the intellectual superior. Agatha Christie narrowed the intelligence gap between public and private investigators. Comparing a murder in Christie's *Evil under the Sun* to one committed earlier in a nearby district, Chief Constable Weston concludes, "This isn't one of the 'lonely copse' murders" (100), but Hercule Poirot proves him wrong by ferreting out the murderous married couple, the very same perpetrators Weston ruled out in advance. The detective-police relationship is marked by incongruity and forced at best. The logic of both sides working together is obscure. The most we can expect of the police in the typical golden age narrative is that they are not corrupt. For Symons, "The police were the representatives of established society, and so ought not to be shown behaving badly" (104).

There were precedents in the United States as well. As was mentioned earlier, S. S. Van Dine's Holmes-like detective, Philo Vance, typically counts on the assistance of two duly appointed officers of the law; Van Dine characterizes a police sergeant, Ernest Heath, and the Manhattan district attorney, John F.-X. Markham, as barely capable and consistently unimaginative assistants to the master sleuth, Philo Vance. Having the district attorney take part in such investigations is a major flaw in Van Dine's plotting, but Vance's partnership with Markham is based on friend-

Four. Marlowe and the Police

ship and equality of class: only a college-educated man high up in the criminal justice hierarchy would be a logical match for Vance. The arrangement is clearly of practical value by allowing Vance access to witnesses, crime scenes, and detectives such as Heath. Neither Markham nor Heath, however, provides much in the way of information or insight, so supreme are the abilities of the amateur detective. These abilities extend to the power relationships.

In *The Casino Murder Case* (1934) a number of poisonings in an upper-class New York family draw Vance, Markham, and Heath into the case. When the matriarch, Mrs. Llewellyn, complains of her house being overrun by police in general and of being spied upon in particular, Vance spontaneously decides, "There will be no more spying — for the time being at least. The police will be removed from your house, and your family are free to come and go as you please" (167). This is only one of many instances of Vance's superiority and position in the crime-fighting hierarchy. More often than not in the novels, Vance turns to Markham for authorization, usually whispering such requests in his ear. On this occasion, however, Markham asks him, "Aren't you being a bit hasty?" Vance's superior judgment prevails and Markham enforces Vance's command, the narrator reporting that Markham was "chided," underscoring the inferior, almost childish, position of the district attorney. Roger Rosenblatt notes a similar instance in *The Benson Murder Case* (1926), in which, Vance "ridicules the D.A. Markham, his close friend, in front of a suspect" (1).

Early in *The Scarab Murder Case* (1930) the narrator clarifies the relationship somewhat: "Markham and he had been friends for fifteen years, and Vance had aided him in many of his investigations. In fact, he had come to depend on Vance's assistance in the more complicated criminal cases that came under his jurisdiction" (17). The narrator may be intentionally downplaying Vance's superiority; it is Markham, however, who assists Vance, not vice versa. In this novel, for instance, Markham's primary function is to agree with Vance's contention that they have too little evidence to convict the man they both know is guilty of murder (316).[2]

Sergeant Heath's role in this novel is what it is in each novel: a pragmatic, cigar-chewing flatfoot admired by Vance for his pugnacity but used purely as a conduit of authority. Wishing to keep control over all suspects who live in the same house, Vance turns to Hennessey, a homicide detective: "'I wish you'd run up-stairs and take a post where you can watch all the rooms. I don't want any communication between Mrs. Bliss and Salveter and Hani.' Hennessey glanced at Heath. 'Those are orders,' the sergeant informed him" (198).

In *The Casino Murder Case* the usually gruff Sergeant Heath proves unexpectedly pliable:

> Sergeant Heath appeared at the door.
> "The young doc's just coming downstairs. Want to see him, sir?"
> Vance hesitated; then nodded.
> "Yes, ask him to come in here, Sergeant."
> Heath disappeared and a moment later Doctor Kane entered the drawing room [157].

The impression this makes is that by this point the sergeant has been sufficiently trained to follow the orders of someone who has no official power over him but who can achieve this by force of character. We are also reminded of the rigid class distinctions of the British detective novel: Vance's good manners, education, his chumminess with Heath's superior emphasize his aristocratic status.

In *The Kidnap Murder Case* (1936) Vance, Markham, and Heath are involved with what at first appears to be a kidnapping, but proves to be murder. Beat officer McLaughlin reports to Heath, but also fields a question from Vance: "The officer answered emphatically, but with an air of deference which he had not shown to the Sergeant" (61). Much later in the narrative Snitkin, another officer who answers to Heath, echoes the deference paid to Vance: "It is interesting to note that Snitkin addressed himself to Vance and not to either Markham or Heath, although Vance had no official standing in the Police Department" (215). In much the same vein as in *The Casino Murder Case*, Markham's position is not only secondary to Vance, but deferential to the point of puerility: responding to Vance's entreaties to calm his nerves, "Markham obeyed automatically, like a frightened child submitting to his parent" (289).

Chandler never allows any true partnership with duly constituted authorities to sink to this level. The formerly rigid division between bourgeois detective and police detective, or, for that matter, different ranks

Four. Marlowe and the Police

and jurisdictions within officialdom, are carefully problematized in an intriguingly democratic fashion. Marlowe neither condescends to nor ignores these officers of the law, nor is cowed by them. It is far more common to find Marlowe teaching a cop or being taught by one, than it is to find the immediate, aggressive behavior (even hand-to-hand combat) typical of Hammett or Spillane.

There is a distinctly didactic element in all of Marlowe's encounters with the police, though often camouflaged by plot tensions and character confrontations. Ohls implies that Cronjager is a bad cop pure and simple, but this scene serves as a lesson in recognizing the gray areas; to give him his due, Cronjager equates proper procedure with justice, indeed with saving lives, but is nonetheless castigated by an officer of a brother organization for being negligent. By this point in time Marlowe is alone with Wilde, and he takes the opportunity to make clear that he has no illusions that law enforcement is guided by the highest ethical standards, but that he can also appreciate the police perspective:

> I've been in police business myself, as you know. They come a dime a dozen in any big city. Cops get very large and emphatic when an outsider tries to hide anything, but they do the same things themselves every other day, to oblige their friends or anybody with a little pull [*Stories* 674].

By way of contrast, in the one scene in *The Maltese Falcon* in which Sam Spade confronts a district attorney, he does so with the same pugnacity as in his dealings with Lieutenant Dundy, assuming, hot-headedly and illogically, that he's being accused of murder (392). He disparages District Attorney Bryan's reasoned conjectures about Thursby's murder and stalks out, daring Bryan to revoke his license and surprising the D.A. with his vehemence (393–4). In his own eyes, Spade can never be wrong, and those with whom he comes in contact can rarely be right. Hammett is concerned to resist established power but provides no other alternative but rigid self-reliance.

In *The Big Sleep* Marlowe has at one time been fired by D.A. Wilde for what he calls "insubordination," but which in fact is his resistance to police corruption (here defined as operating on the basis of political favors). Yet in his present, private status, he is willing to challenge Wilde, to make clear to him that police ethics are no better and no worse than private ethics and implying that, as a superior officer, Wilde should exert more authority. Thus, as there are good and bad cops, Chandler contrasts good and bad district attorneys. D.A. Grenz in *The Long Goodbye* has been drinking out of the office whiskey bottle and establishes an arrogant tone as soon as Marlowe is brought to him after three days' incarceration, insisting the he — and not the law — makes the rules. In reply, Marlowe reveals his knowledge of the law and his insistence on fair treatment:

> I was booked on suspicion. What the hell kind of legal system lets a man be shoved in a felony tank because some cop didn't get an answer to some questions? What evidence did he have? A telephone number on a pad. And what was he trying to prove by locking me up? Not a damn thing except that he had the power to do it. [*Later Novels* 467].

In *The Little Sister* Marlowe is again held in suspicion of withholding information, here in connection with the death of the mobster Steelgrave. In a fashion similar to what we have seen of D.A. Wilde, District Attorney Sewell Endicott informs Marlowe's client, actress Mavis Weld, that he "doesn't believe in seeking publicity at the expense of people to whom a certain kind of publicity might be fatal. It is my duty to determine whether anyone should be brought to trial for any of these murders, and to prosecute them, if the evidence warrants it" (*Later Novels* 394). This is a straightforward declaration of his duties and, since evidence is insufficient to prosecute Weld, she is allowed to leave with her high-priced lawyer, Lee Farrell.

After they leave, Endicott asks Marlowe if Farrell is representing him as well. "I can't afford him," Marlowe replies, "so I'm vulnerable." He assumes, at least for the moment, that Endicott might be corrupt enough to take advantage of that vulnerability, and his experience with "hard little men in hard little offices" (as he refers to Grenz) justifies his suspicion. Endicott replies with a grin, however: "I let them take all the tricks and then salve my dignity by working out on you, eh?" He makes it clear that Marlowe is also free to go, but criticizes the detective's actions, asking him, "Don't you think you owe a certain obligation to the law?" The answer is, "I would — if the law was like you." Endicott then offers a simple equation, "the citizen is the law," which the immediate proceedings have demonstrated as extremely difficult. And when he adds that "we're a nation of

Four. Marlowe and the Police

cop haters," he underscores the need for all citizens to act in concert to produce justice as opposed to merely expecting it, and emphasizes that it is an ongoing give-and-take involving human fallibility. In this quintessential Chandler moment, Marlowe agrees: "It'll take a lot to change that. On both sides" (*Later Novels* 395). The greatest danger, Chandler implies, is the arbitrary exercise of the power by these duly constituted authorities, a theme that he also examines in *The Big Sleep*.

Chandler has Marlowe embody less than total resistance to often arbitrary, quasi-official power and thus, contrary to Porter's assertion, "puts the law on trial." He is also conscious, however, that he depends on the police to make a living and that achieving order and justice is a communal task that requires constant compromise. He withholds information and acts independently of the police over the short haul, but his ultimate goals are congruent with those of good cops, and his confrontations with bad cops underscore the fallible nature of state power. The passage also makes explicit the fact that Marlowe has worked directly with the police (in the district attorney's office in the unspecified past). He well knows that as a police detective he would be bound by a much more stringent set of regulations; having this "official" experience helps him understand the workings of the police mind, one that he never truly disparages.

Farewell, My Lovely does not merely develop Chandler's investigation into police ethics and behavior: these factors constitute the theme of the novel. Chandler paints a complex, contrastive picture of good and bad law enforcement and even casts Marlowe in the role of police instructor. He also underscores the need for a continuing struggle for ethical behavior by introducing supportive characters who have paid a price of some kind for their ethical stances.

Much has been said of the unique position Anne Riordan holds in this novel as the only woman to make a dent in Marlowe's thick carapace of professionalism and masculinity. Jerry Speier sees her in an idealized light; she is "too good to be true" (103) and Marlowe "desires[s] ... to keep her on a pedestal" (113). Stephen Knight considers her the stereotypic "faithful and plucky sister-type" (146). But it is easily overlooked that Anne's ethos is guided by the figure of her deceased father, Cliff, the former honest police chief of notoriously corrupt Bay City who was hounded out of his job when racketeers, led by Laird Brunette, bought the mayoralty. Anne's more active role is to continue (in a private manner much like Marlowe's) her father's work. She bravely confronts Marlowe at gunpoint at the scene of Marriott's murder (apparently intending a citizen's arrest), far from certain that he is not the killer, and, after Marlowe makes his position clear, prods him into further action by tracing the ownership of the missing jade to the Grayles.

Later in the novel the private eye's access to the gambling ship *Montecito* is made possible by Red Norgaard, who, much like Cliff Riordan, was kicked off the Bay City police force when gangster Laird Brunette took over the city. Despite being treated roughly by a frustrated and angry Marlowe, Norgaard takes a deadly risk in accompanying him for a mere $25 and takes a professional interest in Marlowe's difficulties in finding Malloy. These characters remind the reader that Marlowe can and does rely on others for help. Marlowe's profession is not quite as lonely as Speier, Knight, and others have indicated; he is not an avatar of the solitary gunslinger entering a desperate and needy community from without, but a moderately independent, distinctly fallible investigator able to accept the assistance of others. Marlowe has need of Norgaard's boat because he failed in his first attempt to board the *Montecito*: he brings his gun along and is frisked on arrival. On this second trip out, Marlowe admits to Norgaard that he's "scared stiff" (*Stories* 953) and implies that he is in less than total control when he says he needs a "company of Marines" to get the job done (*Stories* 959). Marlowe is a flawed hero; conscious of his own insufficiencies, he is not too proud to admit fear or to ask for help. There is even a hint of a common identity with Marlowe in Riordan and Norgaard: Anne offers to work for free as his assistant and it would not take tremendous imagination to envision Red going into the same line of work.

In stark contrast, Chandler introduces Detective Lieutenant Nulty, who is responsible for the earlier Montgomery murder investigation, as not so much a foil or engaged colleague for Marlowe, but as a buffoon, a man whose dowdy appearance attests to the fact that he is not corrupt, but who virtually begs Marlowe to help him on several occasions. Nulty is essentially disinterested in the case for racist reasons: the murder of a black man is of no concern to him nor to the powers that be, yet he hopes

Four. Marlowe and the Police

that Marlowe's superior talents will help him get written up in the newspapers, which, in turn, will make him look good to his superiors.

Nulty claims on several occasions to have Malloy cornered, but it is clear in each case that he has the wrong man. Marlowe attempts to keep his scorn in check so as to maintain good relations with the police, but Nulty's helplessness makes it impossible for Marlowe to suppress his disdain. Before long Marlowe criticizes the policeman for lack of zeal in implementing quite basic detecting skills, such as tracing and interviewing the wife of the former owner of the bar, Jessie Florian. After Marlowe provides him with substantial evidence and intelligent conjecture, Nulty answers his benefactor by suspecting him of having taken a bribe from Florian. At the other end of the law enforcement spectrum is Lieutenant Randall of Los Angeles Central Homicide, who is investigating Lindsay Marriott's murder. In stark contrast to Nulty's pathetic helplessness, Randall reasons immediately in terms of probability and plausibility, questioning the suddenness and vagueness of Marriott's hiring Marlowe in the first place. Since the $8,000 payoff, entrusted to Marlowe, is missing, Randall has all the more reason to suspect the private eye.

Randall, like Marlowe, possesses the patient talent of suspending judgment and he quickly shifts his tactics to elicit Marlowe's views on Marriott's possible intended theft of the cash. He is skilled enough to reject his initial hypothesis and constructs a thorough scenario of Marriott's duplicity in using Marlowe as a fall guy for his (Marriott's) own scheme. Marlowe is quick to disparage Randall's theory, sarcastically insinuating that Marriott "beat his own brains out," to which Randall coolly posits the existence of an accomplice, one who double-crossed Marriott and took the money (*Stories* 825).

The intricate dovetailing of these crime experts' theories belies the critical consensus that Chandler was poor at plotting. More significantly in our context, it demonstrates that the private investigator/police encounter is fraught with potential antagonism but need not degenerate into conflict. Before long the two men are speaking in collegial terms, together puzzling out the murder, showing teamwork that is quite rare in Hammett. Chandler even allows his hero to be mistaken or to lag behind the police at any given time. It is Randall, not the private eye, who makes the initial, crucial connection between Jessie Florian and her landlord, Lindsay Marriott, and Marlowe explains to Anne Riordan at the end of the novel that the greatest concern the police detective had was that he, the private eye, would upset the carefully developed police investigation. Marlowe shows no resentment. Indeed, he makes clear in each novel that the police have the manpower and other resources to do a superior job; they do sometimes lack the will to do so or are prevented from working cooperatively for political reasons.

In stark contrast, cooperation is not something Marlowe can expect from the Bay City Police Department, which is more likely to be corrupt than Los Angeles since it's easier for gangsters to control a smaller civic unit. In search of information regarding the Grayle gems, he confronts Jules Amthor, a self-proclaimed confidence man who enjoys considerable police protection. In order to dispose of the nosy private eye, Amthor summons two Bay City cops, Captain Blane and Detective Sergeant Galbraith, police detectives who not only exceed their jurisdiction by taking Marlowe into custody in Los Angeles proper, but who beat him and deposit him with the proprietor of an illegal clinic.

Afterwards it comes as no surprise that the chief of police of Bay City, John Wax, is as corrupt as his men. Since Marlowe, however, now enjoys the clout of Grayle's influence, Wax calls Galbraith in to smooth things over with the private eye. Expecting, as might the reader, that Marlowe will seek revenge, Galbraith is surprised that Marlowe is willing to "trade" for information. Galbraith attempts to justify his position as one who is squeezed from above and below: "Cops don't go crooked for money.... They get caught in the system.... A guy can't stay honest if he wants to.... He gets chiseled out of his pants if he does. You gotta play the game dirty or you don't eat" (*Stories* 938). Galbraith's solution, half-heartedly proffered, is that of the religious, anti–Communist Moral Re-Armament program that was popular at this time and that, in Tom Driberg's words, "is summed up in four absolutes: Absolute Honesty, Absolute Purity, Absolute Unselfishness, and Absolute Love" (12). It is at this key juncture that Stephen Knight misinterprets Chandler's design inasmuch as he claims that Galbraith's talk "turns into a thinly-veiled sermon by the *author* on corruption, one that increasingly moves away from any social, interactive

Four. Marlowe and the Police

view of urban problems" (146, my emphasis). Knight thus transposes Galbraith's belief in Moral Re-Armament onto Marlowe and Marlowe's creator.

Quite the contrary; it is a sign of Chandler's willingness to compromise with the enemy (to understand police motives and actions at their worst) that Marlowe strikes up a tenuous professional alliance with Galbraith. Marlowe condemns police corruption, yet sees how and why corruption can exist, and indeed elicits further information from the policeman, who himself criticizes his superior officer's even greater complicity in Bay City–style police procedure. Galbraith's philosophy can be read as either sneeringly sarcastic or utterly hypocritical (since his actions belie purity and love of any kind) but Chandler succeeds in portraying the social background such that Galbraith's words are believable and even sympathetic.

Marlowe's increasing consciousness of his societal role is borne out in *The Little Sister*, the closest Chandler would ever come to writing a Hollywood novel. Chandler's aim was to use the film capital metaphorically: in having Marlowe refer to police detectives Christy French and Fred Beifus of the LAPD as a kind of hard-boiled Laurel and Hardy, Chandler underscores role consciousness on the part of these policemen. They are able, as is Marlowe, to step back and analyze their profession, determined to play out their roles in the best manner possible, despite the faulty quality of the "script." Although French bemoans the fact that the system relegates conscientious cops to dangerous and degrading work, his willingness to work with Marlowe expresses a hope that some degree of improvement can be achieved within the system.

French and Beifus investigate a murder in the Van Nuys Hotel where Flack, the house detective, serves as a bumbling contrast to the capable Marlowe vis-à-vis the police, much like the clownish Nulty in *Farewell, My Lovely*. The police brush off Flack's ill-conceived conjectures as to the possible killer and praise Marlowe's observational and analytical skills. Good relations with the police begin to deteriorate, however, once French feels that the spirit of cooperation is not mutual: he calls Marlowe the next day to let the detective know that he has been caught withholding valuable information.

Marlowe next meets French and Beifus in their office. By now Orrin Quest has been murdered and, indeed, has died in Marlowe's arms. As the detective well knows, he has been at murder scenes far too often to please the police. His role for them has shifted from that of responsible citizen and trusted professional to that of murder suspect. He is introduced to Lieutenant Moses Maglashan of the infamous Bay City police, who makes no bones about what he wants and to what extent he is willing to go to get it. He pulls a glove over his right hand and comments, "Some guys are more voluntary than others.... Something to do with the kidneys, they tell me" (*Later Novels* 345).

Just as Chandler has constructed his story such that Flack plays the foil for Marlowe, here Maglashan demonstrates — in his increasingly clear intention to use third-degree methods — the lapse in professionalism that characterizes police corruption. This three-way critical encounter goes far beyond simplistic good cop/bad cop contrasts often found in hard-boiled fiction. The L.A. cops distance themselves from Maglashan; they are clearly unwilling to go to the extremes of the third degree. They cite delaying tactics rather than coercive measures.

French and Beifus make it clear to Marlowe that he is by no means out of trouble with them, but they emphasize law enforcement concerns and techniques that, if not ideal, are more within legitimate spheres. The focus shifts to a discussion of police procedure and mutual wrongdoing. French insists that Marlowe either talk or be booked as a material witness. Marlowe's response is:

> "Ask the questions, ... If you don't like the answers, you can book me. If you book me, I get to make a phone call."
>
> "Correct," French [says], "*if* we book you. But we don't have to. We can ride the circuit with you. It might take days....
>
> "Strictly speaking, it wouldn't be legal, ... But we do it all the time. Like you do a few things which you hadn't ought to do maybe. Would you say you were legal in this picture?" [*Later Novels* 346].

Maglashan, by contrast, has asked why French and Beifus are talking to Marlowe "like he was human," told Marlowe that the Bay City force could murder him for his transgressions, and lashed Marlowe's face with his glove (*Later Novels* 349). Despite their suspicions, the L.A. detectives are anxious

Four. Marlowe and the Police

to hear Marlowe's theories; they are able to reconcile their anger at his actions with respect for his civil rights and his utilitarian value. Marlowe navigates the extremely narrow channel between accurately reporting what has occurred and revealing everything that he knows. Not unlike other good cops and district attorneys in other Chandler novels, these men serve to challenge Marlowe's sense of duty and ethics. Neither side has a monopoly on virtue, but each strives to achieve a just result.

When Sam Spade is confronted in much the same manner by Tom Polhaus in *The Maltese Falcon*, he reacts egotistically and evasively, emphasizing that the police have achieved nothing in their efforts to coax information out of him (389). There is always, however, a dialectic at work in Chandler, a give-and-take that has the potential to produce a synthesis of ideal detective work, which in turn can stand for the ideal community. Maglashan's unquestioning reliance on his own sense of right and wrong excludes not only his enemy (as he defines Marlowe) but his allies as well. Galbraith represents a "Maglashan" who, when given the opportunity, can be brought to at least express his own self-consciousness of the untenable state of affairs vis-à-vis the criminal justice system.

Towards the end of the novel Marlowe summons French and Beifus to a house in Stillwood Heights where another man has been killed. He is now protecting his new client, Mavis Weld, and although he casts the police as a comedy team "opening up the act" (*Later Novels* 380), they are decidedly grim when they arrive. Well aware that their patience has run out, Marlowe insists that his new client remain nameless and is handcuffed for his troubles. In a revealing speech French bitterly plays on the theme of political interference from above that is paradigmatic of Chandler's "good" cops:

> As if we didn't get pushed around enough by the guys in the corner offices, the City Hall gang, the day chief, the night chief.... As if we didn't have to handle one hundred and fourteen homicides last year out of three rooms that don't have enough chairs for the whole duty squad to sit down in at once.... If we get a confession, we beat it out of the guy, they say, and some shyster calls us Gestapo in court and sneers at us when we muddle our grammar. If we make a mistake they put us back in uniform on Skid Row ... [*Later Novels* 382–83].

French is spoiling for a fight, taunting Marlowe to say something that will justify the kind of punishment that is typical of Maglashan. Marlowe, however, refuses to be baited: "Any private eye wants to play ball with the police. Sometimes it's a little hard to find out who's making the rules of the ball game. Sometimes he doesn't trust the police, and with cause" (*Later Novels* 383). French is ready to punch Marlowe, but Beifus, keeping a cool head and remembering what proper procedure dictates, steps between the two men and himself takes the punch. Thus the earlier portrayal of the police as a comedy team culminates in Keystone Kops–like slapstick, an absurdity not lost on Beifus: "It's a new kind of third degree ... the cops beat hell out of each other and the suspect cracks up from the agony of watching" (*Later Novels* 384).

This has, like all good comedy, a serious foundation. Camaraderie, not retaliation, is Beifus' response as he offers French a cigarette and claims that no one has hit him, that the incident never occurred. Although he is still quite determined to arrest Marlowe, French's punch has had a cathartic effect. While William Ruehlmann finds that this novel "is the account of a Marlowe on his way to becoming a Maglashan" (87), the transformation happens to a different character. It is as if transferring his anger and violence to Beifus has driven the "Maglashan" out of French's system and he is able to resume the proper police attitude. French's frustration is that of a man placed in an untenable position, that of a policeman who resists — as we might imagine Cliff Riordan to have done — the siren song of graft and corruption, but who is caught nonetheless in the same web as those who abuse their positions.

Chandler has constructed an arena within which both police and private eye can establish a dialogue: all participants are in their way "tarnished," but clear boundaries are drawn to define and limit inappropriate behavior, here, specifically, preventing third-degree methods of interrogation. No pretense is made to a completely democratic relationship: Marlowe is, to an extent, in the power of the L.A. police and would be utterly at the mercy of Maglashan, but the anarchic conditions of *Red Harvest* do not obtain in Chandler's world. A just order is lacking, but not altogether missing, as long as dedicated individuals work in concert.

In having Philip Marlowe confront the police to the extent and in the manner that he does, Chandler added a key element to hard-boiled fiction, one that would later be drawn upon, for example, by Ross Mac-

Four. Marlowe and the Police

donald in his Freudian tales of familial crime in Southern California. But so far-reaching is Chandler's influence that it can even be traced in the sadistic, reactionary fiction of Mickey Spillane, whose work Chandler derided as "a mixture of violence and outright pornography" (*Letters* 311). Spillane found his theme in the rugged individualism of Hammett, and indeed, capitalizing on post–World War II American anti–Communist paranoia in books such as *One Lonely Night*, pushes the one-against-all ethos to the utmost limit. But for all the egregious violence of his plots and the two-dimensional self-righteousness of his protagonist, Spillane manages in select moments to portray private eye/police encounters in a manner closer to Chandler than to Hammett.

In *Kiss Me, Deadly* Spillane has his detective, Mike Hammer, reserve for law enforcement agents the kind of derision Sherlock Holmes holds for Inspector Lestrade, especially after FBI men and local police lose a valuable prisoner Hammer has captured. The single exception is his friend, police detective Pat Chambers, the long-suffering good cop who warns, cajoles, chews out, and sympathizes with Hammer. The private eye is, in rare instances, even willing to cooperate with the law as long as it is represented by Chambers.

Aware of his propensity for rash behavior, Chambers tries to rein Hammer in by eliciting the private eye's cooperation and volunteering key information, knowing full well that Hammer's skills are valuable. He eventually hammers out a "two-way deal" with Mike (44) because he realizes, like good cops in Chandler, that political interference — including that which protects the Mafia, which has "political cover so heavy you can't bust through it with a sledge hammer" (43) — is a far greater danger than a single private eye's excesses. In Spillane's world, corruption is pervasive, but neither the private eye nor, at least, one policeman have given up the fight, and this extremely limited, even perverse, optimism recalls the more constructive optimism of Chandler. It is even possible for Hammer to express remorse for not living up to his obligations to Chambers, although it takes the most frightening threat imaginable, the torture of his beloved secretary, Velda, to make him see it.

Hammer's willingness, however, to cooperate only with Chambers greatly limits his interactive potential in the sense that Chandler displays in his far more complex tales. The latter's decision to confront Marlowe with a variety of enforcement agents allows him to paint a quite extensive picture of appropriate and inappropriate police behavior and a private citizen's response to it. When all is said and done, Spillane buries the attempt at cooperative work under a landslide of right-wing ideology and unembarrassed violence expressed through the actions of a man so utterly sure that he is right that no real dialogue can take place. In *One Lonely Night* his overwrought imagination leads him to "address," in an interior monologue, a judge who had previously censured him for acting recklessly on his own. Hammer insists that the members of the Communist conspiracy he has discovered have (like all other of his opponents) forfeited their civil rights, and his idea is to essentially eliminate the police altogether:

> Want to hear that philosophy? It's simple enough. Go after the big boys. Oh, don't arrest them, don't treat them to the dignity of the democratic process of the courts and law ... do the same thing to them that they'd do to you! Treat 'em to the unglorious taste of sudden death [102].

This is an ideological position unthinkable in Chandler. Spillane carefully avoids any real political debate, preferring to have his hero react viscerally, almost literally foaming at the mouth at the prospect of eliminating, as gruesomely as possible, the Communist vermin threatening the fabric of American society. Spillane's right-radical solution can be traced to the Hammett of *Red Harvest*, for whom being right is a function of self-indulgence and having a faster trigger finger.[3]

Chandler, however, emphasizes political debate. Marlowe proceeds from the premise that intellect, not physical force, must be brought to bear on these problems, and his words and actions are practical examples of John Dewey's emphasis on intelligence to effect social change. In Cornel West's words, "the aims of [Deweyan] critical intelligence are to overcome obstacles, resolve problems, and project realizable possibilities in pressing predicaments" (97), an apposite description of Marlowe's modus operandi. "Realizable possibilities" must be emphasized: Chandler's detective works pragmatically, attempting to negotiate on the case-by-case, person-to-person basis that his chosen profession insists upon, usually suspending judgment because his understanding of the grave difficulties the police encounter in *their* day-to-day labor dictates just such a solution.

Four. Marlowe and the Police

Much of what Marxist or Marxian critics object to in Chandler is just this relativist stance, but they are too quick to condemn Marlowe for his compromises. It is, doubtless, easier to place faith in the fire-and-sword solutions portrayed by Hammett and Spillane, but the slow process of negotiation Marlowe utilizes is superior, from a Deweyan perspective, in that it avoids the pitfalls Hammett and Spillane stumble into and upholds the idea that violence is no solution to problems in a democracy. Dewey insists on the need for openness in the democratic political forum. He sees violence as the principle enemy to constructive dialogue and, indeed, that resorting to violence is to maintain the status quo under a new banner: "those who propagate the dogma of dependence upon force have the sanction of much that is already entrenched in the existing system. They would but turn the use of it to opposite ends" (*Later Works* XI:46).

We have seen how the police/private eye interactions in Chandler reveal negotiation skills on Marlowe's part that are, to some extent, echoed by responsible police officers. The next chapter investigates how the private eye produces and elicits similar dialogue and actions in his dealings with the criminal world.

Chapter Five

Marlowe and the Criminals

For Giles Gunn in *Thinking Across the American Grain*, the politics of pragmatism is "distinguished by the democratic preference for rendering differences conversable" (37). Philip Marlowe's key trait — one that distinguishes him from the heroes of previous and contemporary detectives and that serves as the motivating force for Ross Macdonald's Lew Archer — is his willingness to converse with his contemporaries: to discuss, to argue, even to teach and to learn. He is also, in stark contrast to the Continental Op and Mike Hammer, an attentive and considerate listener, on the lookout for possible compromise, resistant to knee-jerk violent solutions reminiscent of the rough justice of the frontier that undermine negotiation. Dennis Porter feels that private eyes, while "authentic representatives of the phenomenon of social protest," can change society only inasmuch as they strive to return society to the traditional status of "the innocent young Republic and its frontier" (181), but Chandler's efforts are forward-looking; although his optimism is fragile, he sees opportunities for improvement through dialogue among clients, criminals, and cops.

As for Marlowe, the same consciousness of his own shortcomings that aids him in understanding the police is also brought to bear on criminals. Marlowe's relations with criminals are even more complex and less predictable than his interactions with police. While Chandler presents the demands and desires of law enforcers often as corrupt (and thus similar to the "tarnished" actions of his hero) the line between official law enforcer and private eye is always explicitly clear. For one thing, Marlowe never operates under any illusion that he has as much power as the police, who can harm his career by suspending or revoking his license, and he is thus often just as much at the mercy of the ethical cops as the sadists.

The private eye interacts with criminals, however, on a more equal

Five. Marlowe and the Criminals

footing. Though at times intimidated by members of the underworld, more often than not he is able to use his intelligence and negotiating skills to neutralize their power. Without any illusions as to implementing an ideal system of justice, he nevertheless strives for social accommodation and incremental improvement. Of equal importance, Chandler rigorously questions just what it means to be beyond the law. His unflinching treatment of law enforcement officers problematizes the law itself on ethical grounds, and logic dictates that he question received definitions of criminality as well.

Although socially critical utterances outside his fiction are few and far between, Chandler does at times provide clues that help in understanding his ideology. In a letter to Frederick Lewis Allan, for example, he rejects W. H. Auden's critique of his work as "serious studies of the criminal milieu" as too narrow: "Is this a criminal milieu? No, just average, corrupt living" (*Letters* 114–15). He refuses to recognize facile social divisions of good and evil, but instead perceives these qualities as intermingled, strives to understand people on an individual basis, and forces the complacent reader to identify, at one time or another, with all his characters. His writing implicitly rejects the two-dimensionality of Mickey Spillane, who characterizes his criminals as subhuman who may thereby be executed by his vigilante hero, Mike Hammer. Ultimately a deeply ingrained sense of tolerance is the detective's touchstone. Although burdened with his share of prejudices, Marlowe strives to understand criminal behavior in light of his own shortcomings; his consistent self-consciousness, most often expressed in self-denigrating, wry humor, functions as a self-humbling mechanism. As a rule the detective withholds judgment whenever possible, and the antithesis here is Spillane's self-righteousness and swift reciprocity.[1]

Shortly before he died Chandler wrote an article for the *Sunday Times* of London on the famous American gangster Lucky Luciano, and wrote to the deported crime boss in Italy that "the object of my life is to understand people, their motives, their origins, how they become what they are and not ever to judge them" (*Letters* 475). Chandler may be excused for exaggerating, given his zeal to achieve an "audience" with the crime czar, for he does bring an ethical standard to bear in his novels. But the principle runs very deep: there is a consistent pattern, from *The Big Sleep* (1939) to

Playback (1958), of the private eye's delaying of judgment of both the ostensibly legitimate motives of his clients and the supposed illegitimate activities of criminals.

There is even faint recognition in these novels of a concept that still seems radical in contemporary America: that crime is normal and even useful to society. In *Ideology and Crime* Leon Radzinowicz draws on Emile Durkheim's analysis of crime within society in a chapter aptly titled "Towards a Pragmatic Position I." Durkheim not only thought the elimination of crime impossible; his much-attacked assertion was that, as deviation, it worked toward improving society, for

> without deviation there could be no adaptation, no change, no progress: a society could not survive. Crime, claimed Durkheim, is "bound up with the fundamental conditions of all social life, and by that very fact it is *useful*, because these conditions, of which it is a part, are themselves indispensable to the normal evolution of morality and law [73].

Chandler intuitively grasped that keeping an open mind towards definitions of criminality was a prerequisite for social change and was thus needed for the genre to have any validity at all. Most of his 1944 essay "The Simple Art of Murder" is a diatribe against what he considered the staid, artificial British whodunit, predicated on the belief that nothing really matters in these works; they are merely intricate puzzles that need solving. It was in exploiting the potential of the hard-boiled novel for social criticism, primarily through the figure of the detective as social connector and catalyst, that led him to develop his detective not merely as a chaser of felons and murderers, but a responsible man who wonders aloud how and why these men and women came to commit such acts, how such acts became criminal in the first place, and to what extent and in what manner they should be punished. Chandler's grasp of the gray areas of social behavior and "legitimacy" enabled him to portray criminals as having recognizable motives, and in some cases even as eliciting empathy and understanding from the reader.

In *The Long Goodbye* Marlowe defines the border between the legitimate and the illegitimate as "the shadow line" while looking for the doctor who treated the writer Roger Wade for alcoholism. He describes the offices of quacks and abortionists as merging imperceptibly with those of merely

Five. Marlowe and the Criminals

unsuccessful lawyers, doctors, and dentists (*Later Novels* 523–4). In doing so he himself crosses the line, is labelled a "cheap grifter" by one of the suspected quacks (*Later Novels* 526). Here and in other novels the fact that Marlowe's occupation is based on gathering information makes him vulnerable to the accusation of misusing his power, primarily through blackmail. Conscious of this status, he brings considerable understanding of the motives of others to his cases.

When Mrs. Elizabeth Bright Murdock hires Marlowe in *The High Window*, she insists that her daughter-in-law, nightclub singer Linda Conquest, has stolen the valuable Brasher Doubloon simply because "you know what these night club people are." Marlowe's cool response is that they are "all sorts of people — like the rest of us" (*Stories* 996). As is often the case in hard-boiled fiction, a well-heeled member of the middle class is far too quick to assume the guilt of someone with a smaller bank account. Marlowe's experience, however, has taught him that superficial labels and appearances can be deceptive. Linda Conquest indeed works for Alex Morny, a member of the underworld, but there is no sign of anything illegal in her actions. One of Chandler's more praiseworthy female figures, Conquest proves to have far higher ethical standards than her accuser. In addition to defending herself, she takes up the cause of Murdock's personal secretary, Merle Davis. She recognizes (and makes Marlowe see more clearly) how Murdock is psychologically torturing Davis and that something has to be done about it.

In his war on intolerance midwesterner Chandler typically casts a "legitimate" figure from the Midwest as a vehicle to incorporate and elucidate rigid mainstream virtues that are no longer fully responsive to current events. While searching for Moose Malloy in *Farewell, My Lovely*, Marlowe questions one Mrs. Morrison, who is helpful with information until she smells liquor on his breath. Marlowe mollifies her somewhat by complimenting her on the beauty of a sideboard she has transported from her native Iowa. Mrs. Morrison represents an intolerance that impedes true neighborliness. She spies on the alcoholic Jessie Florian (hence Marlowe's nickname for her, Old Nosey) and indulges in gleeful Schadenfreude when she learns that Florian may be in trouble with the law. Chandler was an alcoholic and was well aware of its ravages, but his concern here is not that abstention produces a healthier lifestyle, but that leftover Prohibition narrow-mindedness only further tears the social fabric inasmuch as it fragments communities.

In *The Little Sister*, Orfamay Quest, Marlowe's initial client, is a midwestern teetotaler as well. Like Mrs. Morrison she proceeds in terms of rigid, incurious, and unquestioning ethical standards, as when she states, "I don't think I'd care to employ a detective that uses liquor in any form. I don't even approve of tobacco." When Marlowe responds by wisecracking, Orfamay lectures him, invoking the godlike authority of her employer:

> "If I talked like that to one of Dr. Zugsmith's patients," she said, "I'd lose my position. He's most particular how I speak to the patients — even the difficult ones."
> "How is the old boy? I haven't seen him since that time I fell off the garage roof."
> She looked surprised and quite serious. "Why surely you can't know Dr. Zugsmith" [*Later Novels* 204–5].

Orfamay so lacks a sense of humor that she doesn't even know when she's being kidded. Her world is quite settled, quite limited, and quite intolerant, and what brings tears to her eyes is the hypocritical fear that her search for her missing brother Orrin will be reported in the Manhattan, Kansas, newspaper (*Later Novels* 211).

In response to one of Orfamay's many complaints about the evils of Los Angeles, Marlowe simply says that "we have to take the bad with the good in this life" (*Later Novels* 231), an offhand, sarcastic comment, yet one that neatly sums up the detective's philosophy. Marlowe eschews confronting problems idealistically, but he pragmatically confronts them daily on a professional and personal basis. And by guardedly engaging the citizens of the city, he avoids the opposite extreme of nihilism as found in Hammett, whose Continental Op in *Red Harvest*, for Sinda Gregory, "is made to appear as guilty and morally reprehensible as the rest of the gangsters" (37).

Orfamay's puritanical response is to criticize Marlowe for not putting in what she feels is a full day's work. After proving herself utterly ignorant as to the harsh realities of the big city and the difficult job Marlowe has (and overestimating Orrin's ability to cope with them), she once again

Five. Marlowe and the Criminals

attempts to impose upon the detective a narrow and strict code of behavior. If Orfamay's greatest concern is for money (something "I never make mistakes about" [*Later Novels* 397]), the ultimate taboo is sex; she comes from a town where, she claims, kissing in public is illegal (*Later Novels* 235), and she is both repelled by and attracted to the hard-boiled dick's continual challenges through sexual innuendo. While his wisecracking seems at first gratuitous, there lurks behind it the desire to force Orfamay to see her own hypocrisy, to shock her into recognizing that there exist other equally valid systems of value.

Chandler develops here the kind of role reversal he hinted at with Mrs. Murdock and Linda Conquest in *The High Window*. Like the former, Orfamay has no ability to look beneath the surface, and she denigrates the acting career and concomitant lifestyle of her half sister, Mavis Weld, labelling her the black sheep of her family. However, although Weld, like Linda Conquest, consorts with gangsters, there's no evidence of any wrongdoing on her part. Far from it; she has tried to help the murderous Orrin and she's willing to take responsibility for Steelgrave's murder in order to protect Orfamay. It is hardly accidental that Orfamay turns out to be one of the novel's true criminals. She and Orrin have both blackmailed Mavis Weld, and the little sister in turn betrays Orrin when she sets him up for murder. It is this ostensibly "good" citizen, and no professional criminal, who is the recipient of Marlowe's scorn: "I guess you and Orrin belong to that class of people that can convince themselves that everything they do is right" (*Later Novels* 400). In Chandler's ethical universe a criminal who makes no bones about his illegitimate actions is superior to ostensibly law-abiding hypocrites. Marlowe feigns betrayal of his new client, Weld, in order to confirm Orfamay's duplicity, and condemns the little sister far more than he does Dolores Gonzalez, Orrin's actual killer.

Marlowe knows what Orfamay doesn't, that no one can always be right, and he strives to make sense of a less-than-perfect world — one in which laws are passed and enforced for political, not ethical, reasons — inhabited by police, rich clients, naive or unlucky victims, all of whom come to terms of some kind with it. Such compromises are defensible, even preferable, given the unflinching view Chandler takes: "It is not a very fragrant world, but it is the world you and I live in," as he emphasizes in "The Simple Art of Murder" (*Later Novels* 991). Even at its worst, at its most intrusive, manipulative, and violent, he suggests, the world is of our making and thus of our improving.

In a letter to James Sandoe, Chandler provides a personal reminiscence that serves as a keen example of his social concern and his recognition that law does not always equal justice. A banker he knew had provided desperate ranchers with unsecured loans during the Depression with the result that the banker served at least two years in federal prison and the bank was forced to close.

> But who was he defrauding? The stockholders of the bank? He was one himself and the others were all men of property in the neighborhood.... He was attempting by the only means he saw to keep the bank's source of income from collapsing.... There is something tragically wrong with a system of justice which can and does make criminals of honest men and can only convict gangsters and racketeers when they don't pay their taxes [*Letters* 140–41].

By 1920, the year after Chandler's return to the United States from England, traditional respect for law and order had severely eroded. The unpopular and unenforceable 18th Amendment and the law to enforce it, the Volstead Act, had unleashed a crime wave based on rum-running, and Prohibition inculcated disrespect for the law and made criminals out of heretofore law-abiding citizens unwilling to give up their "wet" lifestyles. James T. Kloppenberg reminds us that such discontent had earlier roots. The political system during and after the Civil War was subject to "persistent corruption," so much so that "an electorate incensed by recurring scandals and incompetent politicians finally lost confidence — and interest — in electoral politics" (363). Whether or not Chandler was aware of this history, his fiction reflects the direct experience of Prohibition, and we may speculate that a hard drinker like Chandler felt himself personally implicated in its hypocrisies.

Chandler at his most radical forces difficult ethical and social decisions on his readers. His characterizations underscore the fact that old-fashioned reliance on stereotypes established by detective writers is impossible; he turned the stock characters of the indestructible gumshoe, the cold-blooded or deranged killer, and the beautiful but untrustworthy femme fatale inside out, convinced that a new, more flexible stance that is critical

Five. Marlowe and the Criminals

of received standards was needed to realize the social potential of the genre. While Chandler's protagonist assumes the role of social delineator and connector, his more successful criminals, the entrepreneurs, resemble Hammett's heroes as models of rugged individualism, and are ultimately criticized for it.

Chandler risks downright caricature in his portrait of Mendy Menendez, the entrepreneurial gangster and supposed war comrade of Terry Lennox in *The Long Goodbye*. Menendez appears in Marlowe's office soon after the detective has returned from three days in jail for helping Lennox escape, and he verbally abuses Marlowe long before he identifies himself: "You're small time.... Very small time.... You're a piker, Marlowe. You're a peanut grifter. You're so little it takes a magnifying glass to see you." Menendez protests far too much: he criticizes Marlowe for his befriending Terry Lennox, illogically stating that doing him favors means that the detective has "sold out to him" (*Later Novels* 478–9) and he sings his own praises as a man who possesses all the trappings of modern American success:

> I'm a big bad man, Marlowe. I make lots of dough.... I got a place in Bel-Air that cost ninety grand and I already spent more than that to fix it up. I got a lovely platinum-blond wife and two kids in private schools back east. My wife's got a hundred and fifty grand in rocks and another seventy-five in furs and clothes.... I got a place in Florida and a seagoing yacht with a crew of five men. I got a Bentley, two Cadillacs, a Chrysler station wagon, and an MG for my boy [*Later Novels* 479–80].

Marlowe is just as forthcoming with evidence of his relative poverty, and even lets Menendez slap him before his patience is exhausted. He waits just long enough to learn what Mendy knows about Lennox and just long enough to develop a fairly good picture of the man's character before he strikes back. Even with so obvious and unreceptive an interlocutor, Marlowe gleans what he can from the dialogue.

The detective never allows his disagreements with criminals to get in the way of appreciating their humanity. Towards the end of *The Long Goodbye* Marlowe is pistol-whipped by Menendez. By this point in time, however, the gangster has made too many enemies among the police and Bernie Ohls shows up in support of Marlowe when the detective retaliates. The police detective (one of Chandler's more perceptive policemen) interprets Menendez' being overpowered by the private eye as weakness: "Soft ... soft as mush." But Marlowe, having himself just been brutalized, nevertheless corrects Ohls: "He's not soft ... he's hurt. Any man can be hurt" (*Later Novels* 708). Far from holding a grudge, he identifies, on the visceral as well as intellectual level, with these men.

If Menendez is an extreme case, Marlowe's first encounter with Eddie Mars in *The Big Sleep* is more typical in its rendition of negotiation. Mars is suspicious of Marlowe's presence in blackmailer Arthur Gwynn Geiger's house and is alarmed when he finds blood under the carpet. When he threatens Marlowe ("We'll have some law") the detective readily agrees, and though "he didn't like my agreeing with him" (*Stories* 641) Mars asks for Marlowe's opinion as to what has happened, and a potentially constructive dialogue has been set into motion.

More subtle, but clearly discernable, evidence of the gangster's sense of superiority is presented. Mars attempts to overwhelm Marlowe with his political connections and with the presence of two gunmen waiting outside, but the detective remains unaffected. Instead he quite voluntarily offers to help Mars clear up the mystery, as long as, we discover later, such assistance coincides with protecting his client. What rescues Marlowe from the nihilist attitude typical of Hammett's Continental Op in this case is the fact that Mars truly has had no hand in this murder. Marlowe neither colludes with Mars nor caves in to the gangster's threats. Knowing full well what Mars represents, the detective nevertheless refuses to jump to conclusions regarding Geiger's murder; he reserves judgment as to Mars' possible complicity in the crime. Mars' powers of judgment are inferior to Marlowe's: the private eye sizes up the gangster accurately, emphasizing the protection Mars has bought from the police, but when Mars counters that "you need a little protection yourself" (*Stories* 644), he's off the mark. Implicit in Mars' attitude is that Marlowe is a grifter, and that he needs the gangster's connections with the police to protect himself. Doing so, of course, would make him dependent on Mars. Protection for an entrepreneurial criminal is an assertion of his superior position in the hierarchy, but we have already viewed Marlowe's abilities to fend for himself vis-à-vis law enforcement in the last chapter and his intelligence and talents here serve as a sufficient counterforce to Mars' siren song.

Five. Marlowe and the Criminals

In *Farewell, My Lovely*, Marlowe's quest for Moose Malloy leads him to the gambling ship *Montecito* and its owner, Laird Brunette. Before the actual confrontation, Red Norgaard, a former policeman who assists the detective, echoes Marlowe's attitude about the traits of criminals—that they are "like the rest of us":

> These racketeers are a new type. We think of them the way we think about old time yeggs or needled-up punks. Big-mouthed police commissioners on the radio yell that they're all yellow rats, that they'll kill women and babies and howl for mercy if they see a police uniform. They ought to know better than to try to sell the public that stuff. There's yellow cops and there's yellow torpedoes—but damn few of either [*Stories* 955].

Norgaard continues to distinguish criminals in mainstream societal terms, specifically as successful members of capitalist society: "And as for the top men, like Brunette—they didn't get there by murdering people. They got there by guts and brains—and they don't have the group courage the cops have either. But above all they're business men. What they do is for money" (*Stories* 955).

Like Mars and Morny, Brunette is distinguished by good English and good manners, and his surroundings reflect no-nonsense wealth. Brunette's office on the *Montecito* is described primarily in business terms, with "business-like papers on the desk, with columns of figures, done on a bookkeeping machine" (*Stories* 962). Brunette has Marlowe's gun taken from him, but the subsequent dialogue indicates that this is a safety precaution: there will be no Hammer-like egregious violence here.

Chandler makes the most of his opportunity to analyze entrepreneurial criminals, who are more representative of the larger community than the police who, as public officials, are at one remove from the ultimate source of power: money. The fact that these captains of illicit industry can buy off the police (Menendez has on his payroll a police detective named Big Willie Magoon) further defines their powerful status. Brunette is powerful enough to buy influence with the corrupt politicians of Bay City; police detective Randall claims that Bay City is "Brunette's town," and, more specifically, that "they say he put up thirty grand to elect a mayor" (*Stories* 917). Accepting these men as representative of the hierarchy of the nation as a whole, Marlowe refuses to deny or ignore their significance.

Raymond Chandler's Philip Marlowe

As much as Marlowe displays his reserve of sympathy for the criminals he encounters, however, he is never guilty of excusing wrongdoing. Towards the end of *The Big Sleep*, after the detective has been captured by Canino and has met Mona Mars, he rejects her defense of her racketeer husband as merely an entrepreneur providing a public service, since, in her words, "as long as people will gamble there will be places for them to gamble." He replies,

> That's just protective thinking. Once outside the law you're all the way outside. You think he's just a gambler. I think he's a pornographer, a blackmailer, a hot car broker, a killer by remote control, and a suborner of crooked cops. He's whatever looks good to him, whatever has the cabbage pinned to it [*Stories* 735–6].

The detective as information-gatherer has compiled a complete dossier on Mars and he condemns the rapacity of the entrepreneur, and, by extension, the excesses of the capitalist ideology. Knowledge is, itself, on the other hand, a progressive tool: Marlowe attempts to make Mona admit that she knows full well what her husband is; ignorance is worse than useless, it is deadly. Marlowe does not question the appropriateness of Mars' entrepreneurial activities; they are perfectly in keeping with the money orientation of the nation at large. He implies, however, that an ethical border has been crossed, especially inasmuch as Mars hires Canino to do his killing for him. Ultimately, Marlowe's dealings with entrepreneurial criminals reflect a pragmatic stance that is neither defeatist nor carelessly optimistic. He is too well aware of their political power to imagine that he can oppose them head-on, yet he is actively (even daringly) engaged in resisting their more extreme, more socially damaging, actions.

Chandler's and Marlowe's sympathies are far more often with those who have had no real chance to escape the social roles into which they have been born. One might then expect Chandler's class bias to have endeared him to a Marxist critic such as Ernest Mandel, who, however, feels that Marlowe, among other detectives, is a sentimentalist who wastes his energy on pursuing criminals who wield only "limited clout" (35–36). It is doubtless Chandler's reluctance to make any global condemnation of the capitalist system that bothers Mandel. Chandler was uncomfortable with politics on any theoretical level and did not question his own motives

Five. Marlowe and the Criminals

for sympathizing with the disenfranchised. But he consistently and symbolically sought redress for social ills within the democratic system as he knew it in the United States, within the liberal tradition.

In "The Simple Art of Murder," for example, he insisted that no social or political hierarchy is truly divorced from the "rank and file" in a democracy, and thus cannot be completely blamed for its failures: since Americans get the social order they deserve, it is within their power to change their society, no matter how bleak the outlook. Each individual has his share of responsibility in realizing a just society, since "law and order are things we talk about but refrain from practicing" (*Later Novels* 991).

It is unfortunate that Chandler did not elaborate on this point in the essay, but his fiction makes it clear that social consciousness and social action of the individual are indispensable in a democracy, and he utilizes Marlowe's unique position as shuttle diplomat between the "legitimate" and "illegitimate" worlds to model such behavior. Marlowe has no breathtaking skills, boundless energy, or incredible good fortune, as do Mike Hammer and the Continental Op. Chandler has stripped away these superhero elements; aside from his intelligence and skill, the detective is remarkable only inasmuch as he is conscious of his social position and his responsibilities. Chandler has also stripped his hero of the rugged arrogance of the aforementioned detectives, who give little if any thought to how their actions will affect those around them. Marlowe is prepared to listen to criminals, willing to learn and even to teach.

The less successful criminals are the petty thieves, con artists, and near amateurs such as Joe Brody in *The Big Sleep*, who holds down a legitimate job as an insurance agent, but is ready to indulge in blackmail when the chance arises. Brody's dilemma is that he has neither sufficient muscle to intimidate Eddie Mars nor enough intelligence or skill to outmaneuver him. Marlowe actually corrects and instructs Brody, who has taken over Geiger's cache of pornography, telling him that "that play with Geiger's books was terrible" since Geiger was under Mars' protection. The detective thus demonstrates his superior grasp of the criminal hierarchy. Brody's insecurity leads him to refer to himself in the third person as compensation: "Joe's watchin' his step plenty" (*Stories* 648). He is, nevertheless, clearly out of his league. Marlowe's advice consists of recommending to Brody that he resume Geiger's business of lending out his pornography (which had tacit protection from the police) instead of resorting to blackmail, a substantially more harmful activity.

Marlowe's first duty, however, is to his client, and in order to get the negatives of the nude photographs of Carmen Sternwood, he threatens Brody with Carmen's witnessing of Brody's supposed killing of Geiger. Every time Brody tries to wiggle out of giving Marlowe the photos, the detective is ahead of him, since Brody's intelligence is "just average, for a grifter" (*Stories* 651). Although Marlowe exerts considerable pressure on Brody, he also maintains a reserve of respect for the man; he explains his situation calmly and truthfully, admitting to Brody that he was outside Geiger's house and heard the shots.

Joyce Carol Oates has faulted Chandler for the two-dimensionality of his characterizations, a charge that Chandler elicited through his use of grotesque description.[2] One prime example is Moose Malloy, another lower-echelon criminal, introduced on the very first page of *Farewell, My Lovely*: "He was a big man but not more than six feet five inches tall and not wider than a beer truck." Dressed in garish clothes, "he looked about as inconspicuous as a tarantula on a slice of angel food" (*Stories* 767). What lies beneath this comic-book exterior, however, is a gangster just out of prison on a romantic quest — the "knight" indeed that Philip Durham sees incorporated in Marlowe — whose love for Velma Valento is undiminished despite suspicion that she had betrayed him. Malloy's rash and racist actions in a black bar, culminating in murder, are never presented as justifiable, but while Marlowe condemns Malloy's actions, his sympathy and understanding for the man grow.[3]

When Marlowe and Lieutenant Randall discover Jessie Florian's body, they surmise from the spacing of the finger marks on her neck that Malloy is the killer. Marlowe partially comes to his defense: "He probably didn't mean to kill her, though. He's just too strong" (*Stories* 925). His sympathy for the brutal giant is not merely sentimental; he also makes it clear to Randall that understanding Malloy's motive in the killing (he grew desperate while grilling Florian for information about Velma) is needed to solve the case. His sympathy never extends to support of what Malloy has

Five. Marlowe and the Criminals

done. Rather his pragmatic approach helps Randall connect Malloy's actions with the Lindsay Marriott murder.

Marlowe later takes a considerable risk when he searches for Malloy on Laird Brunette's gambling ship, the *Montecito*. Brunette is puzzled by Marlowe's stubborn pursuit: "You risk your hide to come out here and hand me a card to pass on to some thug I don't even know. There's no sense in it" (*Stories* 965). It is never specified just what the note says, but the implication is that it informs Moose (whom Marlowe refers to as "probably the nicest man I ever met" [*Stories* 969]) that the detective knows where Velma is, and it draws Moose to Marlowe's apartment for the denouement. He chides Moose for killing Florian, implying that his earlier killing of the bar manager was in self-defense, but that he has irrevocably crossed the line: "You're no killer. You didn't mean to kill her." Malloy warns Marlowe about broaching the subject at all, but his passive attitude underscores the fact that Marlowe has been right all along in his judgment of character. "It's about time you learned your own strength," Marlowe says, pointing out the immaturity of the man and his actions, and Moose, more aware, perhaps, than Marlowe realizes, answers, "It's too late" (*Stories* 971). Malloy is, on the emotional plane, Marlowe's alter ego. For all his thugishness and childlike lack of control, Moose has what Marlowe does not allow himself: passion. Marlowe's admiration is for a man who is "softhearted in spots," someone who "wanted his Velma pretty bad" (*Stories* 850). Malloy's quest stands out in sharp contrast to Marlowe's insistence that Anne Riordan is too good a woman for him, that the requirements of his job prevent him from committing to any deep emotional relationship. Despite Marlowe's sympathy, however, the Florian murder turns Marlowe's struggle to help Malloy into his need to capture him. Malloy has been hiding out on the *Montecito*, and "from there you could get clean away. With the right help" (*Stories* 971). But Marlowe is able to produce Moose's "Grayle," Little Velma, as bait, and thus able to prevent Moose's escape.

Marlowe can even sympathize with the venomous Mrs. Grayle. After establishing the fact that she killed Marriott and after narrowly escaping death at her hands, the detective posits that her last act, killing herself, was a final gesture of selflessness. Although Velma must have known that a good lawyer would probably have gotten her off on the Malloy murder,

Marlowe's interpretation is that she has chosen to spare her elderly husband the shame of the trial, that she has given "a break to the only man who had ever really given her one" (*Stories* 984).

Chandler's detective, unlike most hard-boiled protagonists, is capable of change, and the most profound lessons he learns come from lower-echelon criminals. When Marlowe finally meets Harry Jones, the man who has been tailing him throughout most of *The Big Sleep*, he is contemptuous of the man's physical stature (reflecting that he was "not more than five feet three and would hardly weigh as much as a butcher's thumb") and his tough pretentions ("he had tight brilliant eyes that wanted to look hard, and looked as hard as oysters on the half shell") (*Stories* 711). Jones, as if aware of the impression his appearance makes, overcompensates by bragging; without any apparent reason he praises his former activities as a rumrunner.

It develops that Jones is connected to Agnes Lovelle and learns through her of Brody's blackmailing attempts and subsequent murder. Jones comes to the detective's office in the role Marlowe usually assumes, representing Agnes in negotiations with Marlowe for information on the case. Marlowe, however, grows only nastier, telling Jones that Agnes "is too big for you.... She'll roll on you and smother you," but seems to regret it when Jones remonstrates "with something that was near enough to dignity." Marlowe tells Jones to leave because he has work to do, but Jones stands his ground in true Marlovian fashion: "It ain't that easy. I came here to speak my piece and I'm speaking it" (*Stories* 713).

Marlowe gradually comes to appreciate Jones, first for his intelligence ("a three for a quarter grifter wouldn't even think such thoughts, much less know how to express them" [*Stories* 714]), which enables serious negotiation. Jones provides thorough information on interrelationships among Regan, Mars, Brody, Canino, and Vivian, and his trump card is that he knows where Mona Mars is hiding out. Marlowe, oddly, continues to act as if this were not significant, cutting off communication instead of fostering it, and disparages Jones' courage and Agnes' charms. Jones' reply effectively reverses the teacher-student polarity Marlowe had with Brody. He admits to being a grifter and proposes what in his society is an honorable exchange of information for money, and then chastises Marlowe for

Five. Marlowe and the Criminals

not dealing in kind. "I haven't pulled anything in here.... I came in talking two C's.... I come because I thought I'd get a take it or leave it, one right gee to another. Now you're waving cops at me. You oughta be ashamed of yourself" (*Stories* 716). Marlowe's usual willingness to suspend judgment about the ethics of members of the underworld and to accept a foreign standard of values wavers here as he treats Jones contemptuously, as he might treat a violent criminal whose actions ban him from negotiation. His stance is quite cowardly, comparable to the bullying tactics of Mike Hammer or the Continental Op.

Were this Marlowe's consistent stance, we might be forced to agree with Stephen Knight, who posits that, because Marlowe speaks "demotically" to underworld figures and the police, he is guilty of a two-faced "linguistic camouflage" inasmuch as he condescends to those of lesser education and taste (142). In the long run, however, the detective's linguistic variability is a sign of social flexibility. At the very beginning of *Farewell, My Lovely*, for example, Moose Malloy forces Marlowe to accompany him into Florian's bar and Marlowe's response, for Knight, is "childish petulance" (142): "'All right,' I yelled. 'I'll go up with you. Just lay off carrying me. Let me walk. I'm fine. I'm all grown up. I go to the bathroom alone and everything. Just don't carry me.'"[4] Knight, however, reads this dialogue far too literally. There is humor in the discrepancy between Malloy's size and brute strength and his childish yearning for "Little Velma" that is echoed in Marlowe's wisecracking. Marlowe is also developing a sympathy for a man so intellectually challenged yet so strong that he's capable of murder simply because he doesn't know his own strength. At the same time he uses ironic language to fend off Malloy's physical intrusion, he makes sure to use a language that the ex-con will understand, even appreciate.

Harry Jones' significance comes into clearer focus when contrasted to a similar figure in Dashiell Hammett's *The Maltese Falcon*. Aside from the coincidence of the same actor (Elisha Cook, Jr.) having played both screen roles, Hammett's "gunsel" Wilmer is never treated with anything but utter contempt by Sam Spade, who humiliates the young gangster on one occasion by stripping him of his guns and telling Gutman, his employer, that "a crippled newsie took them away from him" (375). Wilmer will later be the fitting candidate for the fall guy, sold out by Gutman to take all the blame for murders and larcenies committed in search of the falcon, and as such is reduced to the status of a nonperson. Marlowe, by way of contrast, ultimately regains his ethical equilibrium. He has reflected, even before he meets Jones, that the man possessed professional skills — is good at "tailing" — and his contempt gradually gives way to respect for someone not merely small of stature, but who is also, metaphorically, a little guy, a man fighting for survival in a world not of his own making.

Marlowe soon has reason to appreciate Jones' courage when he witnesses Jones' confrontation with Lash Canino. Although frightened (he had earlier told Marlowe that Canino was "a boy that is tough like some guys think they are tough" [*Stories* 715]), Jones manages a "brave little laugh" (*Stories* 719) in response to the killer's threats. Jones tells Canino much of what went on during Brody's murder, but balks at telling him where Agnes can be found: "I don't put my girl in the middle for anybody." Without his gun, Marlowe is powerless to intercede and Jones is poisoned to death. Marlowe, finally, is able only to praise the "little gentleman" for his courage (*Stories* 720–3). A subtle indication of Marlowe's debt to Harry Jones is that he spares Agnes (whom he dislikes and who is partly responsible for Jones' death) knowledge of the fact that Harry has been murdered. The tendency toward holding oneself as superior so evident in entrepreneurial criminals and in private eyes such as Spade and Hammer is directly addressed: Marlowe has been reminded of his "tarnished" existence and is more humble for it.

Chandler also has subordinate characters sympathize with lower-echelon criminals. In *The Big Sleep* the privileged and pampered Vivian Regan shows unexpected sympathy for Owen Taylor, the family chauffeur who once eloped with her sister Carmen. Taylor has subsequently murdered Arthur Gwynn Geiger and has himself died under mysterious circumstances. Her rueful comment is that "he was in love with her. We don't find much of that in our circle." Philip Marlowe's comment that Taylor had a police record suggests the insurmountable gap (and class difference) between Taylor and the Sternwoods, but Vivian holds to her opinion of Taylor's basic goodness and then expands on the idea by taking a pragmatic view of Taylor's position in the broader social context: "He didn't know

Five. Marlowe and the Criminals

the right people. That's all that a police record means in this rotten crime-ridden country" (*Stories* 630).

Marlowe's reservations suggest the exacting, encyclopedic critique he brought to bear on Mona Mars, but Vivian's comment is consistent with Raymond Chandler's overall class-conscious depiction of criminals in the detective genre as being very much like other, more "legitimate" citizens; they are, to some extent, the victims of arbitrary laws and prejudicial law enforcement. Vivian's is a statement unthinkable in Hammer or Spillane, who were fundamentally disinterested in the possibilities for human change and the ability of individuals to adapt to the needs of the society. In Spillane's ethical black-and-white world, Mike Hammer's enemies, real or imagined, have ceded any and all civil rights, and as such are fair game for Hammer's egregious brutality. In *I, The Jury* Hammer's verbal and physical abuse of George Kalecki, a suspect in the murder of the detective's best friend, is based on nothing more than the fact that he has a police record. Hammett glosses over ethical questions, focusing on the superiority of his rugged individualist hero.

As he does with Vivian Regan, Chandler has a secondary figure in *The Big Sleep* express a more direct version of his position than Marlowe usually provides. Capt. Gregory of Missing Persons is his most ambiguous cop, a man who seems to be providing Eddie Mars with information but who nevertheless treats the private eye with respect, and shares with Marlowe the trait of self-criticism. Gregory admits to Marlowe that he is as susceptible to corruption as any other cop — that he is one who is only "reasonably honest. As honest as you could expect a man to be in a world where it's out of style"— but he passionately pleads for socially responsible and fair law enforcement:

> I like to see the law win. I'd like to see the flashy well-dressed muggs like Eddie Mars spoiling their manicures in the rock quarry at Folsom, alongside of the poor little slum-bred hard guys that got knocked over on their first caper and never had a break since [*Stories* 743–4].

Gregory remains pessimistic, however; he's sure that no truly equitable system will be instituted in his lifetime because "we just don't run our country that way" (*Stories* 744). Marlowe is no more optimistic than Gregory when considering society as a whole, but the act, soon after, of protecting Carmen Sternwood, even though she has tried to kill him, demonstrates his resolve to improve society on an individual basis. Although a child of privilege, the disturbed Carmen is in danger, if incarcerated, of becoming a hardened criminal. Marlowe forces the family to have her put away in a place where she can receive appropriate care.

Chandler's most radical step is to place Marlowe squarely in the position of the criminal in *The Long Goodbye*. Because he has helped suspected murderer Terry Lennox escape to Mexico, Marlowe himself not only is suspected of being an accessory after the fact, but is booked on suspicion of murder. What follows is a concise yet detailed description of incarceration, including what Marlowe calls "the depth of misery," the drunk tank.

> In jail a man has no personality. He is a minor disposal problem and a few entries on reports. Nobody cares who loves him or hates him, what he looks like, what he did with his life.... The life in a jail is in suspension, without purpose or meaning [*Later Novels* 459–60].

Angered by District Attorney Grenz's superciliousness, Marlowe delivers a plea for the unfairly accused: "I was booked on suspicion. What the hell kind of legal system lets a man be shoved in a felony tank because some cop didn't get an answer to some questions?" (*Later Novels* 467). He emphasizes the fact that petty officials exercise such power merely for the sake of proving that they have it.

The humbling experience of sitting in jail for three days helps Marlowe identify with his ostensible opponents. He credits Dr. Verringer (whom he suspects of exploiting the missing Roger Wade while treating him for alcoholism) as having "a kind of dignity" and the portrait of the doctor (who admits that he's "no longer in practice") is respectful. Verringer reciprocates, helping to defuse a potentially violent situation by commenting, "I realize that in your occupation you often have to be rather intrusive" (*Later Novels* 519–521). Chandler's portrait of Verringer is that of a man made desperate by circumstance. Verringer took the unstable Earl under his wing when the latter's parents died, and had been forced to sell his land to developers when Earl's violent outbursts drove away his "patients." Marlowe is under no illusion as to the doctor's identity as a quack, but he can admire the man's loyalty.

Marlowe consistently refuses to treat criminals (and those that live

Five. Marlowe and the Criminals

along the shadow line) as if they were a race apart; while he condemns criminal acts, especially if they are violent, he knows that to view everything that a criminal does as criminal is to oversimplify, a mistake in judgment that can have deadly repercussion for a man in his line of work. He uses his analytic powers as much to discover the reasons for such acts as to answer the questions of "who," "when," and "where." He is concerned, as Race Williams and Mike Hammer are not, with answering the question "why?" He also knows that this question cannot be answered and that no social solutions can be found until he engages in dialogue with criminals.

In "The Simple Art of Murder" Chandler illustrates how legitimate enterprises, such as hotels and restaurants, can be owned by the same men who run brothels, and he therefore blurs the line as to what really is legitimate. Characters crossing the border between the legitimate and the illegitimate is a constant in the novels and enters into conversations Marlowe has with clients, gangsters, or police; typically, Marlowe's interlocutor expresses a more rigid standpoint. In *The Long Goodbye*, for example, police detective Bernie Ohls sees "the little guy," the average citizen, as the dupe of powerful interests that pander to the individual's yen for gambling, "a disease that is every bit as corrupting as dope." He is critical of the "legitimation" of gambling, such as the institution of state-sanctioned racetrack betting, and favors extreme measures to combat it: "Any time anybody wants to knock off a professional gambler, that's for me" (*Later Novels* 711).

However much he may agree with Ohls' contention that the government contributes to the coffers of the mob by its actions, Marlowe interprets the data less hierarchically and condescendingly. The "little guy," for him, cannot merely become the passive recipient of a benevolent regime. His Deweyan position is that each individual must take responsibility for his own virtues and vices within a broader social context. He tells Ohls that "crime isn't a disease, it's a symptom. Cops are like a doctor that gives you aspirin for a brain tumor, except that the cop would rather cure it with a blackjack. We're a big rough rich wild people and crime is the price we pay for it" (*Later Novels* 712). The "blackjack" solution is insufficient, not only because it is violent, but because it is shortsighted. If crime is a symptom, it is of a condition that lies even more deeply in the national consciousness, the specifically American ideology of rugged individualism, an ideology that has generated great material riches, but whose price is "roughness," a price Marlowe finds too high to pay. If crime is to be effectively fought, he implies, the social conditions that cause it must be addressed.

Ernest Mandel must have given Chandler a cursory reading indeed to assert that modern crime fiction reflects a "Manichaean polarization," that "the crime story is based upon the mechanical, formal division of the characters into two camps: the bad (the criminals) and the good (the detective and the more or less inefficient police)" (42). Mandel also feels that "the detective story is the realm of the happy ending. The criminal is always caught. Justice is always done. Crime never pays" (47), but this is quite superficial, and, in the case of Chandler, simply not true. While it is possible to make these claims for Mickey Spillane and, to a limited extent, for Dashiell Hammett, Chandler's fiction points in the opposite direction: that of a profound problematization of social roles and interactions. Vivian Regan, for example, can be viewed in a positive light since she sympathizes with those not lucky enough to have been born with her privileges; yet, on the other hand, she commits a criminal act in having Rusty Regan buried by Eddie Mars and Canino in order to protect her sister and her father.

Chandler's "criminals" are as often the ostensibly legitimate citizens as the mobster or grifter. In these novels there is hardly anyone who does not at least skirt the border between the legitimate and the illegitimate, and the key distinctions must be made on a basis of degree. Marlowe himself is hardly exempt from this kind of differentiation: he eventually assumes Vivian's role of protector when he tells her to have Carmen put away "where they will keep guns and knives and fancy drinks away from her" (*Stories* 762). Justice will be served to some extent, but crime will not be punished.

Although Ross Macdonald acknowledges Chandler as an important influence on his own work, he does Chandler an injustice when he maintains that "the detective-as-redeemer," as propagated by Chandler, "is a backward step in the direction of sentimental romance, an oversimplified world of good guys and bad guys" (300). Like many critics, Macdonald has been led astray by Chandler's famous and misleading "mean streets" portrayal of Marlowe, the exemplary detective as "neither tarnished nor afraid," and he feels that Chandler has bound his hero in a "moral straightjacket" (300). Macdonald falls into self-contradiction when, in the very next sentence, he grants that Chandler's early novels "include chivalrous gangsters and gangsters' molls with hearts of gold" (300).

It may be the anxiety of influence that motivates Macdonald to distance himself from Chandler by overgeneralizing the latter's sense of the legitimate and illegitimate. In a letter to his publisher, Alfred Knopf, Macdonald claims that Chandler's "subject is the evilness of evil, his most characteristic achievement the short vivid scene of conflict between (conventional) evil and (what he takes to be) good" (qtd. in Bruccoli 48). Quite to the contrary, it is the ambiguity of criminal activity and the self-conscious treatment of it on Marlowe's part that characterizes Chandler's novels. Not only does Marlowe confront criminals and suspected criminals with a pragmatic suspension of judgment, convinced of the need for realistic social cohesion. Other figures, themselves nexuses of conflicting and ambiguous motives and actions, support the detective in his quest for social accommodation not only by defending unjustly accused suspects, but by understanding criminal action as an integral part of society.

Chandler provides a keenly politicized environment for his hero, and the manner in which that hero acts is consonant with the view of civic behavior as posited by key American pragmatists and liberal democrats. In mapping recent developments in this philosophical tradition, Giles Gunn asserts that pragmatism is committed to pluralism, that

> the world [pragmatism] affirms is not only a world of many truths rather than one but also a world in which most things are true only at very definite instants ... a world whose order is only partial and is always being revised in response to what is novel, different, alien, incongruous, other [5].

A constant vigilance is needed to adjust to a changing world, Gunn suggests, and, as Radzinowicz argues, change may assume the guise of that which we would rather not face. Gunn culls from readings of the contemporary pragmatist Richard Rorty the conviction that

> the ideal citizen of this new world of revisionary American liberalism will ... be an ironist who combines an acceptance of the contingency of all political perspectives with a belief that whatever is meant by the good and the true in liberal societies will always be a function of free discussion [103].

Marlowe is this ironist; his job is based not on inciting opponents to violence or on equally violent action of his own, but on discussion that is as free as he can possibly make it. He rejects theoretical constructs that dictate ethical behavior as not possible to live up to, or (as we have seen through the example of Orfamay Quest) as carefully constructed window dressing hiding the worst possible actions. He is a man of acute flexibility, one who can understand and be loyal to General Sternwood, for example, for the paradoxical character he is: a man fully conscious of his less than laudable role in raising two "corrupt" daughters yet also capable of great loyalty towards Rusty Regan.

Dashiell Hammett, on the other hand, emphasizes systems of absolute value: in *Red Harvest*, the Continental Op plays one gang against another and against the corrupt police to save himself the trouble of negotiating among them. Sinda Gregory's interpretation of the Op's blithe attitude toward the Poisonville carnage is that he "depends on the strictness of his code to rationalize his actions and emotionless responses to situations; by obeying rules and regulations, he is freed from the moral responsibilities and ethical choices that inevitably arise with any complex dilemma" (54). Sam Spade picks fights with virtually everyone in *The Maltese Falcon* and, in the end, stands alone, effectively alienated from society.

In *The Public and Its Problems,* John Dewey insists that striking a careful compromise between the needs of the individual and the requirements of a just, democratic community is not only possible, but necessary, and that, since individuals are members of many groups, a high degree of flexibility is needed (*Later Works* II: 327–28). Dewey also makes clear that criminals, by definition, live far more restricted lives:

> A member of a robber band may express his powers in a way consonant with belonging to that group and be directed by the interest common to its members. But he does so only at the cost of repression of those of his potentialities which can be realized only through membership in other groups. The robber band cannot interact flexibly with other groups; it can act only through isolating itself [*Later Works* II: 328].

Criminals in Chandler's novels, for example, differ with their bosses at the risk of their lives, and can only negotiate with the police when the police themselves have been criminalized. Marlowe, by contrast, establishes his

Five. Marlowe and the Criminals

liberal credentials through such flexibility, judging his opponents without recourse to absolute law or morality. His "new" individualism seeks to create rather than restrict, and is capable of negotiating among groups and individuals hardened into inflexible positions.

Geoffrey H. Hartman is one of the keener critics of the American hard-boiled detective as communitarian, and describes Ross Macdonald's Lew Archer as an "ombudsman or public defender" (221). In addition, he rightly identifies a primary concern of Chandler's as "the need for a just system of protection and the inadequacy of modern institutions to provide it" (227). Indeed, "protection" is one of the key concepts in all the novels. In *Playback*, after his talk with Clark Brandon, Marlowe speaks briefly with Major Javonen, the hotel detective who works for Brandon and who has been suspicious of the private investigator throughout most of the novel. Javonen realizes that Marlowe has worked in the best interests of the hotel, and obliquely apologizes:

"You think I'm a bastard, don't you?"
"No. You have a job. I have a job. Mine annoyed you. You didn't trust me. That doesn't make you a bastard."
"I try to protect the hotel. Who do you try to protect?"
"I never know. Often, when I do know, I don't know how. I just fumble around and make a nuisance of myself. Often I'm pretty inadequate" [*Later Novels* 868].

Marlowe is far too self-critical here, but he sees his inadequacies against the perspective of a society in far greater need of reform than he or any single individual can provide. He protects his clients, surely, often at the risk of his license or even his life, but he is also willing to extend what protection he can to the Mavis Welds and even Moose Malloys of the world.

"Protection" is of far greater interest to Chandler than the actual crimes those who buy and sell protection commit. An Eddie Mars or Mendy Menendez, representative of rugged individualism, exploits the potential of protection to solidify his position in a corrupt society, but Marlowe, reminded on occasion by someone like Harry Jones how high the price for it can be, seeks a selfless brand of protection. He strives to serve the community by protecting the individual.

Chapter Six

Ross Macdonald

The successor to Raymond Chandler as a writer of hard-boiled fiction is Ross Macdonald, whose Lew Archer series of novels ran from 1949 to 1973. The comparison to Chandler is inevitable, not only because the setting of these novels is Southern California: Macdonald writes in the hard-boiled style invented by Dashiell Hammett and developed by Chandler. Relations with clients, police, and criminals follow Chandler's pattern, and, most importantly, the private detective occupies the position of middleman/negotiator in his society that we have seen in Philip Marlowe. First and foremost, we will examine Macdonald's relationship to Chandler and focus on his detective's, Lew Archer's, relationship to the police.

Macdonald was acutely aware of his debt to Chandler. Academically trained — he received his doctorate in literature from the University of Michigan — he studied Hammett and Chandler rigorously and published his detective novels with Knopf, with whom both Hammett and Chandler had published. He learned from Chandler the skill of giving historical depth to his characters. As Matthew J. Bruccoli puts it, "past and present are intertwined" (24), but Macdonald developed that skill towards causation, so that deeds in the past motivate, even haunt, the characters. There is also a shared concern with class: money corrupts absolutely for both writers.

Later in his career he consciously broke from Chandler's influence, insisting that he brought greater realism to the genre, and prided himself on his ability to construct plots, something that Chandler was neither good at nor very concerned with. In 1970 Macdonald published "The Writer as Detective Hero" in the collection *The Mystery Writer's Art*. While not as influential as Chandler's "The Simple Art of Murder," it is a succinct and intriguing interpretation of the work of both authors. For Macdonald,

Six. Ross Macdonald

Chandler puts too much of a burden on his protagonist in terms of carrying the plot. We see too much of Marlowe and not enough of those around him. And yet Macdonald describes his own detective in ways that perfectly fit Marlowe: "While he is a man of action, his actions are largely putting together the stories of other people's lives and discovering their significance. He is less a doer than a questioner, a consciousness in which the meanings of other lives emerge" (304). For Macdonald, Archer is thus an analyst; the almost clinical manner in which he deals with clients suggests a doctor making house calls.[1] Chandler can be credited for imbuing his detective with this quality as well and Marlowe provides an example to be followed: in *The High Window* the detective shows sympathy and the depth of his understanding of the psyche when he confronts Merle Davis, his client's secretary, about her panicked reaction whenever a man touches her. He surmises that she had a traumatic experience as a child and promises never to touch her again. He later asks his own doctor, Carl Moss, to examine her when she shows signs of trauma as a result of sexual abuse at the hands of Jasper Murdock. In a sense, the detective even helps to treat her: after the case has been solved he drives the traumatized young woman back to her home in Kansas to recuperate. In the larger scope of things, as we have seen, Marlowe constantly strives to connect disparate individuals and groups and is indeed, first and foremost, a questioner. Due to first-person narration, he is undoubtedly the focus, but he does not dominate.

Macdonald's primary criticism of Chandler is that he is too moralistic; the former strove to keep Lew Archer what he considered a more nonjudgmental figure. He did not succeed, however. Just as there are more detailed observation and overt criticism of Archer's society, his judgments, too, are more clearly delineated. Characters are told point-blank when they have strayed from Archer's rigorous standards, most frequently when their egotism, often expressed as self-pity, has in some way injured those around them. And judgments are not limited to Archer. Most of his clients and many of the people he questions go to great lengths to express disdain for others.

Like other critics, Macdonald misreads Chandler's "The Simple Art of Murder," overemphasizing Chandler's call for "a quality of redemption" as a "central weakness in his vision" (according to Macdonald) in novels.

Raymond Chandler's Philip Marlowe

Chandler isolates his hero, Philip Marlowe, by means of "an angry puritanical morality" (300) and erects barriers, including those of language (or lack thereof), to establish a character who ultimately does not care about anyone else and merely judges them. But for Macdonald this quality of redemption cannot belong solely to one man:

> it belongs to the whole work and is not the private property of one of the characters.... The detective as redeemer is a backward step in the direction of sentimental romance, and an over-simplified world of good guys and bad guys [300].

Macdonald further confuses the issue, however, when he claims, speaking of Archer's role in his novels, that he "is not their emotional center" (304). There is some justice in assessing Chandler's work as over-simplified vis-à-vis that of Macdonald, since he lacks Macdonald's depth of characterization, but the distinction is one of degree, and not a very high degree at that. And as we shall see, Macdonald is at least as judgmental as Chandler, if not more so.

In this essay he does, however, in a rather self-contradictory manner, support Chandler on a very important point: "Chandler's novels focus on his hero's sensibility. Their constant theme is big-city loneliness, and the wry pain of a sensitive man coping with the roughest elements of a corrupt society" (301). We have already seen many examples of this in Marlowe's interactions with clients, criminals, and the police and this is the key transformation Chandler made to the detective novel; he tempered the self-centered yet extroverted hard-boiled hero with Marlowe's willingness to both criticize himself and to use his skills to help others: he is "sensitive" in his heightened perception.

What Macdonald fails to recognize, however, is that his description is just as apt of Archer as it is of Marlowe. Macdonald's hero continues the process of increasing self-awareness: he is painfully aware of the suffering that crime creates, aware of the painful tensions among people that exist even before a crime is committed. In almost every novel Archer must especially negotiate the mutual suspicions and enmities of family members. His introspection and consciousness of the power of the past create a near-obsession with family that distinguishes, more than anything else, his work from that of his mentor.

Six. Ross Macdonald

We see his psychological and familial concerns in the denouement of the early *The Drowning Pool*, published in 1950, when Archer sympathizes with James Slocum, who has broken down under the strain of his mother's murder and his wife's suicide and who struggles with his daughter's anger. Archer is well aware of the man's inadequacies and moral cowardice, but can master considerable sympathy for him, even after being personally attacked. He remarks to Slocum's close friend, Francis Marvell, "if you care about this man, you'd better get him to a damned good doctor" (211). Sympathy is just as central to both character and plot much later in *The Instant Enemy* (1968) in which no less than four generations of the Hackett family are involved in murder. The matriarch of the family, Ruth Marburg, is suspicious of Archer's description of Davy Spanner (whose life is a record of trouble, both physical and psychological) since he has just kidnapped her son: "You sound almost sympathetic." "I almost am," replies Archer. "Davy Spanner didn't make himself" (60). The detective is keenly aware of the social context and, like Marlowe, seeks to negotiate among flawed, alienated characters.

His perceptions of his physical surroundings are quite Marlovian — skies are menacing, cities seen from a distance are sites of anomie. In *The Little Sister* Chandler has his hero sink in spirit to the point of internally grousing about his fellow Southern Californians, upon whom he projects his own self-criticism, only to catch himself and revise his opinion. Macdonald, who, for Julian Symons, views "California as a place of immense beauty made ugly by man" (190), can also be harsh on both his natural surroundings and his fellow men. Arriving at the town of Quinto in *The Drowning Pool*, Archer muses in a manner reminiscent of Marlowe's negative view of Hollywood and its illusions that "the white Spanish buildings seemed unreal, a stage-setting painted upon the solid blue sky. To the left at the bottom of the cross-streets the placid sea rose up like a flat blue wall" (12). Archer's descriptions of Southern California echo those of Chandler in their misanthropy. Contrasting the "cleanliness and freedom" of the water of the Pacific, the beaches are "jerrybuilt" and the cities are "an urban wilderness in the desert." The man-made world is a fallen world that the detective, a redeemer in waiting, chooses to operate in, but on occasion its negative qualities overwhelm him: "there was nothing wrong with Southern California that a rise in the ocean level wouldn't cure," muses Archer (21). In *The Way Some People Die* (1951) Archer assesses the Los Angeles traffic, opining that "[h]alf of the lemmings were rushing down to the sea and the other half had been there and decided not to get wet" (30). The outlook is bleak, yet these "lemmings" are sentient: it is not that they cannot feel but that they are cowed by their environment, reduced by forces they fail to understand. In *The Underground Man* (1971) the detective takes note of a client's apartment: "The walls were lined with books, many of them in foreign languages, like insulation against the immediate present," which is too painful to bear (13). Archer's disdain for the community turns as sour, as sometimes Marlowe's does in Chandler, when in *The Ivory Grin* (1952) he tails a doctor's assistant into a bar which is

> packed with Saturday night drinkers: soldiers and shrill dark girls who looked too young to be there, hard-faced middle-aged women with permanented hair, old men renewing their youth for the thousandth time, asphalt-eyed whores working for a living on drunken workingmen, a few fugitives from the upper half of town drowning one self to let another self be born [68].

Despite the significance nature plays in these novels, Macdonald is not a naturalistic writer. The world is ultimately man-made and man-run. Both detectives make it their business to confront the superficiality and corruption of their fellow men, including themselves; traveling by car and (in Macdonald) by airplane, they constantly work to connect people, to make the present more livable.

As much as Macdonald may have protested, Chandler's influence was strong. Lew Archer, like Marlowe, probes far more than motives for crime. Robert F. Moss recognizes that Archer

> functions more as a catalyst for the actions of the other characters. Above all, Archer is not a policeman interested in solving crimes and bringing the guilty to justice; he is, instead a searcher who probes the complex relationships among people and attempts to discover the truth of what has happened and, more important, why it has happened [5].

This is clearly a key part of the inheritance from Chandler, who stressed in the figure of Marlowe these very qualities of ethical probity, curiosity, and human motivation. It is fair to say that Macdonald's psychological approach creates characters with greater depth than Chandler, yet his

Six. Ross Macdonald

detective functions very much like a negotiator and he expands the role of protector that Marlowe has established. The most obvious example is in *The Chill* (1963), in which, faced with Dolly Kincaid's sudden disinterest in her husband, he is immediately attuned to the eponymous chill that has taken hold of her mind, due to childhood trauma triggered by the reappearance of her father, and intuits that she really loves her husband and needs to be reunited with him. He gets her the psychological help she needs and, along with the clinic's director, shields the young woman from a persistent policeman eager to question her. Archer's altruism is underscored by the fact that Dolly is not his client.

Moss offers a constructive way to focus on the differences between Chandler and Macdonald:

> Chandler focused on his detective Philip Marlowe's search for a personal code of conduct, a way to guide his own behavior within a corrupt society. Lew Archer is on a different quest, concentrating not on his own behavior but on that of the people around him, continually seeking to understand why they do what they do [6].

Although somewhat overstated, since each quest is quite similar to the other, Moss' point is well taken. Archer is by nature an extrovert. Macdonald's greater interest in character psychology leads the detective to probe the lives of perpetrators, victims, even bystanders far beyond what is strictly needed to solve a case.

The difference is subtle, but significant. We have seen how Philip Marlowe negotiates among disparate forces in society, eager to earn a living and enforce justice, but just as eager to understand all sides of the debate, searching for compromise. In *The Big Sleep*, Marlowe is called in by General Sternwood to remove an annoying blackmailer and the subsequent complications and investigation stem, in large part, from the detective's sympathy for the old, ailing client. In order to help him, Marlowe assumes the role of the missing son-in-law, Rusty Regan, whose company the general had depended on. He is solicitous of the old man throughout the novel, hiding, for example, evidence of Sternwood's wayward daughter's, Carmen's, involvement in the murder of the blackmailer, Geiger, in consideration of Sternwood's health as much as for Carmen herself.

A similar, if less physically infirm, client in Macdonald is Mrs. Samuel

Lawrence in *The Way Some People Die*. She runs a heavily mortgaged tourist rooming house in Santa Monica on a street that "had lost its claim to pride" (4). Lawrence is much like the street, clinging to her self-respect, whose "vague eyes swam with self-pity," a quality that Archer often recognizes in people and one not found in Chandler (6).[2] At first Archer is skeptical about the job he's offered — to find Lawrence's daughter Galatea — since he feels the mother is exaggerating: the daughter is a 25-year-old nurse and can, after all, look after herself, and the police can do much better with this kind of work. He also, however, acknowledges a mother's concerns, regardless of the age of the child, and ultimately his empathy wins out, in part because Lawrence has been actively looking for her daughter, talking to the nurse's colleagues, and thus earning, in a sense, Archer's professional respect. He is dedicated to the job of reconciling mother and daughter, not only finding her. Indeed reconciliation is given priority over detection.

Thus even at the outset, before detection has begun, there is a slight shift in priorities for Macdonald compared to Chandler. His focus is on the family in a corrupt society, and the family is often the site of corruption.[3] No fewer than eight Archer novels reveal wives killing husbands, husbands killing wives, mothers killing children, granddaughters killing grandmothers, and fratricide. Not only do we constantly view family conflicts; the detective takes on an active role and is himself, in a sense, adopted in *The Instant Enemy*. He symbolically becomes a family member, joining as an equal the missing teenager Sandy in the Sebastian family: "Sandy was middle girl in a tense marriage and at the moment I was middle man" (6). Archer is a more adaptable, even chameleon-like figure than Marlowe. Archer overcomes his repugnance for the cowardly Keith Sebastian, who obsesses with his job and his boss, placing them above his daughter's welfare, and assumes the position of head of the Sebastian household. He does this out of sympathy not just for Sandy, but for the man himself and for the wife/mother, Bernice, even though she criticizes her husband and refuses to show Archer something of great value, her daughter's diary, which, it turns out, would have provided key clues and might have saved lives. Towards the end of the novel, after Sandy has returned home, she is faced with criminal charges due to the kidnapping of Steven Hackett.

Six. Ross Macdonald

Archer does his best to advise Bernice to work with legal authorities, especially probation officers, in Sandy's best interest.

In *The Chill* Archer fights to keep the patronage of his client, Alex Kincaid, when Kincaid's father argues against the younger man using the detective to protect his wife, Dolly, suspected of murder and in need of psychological care. The elder Kincaid insists that the marriage is based on false pretenses and at first succeeds in convincing the confused young man that he's under no obligation to Dolly (the marriage was a "boyish impulse" [89]) and treats him like a child. Archer's reaction is uncharacteristically verbally abusive, calling him, among other things, a "bloodless bastard" (90). Archer attempts to reason with both men, implying that he has greater maturity than either:

> Somebody has to assume responsibility. There's a lot of it floating around loose at the moment. You can't avoid it by crawling into a hole and pulling the hole in after you. The girl's in trouble, and whether you like it or not she's a member of your family [91].

The emphasis on kinship, so prevalent in the Archer series, here casts the detective in the role of substitute father, almost of *both* men, since the elder Kincaid is acting so immaturely. He also extends the definition of family itself. The two young people have been married for only two days when Dolly goes missing, but for Archer the social commitment has priority. Although there is much emphasis on blood ties, the ties that people voluntarily make are just as valid. Marlowe often acts as go-between, but, in addition to Chandler's lack of interest in families, the emotional engagement is generally lacking.

Guided by Macdonald's distinction between Chandler and himself, Michael D. Sharp sees Macdonald's *The Doomsters* (1958) as a pivotal work, one which "suggests a new style of detective narrator, one with a greater focus on the humanity of his clients than Marlowe ever had"; furthermore, "Archer frequently stands in, if only temporarily, as a father figure to young adults in trouble" (413). Of all of Macdonald's novels *The Doomsters* is an odd choice for establishing Archer as a father figure. This novel, like most of the others, focuses on family conflicts, hatreds, and murder, but the children of the rich, recently deceased state senator Hallman and their spouses, some of whom become suspects, are in their 20s or 30s. Nevertheless, Archer is intensely aware of the humanity of these people, some of whom suffer from mental illness. There can be no doubt that the younger writer (Chandler was born in 1888 and Macdonald in 1915) focuses far more on family conflicts and crimes and family history invariably plays a central role in Macdonald's narratives. Suspects and clients (often one and the same character) are often young men and women who have inherited the sins of fathers and mothers and suffer, and make others suffer, because of them. In *The Instant Enemy* Archer is initially called in to retrieve Sandy Sebastian, who has left home with a young man, Davey Spanner, who has done jail time and appears unstable. They kidnap her father's employer, a man, as it turns out, who had raped her the previous summer. As the investigation develops Archer discovers that Spanner's father died under mysterious circumstances many years previously and ultimately four generations of this family are involved in the case. After five people have been killed, one victim of murder proves to be a man killed by his own mother. The past weighs heavily on the present, and although Chandler incorporates past crimes into his present ones, they function for him as exposition. For Macdonald there is a causal relationship.

Sharp's primary point, however, is to prove that Lew Archer is more sympathetic to his clients than is Philip Marlowe, and some examples bear this out. Recognizing a seriously disturbed individual in Carl Hallman, suspected of killing his father and perhaps even his mother, Archer is dogged in his determination to protect the man, Even after it is clear that Carl's wife, Mildred, is the killer, he feels truly sorry for "a human being with more grief on her young mind than it was able to bear" (220). Sharp's interpretation, however, is generally misleading. Certainly the detective can easily summon sympathy for those caught in the middle of conflict, especially when they're young. Sandy Sebastian, at first trapped in Davey Spanner's kidnap/murder plot, is rescued by Archer and returned to her dysfunctional family. Archer quizzes the traumatized girl, hoping to find both perpetrator and victim before the latter is killed. Distrustful now of everyone, she is reluctant to tell him everything she knows. Archer understands her quite well: "I felt a certain empathy with her. The scene was becoming a part of my life, too" (82). Marlowe is certainly capable of empathy, as we have seen, but is never confronted with people of Sandy's

Six. Ross Macdonald

age. Perhaps because he had no children of his own, none of the victims in Chandler's novels are adolescent. Moose Malloy, the ungentle giant of *Farewell, My Lovely*, is childlike in some ways and Marlowe broods over him in a parental way, but he's under no illusion about the man's power and violence and does not protect him when he's shot by Velma.

In many respects Macdonald can be seen as a truer heir than Chandler of the British school of detective fiction, not so much in terms of gathering a group of suspects together at the finale to reveal the perpetrator, a favorite motif of Agatha Christie, but in terms of psychological observation on the part of the detective and attention to the past lives of suspects, also Christie motifs, especially as expressed by Hercule Poirot. In the hard-boiled school, attention is paid to characters' thoughts and feelings, but Macdonald brings a far greater quality of empathy to bear. In a forward by the author in *Cards on the Table* (1936), Christie confounds reader expectations that the least likely suspect in a murder case involving four bridge players will prove to be the villain (a formula she normally excelled in), insisting that any one of the four likely suspects could be guilty. By the end of the novel the "moving finger" has pointed to all four in turn because each has committed murder in the past, and one even admits to the crime in hopes of protecting a sympathetic young woman who she thinks is the guilty party. Christie stresses the psychological makeup of the suspects: "They are four widely divergent types: the motive that drives each one of them to crime is peculiar to that person" (378). She also notes the psychological probing by the detective, since "the mind of the murderer ... is of supreme interest" (378). Thus there is a similarly psychological approach to interviewing witnesses and suspects shared by Archer and Miss Marple and Hercule Poirot.

Quite a bit of the investigation in *Cards on the Table*, in which Poirot essentially assists the able police superintendent Battle, is taken up with investigating suspicious deaths connected to the suspects in the past; even Battle validates this method: "[T]here's only one hope—the past. Find out what crime exactly ... these people have committed—and it may tell you who committed this crime" (455). As he does in other novels, Poirot makes psychology the key factor, in this case utilizing process of elimination: "If we have a person who from the psychological point of view could not have committed that particular type of murder, then we can dismiss that person from our calculations" (409). He then takes each suspect in turn and discovers, despite great differences in character and behavior, that each could have committed the present crime and that only learning as much as possible about his or her past crimes can bring success.

While questioning a young, middle-class Englishwoman, Mary Debenham, in *Murder on the Orient Express* (1934), Poirot establishes the woman's puzzling lack of interest in a murder that was committed the previous night in the same sleeping car. The detective interprets her terse, unemotional reactions to his questions as resentment towards him and his inquiries and explains his method:

> I look first at my witness, I sum up his or her character, and I frame my questions accordingly.... I see at once that you will be orderly and methodical. You will confine yourself to the matter in hand. Your answers will be brief and to the point. And because, Mademoiselle, human nature is perverse, I ask of you quite different questions. I ask what you *feel*, and what you *thought*" [199].

Poirot adapts his approach as much as possible to unsettle his interlocutor, convinced that offhand statements are the most telling. His method is based not so much on a question of motive, then, than of identity. This almost deterministic quality unites Christie and Macdonald. For each detective the perversity of human nature is assumed, so a purely logical approach won't work. Because Christie indulges in stereotype in terms of how a Francophone would act—quite differently from the reserved British—Poirot is thus "warmer" than the very British Holmes or even Miss Marple.

Macdonald's approach is far less didactic, however, probably because his suspects have more freedom of movement and expression; Lew Archer rarely directly elucidates his professional methods and infrequently discusses the psychology of his clients with them, but psychology, especially that of young adults, is always present. In one respect Macdonald harks even further back in the history of the genre to the American Anna Katherine Green, often referred to as "the Mother of the Detective Novel." In his introduction to Green's *The Leavenworth Case* (1878), Michael Sims notes that Green produced "more than three dozen books in the mystery field" and strongly influenced Agatha Christie (xx). Green's detective is Ebenezer Gryce, introduced as a "city detective," not as a private investi-

Six. Ross Macdonald

gator (6). Perhaps because Gryce is immobilized by gout, the real detective work falls to Everett Raymond, who is an attorney and therefore closer in characterization to private eyes.[4]

For our purposes it is Raymond's interactions with Gryce, witnesses, and possible murderers that draw parallels to Macdonald. Perhaps even more class conscious than British detectives such as Sherlock Holmes and possessing far greater instincts to protect women, Raymond passionately states that his "business was to save Eleanore Leavenworth," (100) who is suspected of murdering her uncle and with whom he is in love.

Since evidence at the scene of the crime implies a locked-room mystery, Raymond interrogates the servants, primarily the butler, in a style reminiscent of Hercule Poirot and Philo Vance. When evidence implicates Eleanore, Raymond (demonstrating his amateur status) insists that "if she declares she is innocent I will believe her" (70). Eleanore's surprise at seeing herself suspected in a newspaper report serves to support his conviction of her innocence. He becomes convinced that she's shielding someone and vows to find the "true culprit" because Eleanore "must be saved at all hazards" (93). As the case develops, Gryce, who had been using Raymond as a mere convenience, asks him, "You are, then, intending to make a personal business of this matter?" (103). After establishing that Raymond is not determined to work alone, he forms a partnership with the lawyer, primarily because Raymond is a gentleman who has access to the upper class. The two men cooperate fully until the end of the novel.

There is a similar, if updated, character trait towards women in Macdonald. In *The Drowning Pool* the client, Maude Slocum, engages Archer to find the person sending anonymous letters to her husband, warning him of his wife's infidelity. Since she has been unfaithful in the past, Slocum is quite indecisive about what she wants done and, illogically, resents Archer for intruding in the life of her family, although the detective needs to do just that in order to find the letter writer. Forbidden by her to appear as a detective, Archer manages to visit the family under the assumed identity of a Hollywood literary properties agent, but his client still resents his close proximity. Maude Slocum feels he is spying on her and the detective must insist, somewhat awkwardly, that "[t]his is a very intimate business, there's nothing overt in it like the ordinary divorce setup, and I need to get closer to your life" (20).

Very soon Archer is succeeding in doing just that. At a cocktail party at the Slocum home he is taken aback by Maude's sudden willingness to reveal not the information that might help his investigation, but family intimacies that put him in the role of psychoanalyst:

> Almost a total stranger, I was being asked to approve of herself and her daughter. Her insecurity went further back than the letter she had given me. Some guilt or fear was drawing her backward steadily, so that she had to enthuse and emote and be admired in order to stay in the same place [32].

Out of context, this may read as Archer sneering at his client and trying to establish a distance between them. However, the novel as a whole and most of the other Archer novels are imbued with the writer's sympathies for his troubled characters. Macdonald is willing to risk including subplots and background information that threaten to distract the reader from more important matters and endow the detective with a similar kind of ready sympathy for his clients.

Later on, after Maude's mother-in-law, Olivia, has been found drowned in the swimming pool and murder is suspected, Archer shows sympathy to Maude, getting her to admit that "I suppose I'm a little afraid of a man who cares strongly about something" (139). Archer eliminates her as a suspect, since she stands to inherit none of Olivia's money, but also because of his sympathy for her loveless marriage. After she commits suicide he tells her friend, Mildred Fleming, "I liked her too" (198). After Fleming has left, Archer muses over Maude's disappointed life, generalizing about the human condition:

> Hers was one of those stories without villains or heroes. There was no one to admire, no one to blame. Everyone had done wrong for himself and others. Everyone had failed. Everyone had suffered. Perhaps [Maude's daughter] Cathy Slocum suffered most of all. My sympathies were shifting from the dead woman to the living girl [204].

This is an apt example of what I term "risk": shifting sympathies are hardly likely to result in any significant progress in his investigation, but they underscore his role as analyst.

Archer probes the psyche of Pat Reavis, the newly fired Slocum chauf-

Six. Ross Macdonald

feur who will soon be the suspect in the novel's first murder: "Reavis had quantities of raw charm. But underneath it there was something lacking. I could talk to him all night and never find his core, because he had never found it" (51). What is striking here is not that Reavis is superficial, but that the detective is concerned with his lack of depth in the first place. Macdonald may have faulted Chandler for moralizing, but Archer is far more interested in people's inner lives than Marlowe ever is and does not hesitate to make value judgments.

At the very end Archer reveals to Cathy that he knows that she is the culprit, that she killed her grandmother and framed Reavis. His sympathy remains, however, with the girl. When she says that she doesn't deserve to live, the detective insists that "too many people have died" (213) and that he has no right to judge her. Afraid that she might become mentally unstable, he assumes the psychologist's role. The ending is not unlike that of "The Adventure of the Blue Carbuncle," in which Sherlock Holmes refuses to turn James Ryder, guilty of impulse theft and very unlikely to ever commit another crime, over to the police. In *The Drowning Pool* Archer, in a sense, "hands over" the young woman to an authority figure, but the man is her biological father, Chief of Police Ralph Knudson, who has just resigned his position and will take Cathy away from the site of such trauma. Where Holmes is likely to forget Ryder within 24 hours and displays his class-bound sense of noblesse oblige, Archer's bond with Cathy is ultimately important to the theme of reconciliation.

The Barbarous Coast (1956) is even more explicitly psychological and begins much the same way as *The Chill*. Called in by Clarence Bassett, the manager of the exclusive Channel Club in Malibu, to be his bodyguard, Archer sympathizes with George Wall, a young sportswriter from Toronto, the very man Bassett feels he needs protection from. Wall engages the detective to find his wife, Hester, a character closely connected to Bassett. Having recently been divorced himself, Archer admits that "[i]t seemed very important to me that George should get together with his wife and take her away from Los Angeles. And live happily ever after" (44). The reader might expect irony in his response, but Archer sincerely wishes the couple to do better than he has. The fact that Hester does not live to fulfill his desire gives the narrative tragic dimensions.

Before Archer can find Hester, he hears that a young woman and former friend of Hester's, Gabrielle Torres, was killed two years earlier and that Hester has taken up with Gabrielle's cousin, a former boxer and now film actor, Lance Leonard. Archer discovers a body that he at first assumes is Hester's but runs afoul of studio security agents who attack him and who appear to have connections to organized crime. Leonard is also working for Carl Stern, a mobster, and is murdered. Archer finally finds Hester, tells her that Leonard is dead, and tries to get her to tell him if she's involved in blackmailing a Hollywood mogul and if Gabrielle Torres was ever involved. Archer pressures her to trust him, to accept his counsel, but she refuses. His only consolation is that he revises his judgment of her, decides she's not a hustler, but "straight" (87). In a strikingly un-hard-boiled manner, the detective falls back on emotion, pitying not only the doomed woman, but the human condition itself: "The problem was to love people, try to serve them, without wanting anything from them" (87).

He brings just such sympathy to bear with Isobel Graff, the wife of Simon Graff, head of Helio-Graff Studios and Gabrielle's lover at the time of her murder. Isobel is mentally disturbed and has intermittently been institutionalized. Archer protects her from gangster Carl Stern, who has been beating her, and he grasps the opportunity to talk to her (110). Isobel wallows in self-pity, one quality that usually evokes little sympathy from the detective, but his role of rescuer predominates. Isobel proves the ideal patient for the psychologist in Archer, describing her neuroses in great detail. Archer admits to the reader of being disturbed by someone "teetering on the verge of a psychotic episode" (111) but he continues his conversation with her, half detective, half analyst. At the end of the narrative Isobel admits to being Gabrielle's murderer, but it's shown that she only wounded her and Bassett finished the job. This, of course, does not absolve her, but Archer assures her husband that, due to her mental state, she will at least be spared a public trial.

Just as we have seen in Chandler, Macdonald is greatly concerned with cooperation (or the lack thereof) between private eye and duly constituted legal authority. *The Galton Case* (1959) is typical of most of the Archer novels in its portrayal of the detective and the police. Archer is again engaged with a search for a missing person, Anthony Galton, who

Six. Ross Macdonald

has been missing for 20 years. Fearing her own demise, his rich mother, Maria, yearns for her only child and wants to make amends for alienating him. Before Archer can begin the investigation, Peter Culligan, the houseman of Mrs. Galton's attorney, Gordon Sable, is stabbed to death in an incident that will turn out to be closely related to Archer's investigation. On his way to the scene of the crime Archer is waylaid by a suspicious young man who steals his car and the detective becomes, as a result, the prime suspect for local sheriff's deputies when they laugh at his improbable story of being carjacked.

As is often the case in Macdonald, the subordinates on the police force prove to be inexperienced, rash, and quick to exercise their authority, sometimes exceeding it. Archer exacerbates the situation with sarcasm, claiming to be Captain Nemo, just embarked from his submarine. It is unclear if the deputies even understand the literary allusion; they assume that the detective is a junkie. The officers are inordinately proud of their skills. One of them tells a fireman who was already on the scene, "We're trained to spot these phonies, the way you're trained to put out fires" (29), as if seeing through disguises were his primary task. It slowly dawns on them that Archer isn't taking them seriously and he notes the physical signs of anger: "He balled his right fist on his knee. I could see the packed muscles tighten under the shoulder of his blouse. I pulled in my chin and got ready to roll with the punch" (30). The private eye was once a Long Beach police sergeant and has seen how ugly such situations can get. No violence is forthcoming, however, and Archer muses that "under the circumstances, this made him a good cop" (30). Illustrating a keen insight into the subtleties of corruption, much like we find in Chandler, Macdonald shows that the crucial boundary between proper and improper police method hasn't been crossed.

The situation is defused once the deputies deliver Archer to the Sable house, where the murder occurred, and where the attorney, his client, can identify him. He is met there by Sheriff Trask, who, although he defensively claims otherwise, apologizes for his assistants. Recognizing a good cop when he sees one, Archer immediately engages Trask in finding the real culprit. Macdonald displays his considerable skills in plotting as the seemingly separate cases, disappearance and murder, begin to come together.

Anthony Galton's 20-year-old trail leads Archer to San Francisco and nearby Luna Bay, where Galton was last seen and where the detective gleans much important information from Dr. Dineen, who once delivered a baby boy, John, to Anthony Galton and his wife. Soon after, it turns out, Galton was brutally murdered and the remains of his body have recently been discovered. Enter Deputy Mungan, another good cop, who is in charge of the remains and who establishes the criminal act of decapitation. The identity of the victim is not yet certain to Archer or the reader and the detective and the deputy, who, Archer observes, "talked like a trained cop, and his eyes were sharp as tacks" (65), work together to determine identity, recognizing a mutual benefit. Mungan's value to Archer is in his local knowledge and he relates the history of the Red Horse Inn, a Prohibition center for crime.

Lawyer Sable joins Archer and Mungan in Luna Bay in order to help with the identification of the murder victim, but not before the PI and the cop have sparred over responsibility and jurisdiction. Mungan identifies Peter Culligan as a member of the Red Horse mob. When Mungan asks for Archer's source of information (whom the reader knows to be Culligan's ex-wife) Archer refuses and deflects the conversation to a different issue. Anticipating Sable's arrival, Archer stresses the need for collective work: "This is a big case, bigger than you realize. It's going to take more than one of us to handle it"(88). The fact that the lawyer is coming allays Mungan's fears and salvages his pride, since "working for a lawyer ... lets [Archer] off the hook. It gives you the same rights of privacy a lawyer has" (89).

Much later, after Archer has begun to tie up the many loose threads of the investigation, Trask accuses the detective of irresponsibility for confronting a valuable witness who then left the country, leaving Trask high and dry. Archer admits he was at fault and both men continue cooperating. Archer is now working for Dr. August Howell; Trask confirms his knowledge of this, welcomes Archer's help, and defines the parameters of his own role: "I assume you've been hired to go into the boy's background. Howell wanted me to. Naturally I told him I couldn't move without some indication that law's been broken" (127).

Archer travels to Las Vegas and apprehends two men, Roy and Tommy

Six. Ross Macdonald

Lemberg, implicated in the Culligan murder. He immediately makes it clear to both of them that it's Sheriff Trask they have to answer to. Once they have given their statements, Archer and Trask turn back to a more central problem, the disappearance of John Galton with Dr. Howell's daughter, Sheila. Red-faced with embarrassment, the sheriff admits to letting them get away, but as the two men consider their options and Archer posits Alice Sable as a guilty party, Trask hints at the possibility of political corruption since she's the wife of "one of the top lawyers in the city" (160). Macdonald, however, deflects the existence of true corruption as Archer considers that "the politician latent in every elected official was rising to the surface and blurring Trask's hard, clear attitudes" (160): he values Trask as a fundamentally honest cop and Trask quickly agrees that questioning Alice Sable is important.

In a showdown involving Mr. and Mrs. Sable and Dr. Howell, Archer gets Sable to admit that he killed Culligan and setup Archer, as well as his wife, from the very start in his scheme to get some of the Galton inheritance. Having apprehended the killer, Archer upholds his end of his bargain with the police and hands him over to Trask. Where in Chandler there is greater differentiation of roles — good cops are obviously good and bad cops patently bad — Macdonald insists on ambiguity: the chance that his police may surrender to temptation is always present and sometimes a novel ends with no clear indication of the officer's ethical status.

In *The Chill* a frantic young husband, Alex Kincaid, engages Archer to find his wife, Dolly. There are enough clues to go on to locate her at Pacific Point College, where she is registered under an assumed name, quickly and efficiently, but she at first rejects her husband. Events also proceed quickly as Helen Haggerty, Dolly's college adviser, is murdered, with Dolly insisting that she committed the crime.

Sheriff Herman Crane is called in and he and Archer begin as wary antagonists, Archer revealing his first impression of the man as having "the heavy ease of a politician, poised between bullying and flattery." Crane treats the private detective "with occupational suspicion" and Archer instinctively decides not to cooperate any more than absolutely necessary (54). Crane reveals a mangled sense of ethics when he insists on interrogating Dolly, but Archer, concerned for her mental health, is able to temporarily block him. Crane persists at the nursing home where Dolly is being treated, but Dr. Godwin, her physician, angrily sends him away. Crane is an elected official and Archer succeeds in winning allies who can make him feel politically vulnerable. The significance of politics is reprised towards the end of the novel. Archer is arrested on mere suspicion since he's been seen consorting with a murder suspect and he tries to turn a bad situation into one of cooperation: "You and I could trade information, Sheriff." Crane, however, is adamant and forces the detective to play the political card, claiming, "I have friends in Sacramento," which is enough to grant him his right to call his lawyer, who soon comes to release him (184).

In *The Drowning Pool* Macdonald establishes a good cop/bad cop dichotomy although it isn't immediately clear who stands where on the ethical scales. On the orders of Chief of Police Ralph Knudson, Detective Sergeant Simeon Franks tracks Archer to a local bar right after Olivia Slocum is murdered. Imagining that the detective is trying to escape and eager to prove how tough he is, Franks fires a shot past Archer's hand, handcuffs him and delivers him to the Slocum residence. Knudson is well aware of Franks' incompetence and soothes Archer's anger by indirectly apologizing, explaining that Franks is "a ward-heeler in the Mayor's party, and the Mayor is *ex officio* on the Police Commission" (60). Thus local politics is shown as corrupt and Franks will prove yet more dangerous.

Knudson plays a role far more central to the plot than any other officer of the law in Macdonald. By the end of the narrative he is shown to be the former lover of Maude Slocum and the biological father of Cathy Slocum, but, as this is the family's secret, initially he is introduced as a friend of James Slocum. Knudson questions Archer since he was the last one to see Olivia Slocum alive. As soon as the detective's statement is taken, Archer assumes the role of coinvestigator, displaying his competence by querying Slocum, "What's the physical evidence?" (61). Soon after, Knudson elicits Archer's expertise, asking him "What are you going to do? Help us find Reavis?" (63).

The relationship between policeman and private investigator is vexed, but ultimately they work together to find the truth, that Cathy has murdered her grandmother. There is little coordinated work such as found

Six. Ross Macdonald

between Marlowe and Lieutenant Randall in *Farewell, My Lovely*, but Archer is careful to always report back to Knudson, even under trying circumstances. He trails Pat Reavis, top suspect in Olivia Slocum's murder, to Las Vegas, intending to hand him over to Knudson, only to have him abducted and killed by "oilfield hoods" (135). He reports to Knudson as soon as he returns to Quinto, but, sensing that the officer is either unwilling or unable to follow up (the murder is out of his jurisdiction and he's convinced that Reavis deserved to die), he prods the sheriff into action, especially since Franks, Knudson's deputy, appears to have informed the lynch mob as to Reavis' whereabouts. Feeling professionally threatened, Knudson tells Archer, "When I need a door-knocker to tell me how to conduct my official work, I'll send you a special-delivery letter" (136).

Knudson is not a corrupt policeman like Franks: he reacts in part to the presence of his lover, Maude, and the secret they share. Archer later reveals his assessment of Knudson to Maude as a typical policeman with two consciences, "a public conscience and a private conscience" (139). Macdonald's police generally inhabit a gray ethical area and their (usually resisted) corrupt tendencies stem from years of work at a thankless job.

Archer himself summons the police in *The Ivory Grin* just after he discovers the first murder victim, Lucy Chapman, in a cheap motel room. Archer's immediate assessment of Detective Lieutenant Brake is as someone who "looked as if he had always been a policeman — had teethed on handcuffs, ... pounded out his career on broken pavements, in nocturnal alleys" (46). After that description the reader is expecting a corrupt cop, but Brake is much like Knudson; the narrative develops in the direction of cooperation. When, almost immediately after apprehension, the suspect escapes, he is fired upon by yet another inexperienced, trigger-happy policeman, a type prevalent in Macdonald's novels. Archer manages to deflect the shot, demonstrating his superior professionalism, since "you wanted him alive. If you shot him you'd be in the soup. He wasn't under arrest" (51).

When Brake admonishes the officer and asks him what the suspect's license number is, it is Archer who shows superiority by filling in the man's role and by providing Brake the number. He identifies himself but at first refuses to give Brake the name of his client. This is very much parallel to Chandler's depiction of Marlowe in Bay City, but where Chandler underscores the corruptibility of the smaller city — smaller equals easier for gangsters to manipulate — Macdonald stresses the dichotomy in terms of professionalism. Archer eventually gives up the name of his client because he has been suspicious of her motives from the start. Cooperation between PI and cop is enabled, for instance, by the fact that neither one believes that Lucy Chapman is the victim's real name. Archer's suspicions of policemen in general are far from eradicated, however. He pursues an older crime he thinks is related to the Chapman killing since he found with her belongings a news clipping offering a $5,000 reward for information about a missing person.

He visits Mrs. Charles Singleton, mother of the missing Charles Singleton, and asks her to hire him. Thinking that he wants the reward, she assures him that he will get it if he earns it, but his experience with police corruption informs his decision: "Reward money has a way of slipping into policemen's pockets. It has a homing instinct for authority" (85). This relatively minor instance of corruption serves to underscore Archer's appreciation of the complexities and degrees of unethical behavior on the part of law enforcement officers. Mrs. Singleton decides against hiring Archer, but her companion, Sylvia Treen, who is in love with Singleton, engages him.

Brake accepts Archer's cooperation, saying that he appreciates the help of any citizen: "I like help, from private cops or citizens or anybody" (143), but insists that the private investigator keep him informed. Archer is forthcoming with his new client's name and despite minor squabbling over respective motives the two men together pursue lines of investigation. Archer's suspicions linger, however, and he holds back some of what he knows, fearing that Brake is determined to arraign and convict Alex Norris, Chapman's fiancé, whom Archer knows to be innocent. In one respect, Brake resembles Sergeant Nulty in Chandler's *Farewell, My Lovely*. Where Nulty subsumes racism within his overall lack of professionalism, Brake inherits, as it were, a watered-down version of his racism. His suspicions of Norris are reasonable, considering the fact that the young man was with the victim just before the killing, reappears just after Archer finds the

Six. Ross Macdonald

body, and escapes from custody. Archer, however, already fears that Norris would be "railroaded" by the Bella City police, primarily due to the color of his skin.

Brake reinforces Archer's suspicions by stereotyping blacks as a criminal element: "You don't know these people the way I do." He rolls up his sleeve and shows Archer a nasty scar on his forearm: "The buck that gave me this was trying for my throat" (149). Brake defensively assures Archer that he hasn't used any third-degree methods on Norris, but later shows signs of being not averse to railroading blacks: "What do I do when they go around cutting each other with knives, setting fire to each other? Pat them on the back and tell them to go to it? I say stop them, put them away" (161).

Archer's fears are confirmed when he discovers that Brake has forced Norris to sit in the morgue, handcuffed to the corpse, in order to get him to confess. It is a sign of the power that Archer has gained in the still-young relationship that he has only to ask the policeman to let him talk to the young man to get Norris released. Brake even tells Norris that Archer is his friend and that he should open up to him (152). Macdonald draws a parallel to Knudson when he has Archer sympathize with Brake: "I understood Brake's routine and desperate anger after thirty years of trying to fit human truth into square-cut legal patterns handed down for his use by legislators and judges" (157).

Chapter Four considers how Chandler's novels responded to Dennis Potter's claim that "recognition that the law itself, with its definitions of crimes and its agencies of law enforcement and punishment is problematic" in what he calls "formulaic works" of the hard-boiled genre (121). Chandler built on limited criticism of law and law enforcement in Hammett to tackle these issues head-on, often in virtual debates among police, district attorneys, and Philip Marlowe. One major result was to question simplistic definitions of legitimate and illegitimate actions, revealing the relative and interpreted nature of law enforcement.

In his essay "The Writer as Detective Hero," Macdonald sought to distance himself from Chandler, in part by distinguishing his detective, Lew Archer, as a questioner and social analyst, keenly sensitive to the thoughts and actions of everyone with whom he comes in contact. While

Raymond Chandler's Philip Marlowe

his portrayal of Archer in many novels supports his claim as critic, his distinction is, on the whole, inaccurate, since Chandler's Philip Marlowe essentially pursues the same goals as Archer with much the same results. Nevertheless, we recognize Macdonald's development of social criticism beyond that of his mentor through his increased appreciation of the subtleties of corruption. Chandler's tendency was to counterbalance good cops with bad cops, but Macdonald problematized these crucial definitions more effectively than Chandler by merging the two extremes in several of his policemen.

CHAPTER SEVEN

Cinematic Considerations

A brief investigation of selected film adaptations of the novels of Raymond Chandler illustrates the inevitable changes that occur in such transformations to the screen and sheds light on the relationship between expression of American individualism in fiction and American individualism in film. The economics of the American film industry limited feature film length to 90 minutes, requiring radically abbreviated versions of the novels that served as bases for screenplays, but cuts were never ideologically neutral since industry-based censorship played a large role in what landed on the cutting room floor. Chandler's concept of individualism and Marlowe's role of negotiator are generally retained, but there are significant changes in Marlowe's interactions with criminals and police.

Three of these films, *The Big Sleep*, *Murder, My Sweet*, and *Lady in the Lake*, were made in the period of American cinema when the major studios had a stranglehold on production (roughly 1930–1960). In this period a highly significant factor of production was a self-regulating mechanism, the Motion Picture Producers and Directors Association (MPPDA), whose strictures, commonly referred to as the Production Code, were first instituted in 1927 and subsequently made more and more restrictive. In the 1940s, when the first Chandler adaptations were produced, the Code was still a stringently enforced censoring mechanism that shaped narratives according to perceived mainstream moral values.

The most obvious manifestation of rigid control of narrative is the insistence on a "happy ending," for instance by means of establishing a monogamous, heterosexual, seemingly lasting relationship between protagonists by the fade-out, a sure indication that problems have been overcome and all is well. Yet more crucial to hard-boiled adaptations were strict rules guiding narratives in their depiction of crime and crime prevention. Such narrow restrictions have not always obtained: American film has always appealed to a perceived sensationalism on the part of its audience, but films of the late 1920s and early 1930s especially aroused the vigilance of religious and civic groups such as the Legion of Decency, affiliated with the Catholic Church. For these concerned citizens, Hollywood too often depicted the joie de vivre of loose-living flappers and charismatic, tommy-gun toting gangsters, products of the high-spirited Jazz Age.

Although it encompassed a multitude of sins, the Code was particularly sensitive to gangster films of the early sound era, whose charismatic, blatantly violent, and ambitious heroes parodied the optimistic Horatio Alger model of democratic self-reliance and upward mobility. Thus the Code demanded that "the treatment of crimes against the law must not ... make criminals seem heroic or justified" (qtd. in Schumach 290) and even in cases in which the criminal is captured or killed, the MPPDA was perceptive enough to recognize the allure of such criminal protagonists.

The Code was intentionally vague in defining its moralistic parameters, but the tacit assumption was that all "good" people agree on what is accepted or common. The framers of the Code stood for the rigid social hierarchies and family-bound mores of the 19th century and assumed that depiction of what they considered abnormal behavior would "affect the moral standards of those who, through the screen, take in these ideas and ideals" (qtd. in Schumach 286). These films succeed in transforming not only character and plot, but also the ideology behind such constructs. These films present a simplistic world in which hero and heroine embrace at the end; where good, personified by these characters, triumphs over clearly recognizable evil; where police are, at worst, absent, and almost never depicted as corrupt. They were consciously constructed so as to depict a black-and-white moral universe and to placate civic and religious groups that dictated this sanitized and simplified worldview to studio owners.

In following these strictures, Hollywood gravely misrepresented Chandler's worldview, one which insisted on *not* reducing the moral complexities of modern American life to the convenient mythologizing of America's self-appointed champions of the good. Relativism is inherent in Chandler's individualism; no single set of moral rules could apply to all

Seven. Cinematic Considerations

people; his position, both in his fiction and in commentary, was that differing, even conflicting, systems of ethics could and must coexist and that tolerance was the responsibility of each individual. He resisted compartmentalizing people into convenient categories.

Chandler thus rejected the possibility of an ideal society, preferring a world in which crime exists (and sometimes pays) and where the definition of crime must be constantly reexamined in a world in which the powerful few can dictate for all time codes of behavior to those not as powerful and where root causes of crime are ignored. To some extent Chandler's hero is transformed in film into a representative of rugged American individualism, much like the earlier Western heroes, and tends to exercise superhuman powers and display invincibility. He exudes a sense of moral self-assurance not unlike that of the proponents of the Production Code, brushing aside incompetent police in his pursuit of archcriminals, meting out often very rough justice as he sees fit. While he valued the utility of such a hero for purposes of assailing an oppressive hierarchy, Chandler's principal accomplishment was to turn the hard-boiled genre inside out, to transform a radically extroverted genre into an introspective one. But the medium dictated the message: making the hero an extrovert was inevitable in a medium that does not express introspection very well.

Chandler's deepest concerns — his interest in the community as well as the individual, his hatred of the abuse and the abusers of power, his conviction that ethical conduct cannot be reduced to simplistic formulae and must be continually scrutinized — are inevitably what Hollywood was most concerned to change. In many cases Chandler presents not so much the explicitly subversive narrative that Hollywood censors feared, but a profound skepticism concerning received definitions of proper and improper conduct. He refuses to close his detective narratives with reassurances for his audience that crime is committed only by a distinct social class, and he opens up to his readers the possibility that, even if they are not directly affected by crime, it is impossible not to live within its reach.

Raymond Chandler's novels question societal definitions such as criminal behavior and the role of women, whereas film adaptations of the 1940s seek to contain such criticism by reinforcing mainstream norms of obedience to law enforcement officers and a hearth-and-home role for women.

Raymond Chandler's Philip Marlowe

Chandler's novels are based on a bleak view of a corrupt modern American society, but not without a guarded sense that the society can be improved by personal responsibility informed by skepticism toward received codes of conduct. The intrinsic message in *Murder, My Sweet* (1944), an adaptation of *Farewell, My Lovely*, and the film version of *The Big Sleep* (1946) is that appropriate codes of behavior are already in place. In such texts there are clear-cut and clearly recognizable distinctions between good men and bad, between dangerous femmes fatales and sweet, well-meaning homebodies, but Chandler makes no attempt in his novels to reify such categories.

Edward Dmytryk's *Murder, My Sweet* retains the main plot of Moose Malloy's search, through Marlowe, for his long-lost Velma, and her concomitant cold-blooded and deadly response to being hunted. But while Dmytryk and screenwriter John Paxton accept and elaborate upon such male, action-oriented scenes as Marlowe's confrontation with the self-admitted charlatan Jules Amthor and his escape from Dr. Sonderborg's clinic, they take great liberties in adapting female characters.

In the novel, Ann Riordan is a self-assured, independent working woman. She and Marlowe first meet after Lindsay Marriott has been murdered and the detective is recovering after being sapped. Fearing that he has killed Marriott, she bravely holds him at bay with her automatic and demonstrates her grit by verbally sparring with the detective in his own hard-boiled jargon. Chandler establishes an equality of language when Marlowe moves unexpectedly and Ann comments, "You take some awful chances, mister" (*Stories* 817). Later in the scene, after Marlowe admires the "cool quiet of her voice" and her nerve, he compliments her on her boldness in investigating a dangerous situation, remarking, "You take some awful chances, Miss Riordan" (*Stories* 820). Verbal equality translates to social equality: Marlowe's superiority is limited to his métier, one in which he is a seasoned professional and she a neophyte, but Marlowe recognizes her ability and courage. Ann Riordan is an intellectual match for Marlowe; she admires the detective and strives to aid him in his inquiries, asking to sign on as his assistant, but while a romantic relationship with Marlowe is suggested in the penultimate chapter, it is that and no more: a common future is neither projected nor ruled out. The open-ended nature of this relationship helps keep it from becoming a male-dominated one.

Seven. Cinematic Considerations

In the film Riordan is transformed into the daughter of Lewin Lockridge Grayle, the old, seemingly impotent husband of the deadly Velma Valento. Ann Grayle retains something of the complexity of Ann Riordan, but her prime motivation, initially, is to protect her father. Although she recognizes early on that her stepmother is motivated by greed rather than love and she strives to combat her, she depends on Marlowe, the strong, younger male, to restore the sanctity of the home into which she was born and, ultimately, to establish a recognizably proper new one with her. The familial theme in the novel, in contrast, presents Ann Riordan as the daughter of a deceased Bay City policeman, whose courage and high ethical standards she has inherited, but she is not placed in a subservient position to him or any man. In the film it is Marlowe who asks, rather insincerely, "How would you like to work for me?" and not Ann who takes the initiative. The filmmakers deftly tease the viewer with romance throughout the narrative, and the obligatory happy ending is established in the final shot when Ann and Marlowe drive away, embracing in the back of a taxi. So complete are the transfer of Ann's loyalties and the transformation of her world that she shows no sign of mourning for her dead, ostensibly beloved, father. Love not only conquers all, but erases memory.

The often stunning, high-contrast black-and-white cinematography of *Murder, My Sweet* is paralleled by the polarized characterization of the film's heroes and villains. While Velma Valento/Mrs. Grayle is a prototypical film noir femme fatale, and, as such, well worthy of study, her character is quite black and white in contrast to Chandler's Velma. Introduced sketchily by Ann before we meet her, the characterization is one of unrelenting selfishness and greed. Her duplicity is underscored by a transparently false English accent, and her "bad girl" credentials are established, when Marlowe and the viewer first meet her, by provocative dress (an errant hemline and a bare midriff) and a lascivious posture when seated. Confident in her sexual allure throughout the narrative, she attempts at the climax to inveigle Marlowe into doing her killing for her, and only after Marlowe lets slip the fact that the intended victim, Jules Amthor, is already dead does she make clear her plans of killing the detective. After her father kills Velma to prevent her from killing Marlowe, Ann Grayle makes explicit that which is implicit in every facet of the scenario: "She was evil, all evil."

In stark contrast, the novel ends with Marlowe and police detective Randall ruminating on Velma Valento's suicide. Cornered by a Baltimore detective three months after shooting Moose Malloy, Velma mortally wounds him and then turns the gun on herself. When Randall points out the senselessness of the act — that she could have easily won her murder trial — Marlowe suggests an answer that opens the narrative to further interpretation: it wasn't fear of arrest and trial that motivated Velma; she killed herself to avoid mortifying her husband with a trial, to "give a break to the only man who had ever really given her one" (*Stories* 984). The erstwhile femme fatale of film noir (the ostensible embodiment of evil in the form of a manipulative, egotistical woman) proves to have a sense of pride and a system of ethics that extends beyond her purely individual needs and desires. Unlike the Velma of *Murder, My Sweet*, this character has a palpable, if limited, appreciation of at least one other person, and her last act impels the reader to reconsider the motives of her criminal actions. Chandler thus resists the all-too-neat closure that had become standard in the Hollywood film. The purely manipulative (and, indeed, predictable) Velma of Dmytryk's film, who, unlike Chandler's original, attempts to distract Marlowe by making him her lover and accomplice, is, in the original, an ambiguous character worthy of reader empathy.

Another striking difference between the novel and the film can be seen in the treatment of the police. Chandler often expressed his lack of interest in — and even condemnation of— the whodunit tradition of crime fiction, which challenged the reader to assess clues and attempt a solution alongside of the detective. His interest lay in the critique of society in terms of its power structure, and he found in crime the ideal means by which to illustrate societal tensions. Thus, most specifically and consistently, his portrayal of the police and the private detective's interactions with them constitute the core elements of his novels.

In *Farewell, My Lovely* Chandler locates extreme police corruption in Bay City, on the theory that gangsters can only purchase parts of a big city, but can buy a town outright. There Marlowe's protection is provided by the financial and political clout of his client, Mr. Grayle, but not before he is beaten by Bay City detectives Blane and Galbraith, who deliver him into the sadistic hands of Dr. Sonderborg, a quack who incapacitates

Seven. Cinematic Considerations

"patients" with dangerous drugs and provides a safe haven for criminals on the run. Chandler's strategy in less easily corrupted Los Angeles County is to contrast an incompetent police detective with one whose intellectual abilities and high ethical standards match Marlowe's own.

As we have already seen, Lieutenant Nulty, who is in charge of the Montgomery murder, recognizes Marlowe's interest and intellect and soon depends on the private eye to do his work for him. In stark contrast to Nulty, Lieutenant Randall of Central Homicide, investigating the Lindsay Marriott murder, establishes his professionalism by initially questioning Marlowe, who is under suspicion for having been at the crime scene. Before long, convinced of Marlowe's innocence, he elicits the detective's theories as to what happened, and provides an important piece of the puzzle by making the crucial Jessie Florian–Lindsay Marriott connection that Marlowe has missed. In a town where "law is where you buy it" (*Stories* 868), Marlowe pays Randall a high compliment, stating "twenty million dollars wouldn't scare you. But you might get orders" (*Stories* 908).

Throughout all of Chandler's novels, police corruption is examined as closely as any crime scene clue in whodunit narratives. In *Farewell, My Lovely* the good cop/bad cop contrast underscores Chandler's observation that all is not well with the American system of justice, in opposition to the Production Code insistence that the public be presented with efficient, irreproachable agents of law enforcement.

In Dmytryk's film all of Chandler's social criticism is erased. Blane and Galbraith do not appear at all (Moose Malloy and Amthor's goon-like chauffeur deliver Marlowe to Sonderborg's clinic). Unable or unwilling to tackle issues of race, the filmmakers transformed Florian's into a white bar where Malloy only roughs up the manager, and Nulty's role is substantially reduced: he's now Randall's colorless assistant. Clearly, Chandler's social critique — even merely his concern for realism — was incompatible with the spirit of the Production Code, which stipulated that "law — divine, natural or human — shall not be ridiculed, nor shall sympathy be created for its violation" (qtd. in Schumach 280). It was therefore excised, and an important aspect of Chandler's concept of individualism went with it.

Compared to *Murder, My Sweet*, Howard Hawks and his screenwriters

(William Faulkner, Leigh Brackett, and, later, Jules Furthman) took fewer obvious liberties in their 1946 version of *The Big Sleep* (1939). However, although Hawks' stoic masculine ethos (where groups of men are bound by an unspoken code of conduct and honor) more closely matches the ethics of hard-boiled fiction and promises, at times, to reflect the introspective, open-minded ethos of Chandler's world, his film ultimately presents a hermetically sealed Hollywood world where conventional mores triumph.

Where Dmytryk's radical changes to *Farewell, My Lovely* involve a deadly crossfire between Moose Malloy and Mr. Grayle, Hawks' subtler, but no less significant, transformation also involves a climactic shootout not found in the novel on which it was based. In a closely related change, Hawks shifts responsibility for the death of Rusty Regan (Shawn Regan in the film) from Carmen Sternwood to the now stereotypical underworld figure Eddie Mars. In the novel, the mentally unstable younger Sternwood daughter murders Regan because he has resisted her sexual advances, and Marlowe convinces Vivian Regan (Vivian Rutledge in the film), her older sister and Regan's estranged wife, to institutionalize Carmen in hopes that she will be eliminated as a threat to society and receive proper psychiatric treatment. The film's conclusion, however, scrupulously avoids such thorny issues as psychological versus legal culpability and reveals that gangster Mars has killed Regan.

In this final scene of retributive justice, Marlowe tricks Mars into arriving at Geiger's house after he and Vivian have arrived, and thus gets the drop on the gangster. Marlowe intimidates Mars by shooting him in the arm. Mars attempts to escape, but he is unsuccessful in countermanding his own order to his men to shoot the first man out the door, and they summarily execute him.

The tortured logistics of this scene underscore its struggle to tie up the narrative into a neat thematic package: Mars could more easily and more logically have given his henchmen the order to shoot Marlowe as he left the house, but then he himself would not have been killed by them and "justice" would not have triumphed. The censors were concerned not with narrative credibility or aesthetics, but solely with placing the white and black hats firmly on the appropriate heads. In similar fashion to the

Seven. Cinematic Considerations

treatment of Velma in *Murder, My Sweet*, it is much simpler to identify a character as evil and then eliminate that character in order to preserve the social fabric.

In the novel Mars is not Regan's killer, and a kind of rough, if less-than-satisfying, justice is achieved by *not* having him killed or even arrested. This is not to say, however, that Chandler absolves Mars, that no ethical stance is taken. Marlowe is never under any illusion as to Mars' character. When he discovers Mona, the gangster's wife, at the Rialito hideout, he castigates her for excusing her husband's actions by enumerating his vices: "You think he's just a gambler. I think he's a pornographer, a blackmailer, a hot car broker, a killer by remote control, and a suborner of crooked cops" (*Stories* 736). Mars especially earns Marlowe's contempt by hiring Lash Canino, who poisons Harry Jones while in Mars' pay; but in the novel Mars has helped Vivian Regan dispose of her late husband's body and then blackmails her: he has nothing to do with Regan's death. As guilty as Mars is in the broader context, Chandler leaves him untouched by the law or forces of divine retribution (as implied in the film). He refuses to provide a convenient scapegoat and leave his audience with the assurance that justice always prevails: he prefers to challenge, even disturb, his readers' sense of justice.

In all of Chandler's novels, upper-echelon criminals like Mars are viewed as morally more culpable than petty crooks like Harry Jones, because Chandler recognizes the social pressures that force the "little guys" into a life of crime. In *The Big Sleep* he has Captain Gregory of the Missing Persons Bureau state explicitly that which is implicit in Marlowe's motivation:

> I like to see the law win. I like to see the flashy well-dressed muggs like Eddie Mars spoiling their manicures in the rock quarry at Folsom, alongside of the poor little slum-bred hard guys that got knocked over on their first caper and never had a break since. That's what I'd like. You and me both lived too long to think I'm likely to see it happen. Not in this town, not in any town half this size, in any part of this wide, green and beautiful U.S.A. We just don't run our country that way [*Stories* 743–4].

Gregory is one of Chandler's ethically ambiguous cops. Eddie Mars appears to have information only Missing Persons could provide, suggesting that Gregory is on his payroll, and Marlowe even hints to Gregory that he suspects this. Yet once Gregory has called Bernie Ohls, Marlowe's friend and chief inspector for the district attorney, to check Marlowe's credentials, he is willing to help Marlowe and is very forthcoming with information concerning Rusty Regan's disappearance. It is, however, this very ambiguity that seems to have bothered filmmakers and/or their censors, since Gregory is never even mentioned in the film. Gregory admits to Marlowe that he's "reasonably honest. As honest as you could expect a man to be in a world where it's out of style" (*Stories* 743), but this is far too pragmatic an answer for Hollywood, too far removed from a clear, booster attitude toward policemen as immaculate guardians of the system. The ironic tone in Gregory's speech illustrates Chandler's resistance to any codified view of American history or society. Whatever the motivation, Chandler is careful to expose societal inequities that Hollywood typically glosses over.

William Luhr also focuses on the transformation of the novel in terms of the "happy-ending" convention of mainstream Hollywood film: "In the film ... Marlowe has everything. He has defeated, not only Canino, but also Eddie Mars, and he is in love with a woman who is 'good.' His relationship with her would also, since her sister is mad and her father dying, give him access to the Sternwood fortune" (135). This last supposition seems too far removed from one of the sturdiest of hard-boiled conventions — that the detective resist any temptation of riches or domesticity — to be valid, but Luhr is correct in indicating the economic bent of the adaptation, reducing the roles of Carmen and General Sternwood, so that "the focus becomes Marlowe, Vivian, and Eddie Mars" (135). Ronald S. Librach similarly suggests a triangle, one that helps establish a suitable and unambiguous villain: "In opting not to punish Carmen, Hawks has exonerated her, and given the transformation of Vivian into a suitable love-interest for the hero, Mars remains the only candidate" (172). Thus, while the reduction of elements paves the way for the external limitation of the standard 90-minute form, the complexity of Chandler's novel, notably in its social critique, gives way to a neatly constructed romantic triangle. Eddie Mars is presented as a possible surrogate for Vivian's absent husband: the mysterious quality of the Vivian Rutledge-Eddie Mars relationship and Marlowe's repeated question to the former, "What's Eddie Mars got

Seven. Cinematic Considerations

on you?," subtly suggest a romantic liaison, and the detective himself replaces Mars in the equation at the end.

A dramatic crisis is achieved in both novel and film after Vivian has won at Eddie Mars' roulette wheel and is the victim of a supposed armed robbery acted out for Marlowe's benefit. The novel underscores Marlowe's and Vivian's mutual antagonism: after a brief kissing scene in a parked car, Marlowe insists on returning to professional duties and resumes his inquiries into Vivian's dealings with Mars. Vivian can no more abide refusal of her sexual favors than can her sister; she threatens Marlowe with violence (presumably from her gangster friends) and dismisses him angrily.

Hawks does not present quite so idyllic an ending as Dmytryk: in place of Ann Grayle's oblivious attitude to the death of her father, there is a palpable sense of the loss of human life. He manages to suggest, however, the superiority of the intimate, self-constructed, closed world of romance over the dangerous, indeterminate world "outside." Vivian has acted mysteriously throughout, especially when Marlowe repeatedly asks about her connection to Mars. After one refusal to cooperate, she claims that Shawn Regan has been located in Mexico and that she's flying down to meet him. Marlowe next sees her in Rialito. Where, in the novel, Mona Mars saves him from Canino, here the trussed-up detective is flanked by Mrs. Mars and Mrs. Rutledge. In terms of any narrative logic, the latter's presence in Rialito is left unaccounted for: her function is to aid Marlowe in his escape and thereby solidify the romance. After Marlowe kills Canino, he compliments her on her courage under fire, but, in a rather blatant move to paper over holes in the plot, Marlowe cuts her off when she tries to explain what she's been doing. Both hurry to Geiger's house in order to arrive before Mars does, and all subsequent dialogue involving Vivian is focused on the dangers of the anticipated encounter.

After Mars is shot, Marlowe calls Bernie Ohls to inform him of recent events, notably that Mars "killed Regan. I'll tell you about it when you get here." Unsure if Mars' thugs are still lying in wait for them, the lovers nevertheless are utterly committed to one another, threatened from without but unified in their common "goodness" as they wait for deliverance from a police force far more incorruptible and benevolent than ever in Chandler.

Raymond Chandler's Philip Marlowe

While classics of film noir and exciting, entertaining narratives in their own right, Dmytryk's *Murder, My Sweet* and Hawks' *The Big Sleep* not only simplify Chandler's novels but also defuse Chandler's social critique, transforming plot and adapting characters when not eliminating them outright. Dmytryk's film turns a figure in Chandler who matches wits with the detective and proves herself to be that rare creature in hard-boiled fiction — the strong, independent woman — into hardly more than an infatuated schoolgirl. Hawks' film is a more complex crime narrative, but ultimately his story emphasizes the growing love between the detective and the daughter of his client, and much of the director's scenario is concerned with keeping the viewer guessing as to how and when the lovers will unite.

Both films treat law enforcement in general and the police in particular in a benign manner. Their policemen, when present, are efficient, if unimaginative, investigators; higher-ranked officers, Bernie Ohls in *The Big Sleep* and Lieutenant Randall in *Murder, My Sweet*, ultimately support Marlowe and appear only long enough to reassure viewers that crime doesn't pay. The abuse of power, notably as exercised by the police, however, is a theme highlighted in all of Chandler's novels. In "The Simple Art of Murder" Chandler not only criticizes the prejudicial treatment the less powerful receive from the political hierarchy, but insists that citizens of the United States possess a democratic inheritance sufficient to rectify injustices within the system. He refuses to accept the implied attitude of most other hard-boiled writers of his day that only the exceptional individual, the self-reliant private eye, can correct the situation, but places the responsibility for realizing a just society on the shoulders of each individual. In positing that "law and order are things we talk about but refrain from practicing" (*Later Novels* 991) he urges his readers to carefully analyze their society and to do more than pay lip service to their ideals, lip service that is the superficial and complacent rule of the Production Code.

Lady in the Lake, directed by Robert Montgomery in 1947, is best known for its experimental, first-person point of view. Aside from several after-the-fact scenes of narration with Marlowe addressing the audience directly, the viewer sees all the action through the eyes of Marlowe (played by Montgomery) so that, for example, we only see the detective in occasional mirror images. A rarely used cinematic device, first-person narration places extreme emphasis on the hero while, paradoxically, nearly eliminating him from view.

In the novel Marlowe is brought in to investigate the disappearance of the wife of Derace Kingsley (changed to Kingsby in the film), the head of the Gillerlain Company. His secretary, Adrienne Fromsett, plays a secondary role. Similar to the treatment of women's roles in *Murder, My Sweet*, Fromsett is transformed in the film into the "love interest" for the hero and thereby a major character. Marlowe asserts his autonomy by ignoring Fromsett's insistence on her client — and therefore superior — status; as romantic sparks begin to fly, the detective makes it clear that a woman should not be in business at all and that "his woman" must be a stay-at-home wife. By the end of the film Marlowe has brought her around to his way of thinking.

Far truer to the original is the treatment of the private eye–police relationship, especially in Marlowe's interactions with Bay City's Lieutenant DeGarmot (Degarmo in the novel), in which Montgomery does not gloss over the policeman's corruption or brutality, and Captain Kane (Webber in the novel), the responsible public official portrayed along the lines of Lieutenant Randall in *Farewell, My Lovely*. In the film Marlowe first encounters DeGarmot after being framed by Chris Lavery, a suspect in Mrs. Kingsby's disappearance and, according to DeGarmot, an upstanding citizen of notorious Bay City. The policeman shows a fundamental dislike of private eyes in general and Marlowe in particular. Marlowe investigates the site of the supposed drowning death of Muriel Chess, the wife of Bill Chess, the caretaker of Kingsby's mountain home in Little Fawn Lake, and on his return discovers the murdered body of Lavery in his home.

In Chandler's novel Marlowe is surprisingly forthcoming when interrogated by Webber and Degarmo at Lavery's house, revealing his client's name and his presence at Little Fawn Lake. Alone with Degarmo, Marlowe questions him about Florence Almore, who died in her home just across the street from Lavery under suspicious circumstances a year earlier. It will be clarified later that Degarmo was implicated in her death, but at this juncture Marlowe intimates that police corruption was involved in the Almore case and Degarmo reacts by slapping the private eye's face twice and warns Marlowe to keep his nose out of police business.

Although basically true to the novel, the film has Marlowe taunt Degarmo with information he gathered at Little Fawn Lake that "a tough cop, one like you," one whose description matches Degarmo, was seen there. Marlowe punches the policeman when Degarmo attempts to slap him a third time; Degarmo pulls his gun but is restrained by the returning Capt. Kane. Kane cuffs Marlowe and takes him to police headquarters, where Degarmo again threatens violence before Kane intervenes and learns that Marlowe couldn't have been Lavery's killer, that the Little Fawn Lake alibi checks out.

The novel includes an extensive discussion between Marlowe and Webber about the present case, the Almore case, and the possibility of police corruption. While his forthrightness about discussing the matter is evidence of his own integrity, Webber admits that Bay City has earned its reputation for corruption and that Degarmo in particular has been acting suspiciously, especially since it's no mystery that he was once married to Muriel Chess. When the conversation turns to the Almore case, the two men virtually reopen it, examining evidence that was suppressed in the past. The film greatly simplifies this interaction, but, while Kane resists the odious task of investigating DeGarmot's suspicious behavior as being "the rottenest job a policeman can have," he nonetheless forges a partnership of sorts with the private eye.

Soon afterward Marlowe is tailed by DeGarmot, who forces the PI off the road, pours whisky over his injured body, and anonymously calls the police to report an incident of drunken driving, intending to frame Marlowe. Marlowe evades capture and eventually joins forces with Kane. In the final scene DeGarmot overpowers Marlowe and admits to his crimes of passion. He tells Marlowe that once the detective is eliminated he can go back to being a good cop, "the best cop in the world — be clean." He is about to kill him when Kane comes to the rescue and shoots the crooked cop. None of this is in Chandler's novel, but DeGarmot's statement of intended reform does recall many discussions in Chandler's work that reveal the ubiquity of corruption and possibilities for its eradication.

Marlowe, an adaptation of *The Little Sister* directed by Paul Bogart in 1969, is, with one significant exception, generally true to the novel. One obvious change is to update the narrative to the late 1960s, including mak-

Seven. Cinematic Considerations

ing the up-and-coming movie star Mavis Weld into the television star Mavis Wald. Marlowe, portrayed by James Garner, is still a Los Angeles private detective and very much the lone quester, negotiating among gangsters, clients, and the police.

Aside from the difference in period, characters such as Mavis Wald, her sister Orfamay, her brother Orrin, and her lover-gangster Steelgrave are embroiled in several murders, two by means of ice pick. Searching for Orrin Quest at the behest of his sister, Orfamay, Marlowe is at first stymied, yet he discovers two men, Clausen, a hotel manager and Hicks, a potential blackmailer, who have been murdered. As in Chandler's novel, homicide officers French and Beifus are called in to investigate the second murder and Marlowe initially cooperates with the policemen. French, however, is mildly suspicious and tells Marlowe not to leave town.

Marlowe soon discovers that someone is blackmailing Wald with compromising photos taken of her with Sonny Steelgrave. He offers his assistance, but his knowledge frightens her; she calls Steelgrave, who has his thugs work Marlowe over. A striking bit of casting is that of Bruce Lee as Winslow Wong, demonstrating his kung fu abilities on two occasions, but the fact that he plays a henchman of Steelgrave's keeps him within Chandler's original spirit, so the change is cosmetic. Wong tries to intimidate Marlowe by destroying his office, but cannot convince the detective to drop the case.

As soon as Wong leaves, French arrives and asks Marlowe if he knows anything about the Clausen murder and tells him that they found the detective's business card on Hicks, implying that Marlowe is suppressing information. Marlowe talks himself out of a possible bind when he tells French that he gave a card to Hedy, the hotel detective. When the detective asks French if he knows where Steelgrave can be found, the policeman shows his cooperation by telling Marlowe The Dancers, Steelgrave's club.

When Marlowe finally catches up to Orrin Quest, it's when Orrin's shot and mortally wounded. Marlowe informs Orfamay and they both go to French who, increasingly suspicious of the detective, tells him, just as he does in the novel, "Don't tell me you've been strictly legal" in this matter and Marlowe admits he hasn't. As has already been pointed out in Chapter Four, in the novel French and Beifus are willing, almost equal partners with Marlowe, responsible cops who are cognizant of both outright corruption and gray areas of police procedure that put pressure on people like Marlowe. They are, however, loathe to assert that kind of power. There is more friction in this encounter when Marlowe challenges the lieutenant to book him, but the encounter ends amicably and Marlowe again promises not to leave town.

Soon after, the private eye discovers Steelgrave's body in the latter's house with Mavis Wald sitting near the corpse with a gun in her hand. In an effort to protect her, he forces her to leave, cleans up any possible trace, and calls French. Marlowe, claiming that "I wouldn't lie to you, lieutenant," does just that when he says that no one else was present when he arrived and still refuses to give up the name of his client. In a scene taken directly from the novel, French has reached the limit of his patience and tells Beifus to cuff Marlowe. Growing increasingly loud and angry, French bemoans his situation: as if the danger and the politics of the job weren't enough, he has to put up with "a sharpie suppressing information and concealing evidence." Waiting for Marlowe to "crack wise" and give him an excuse for violence, French punches Beifus, who has gotten between them, instead. This defuses the situation; the handcuffs are taken off Marlowe and he is told to leave.

The film thus shows viewers the police side of the story in a manner much like in the novel, only in abbreviated form. In the novel Marlowe, though uncuffed, is under arrest and has more to say in his own defense: "Any private eye wants to play ball with the police.... Sometimes he doesn't trust the police, and with cause" (*Later Novels* 383). The major change in the adaptation is the absence of Lieutenant Moses Maglashan of the Bay City Police Department, who in the book forms with the private eye and the Los Angeles policemen a kind of ethical triangle. In the novel Maglashan represents the extreme pole of police corruption: despite his presence in French's office, which places him clearly out of his jurisdiction, the Bay City officer volunteers to use third-degree methods on Marlowe and he's even puzzled that the Los Angeles officers would treat the detective "like he was human" (*Later Novels* 349). French and Beifus prevent Maglashan from doing more than slapping the private eye, and after Maglashan has left Beifus reveals that the next move of the Bay City police will be to fake a raid using innocent vagrants as victims.

Seven. Cinematic Considerations

The fact that Maglashan has been excised in *Marlowe* drastically reduces the film's overall critique of the police. The scene barely touches on police ethics with Marlowe insisting on his right to a phone call if booked and French replying that "he could ride the circuit" with him in lieu of a booking. Although the Production Code was on its way out by 1969, it had not lost all its power. Contemporary films like *Bonnie and Clyde* and *Midnight Cowboy* challenged the Code's censorship power, but the filmmakers of *Marlowe* were careful not to imply that the police are corrupt.

In these and in other film versions of Chandler's novels, a limited degree of Chandler's Deweyan individualism is retained, primarily in the detective's role of negotiator. Marlowe's "shuttle diplomacy" among clients, criminals, and police is still palpable. Due to a large extent to the censorship power of the Production Code, however, the detective's role of social critic is severely restricted. One key point is that there are rarely any bad cops; ethical policemen pursue criminals and interact with the private eye. Like many film versions of all possible genres, ethical gray areas are reduced to simplistic extremes that would not draw the attention of the censors.

Conclusion

The figure of the hard-boiled detective holds a paradoxical position in our culture. Reproduced, mimicked, and parodied countless times since his birth in the 1920s, he constitutes one of our most familiar icons: wearing a trench coat and a fedora, wielding an automatic or a revolver, talking "tough" when he talks at all, he represents the lone, honest individual in conflict with urban corruption. And yet, the very familiarity of the icon seems to preclude careful analysis; the critical tendency has been to accept him at face value, to assume not only that his motives and actions are easily grasped, but that he carries the same set of values with him whether his name is Philip Marlowe, Sam Spade, or Mike Hammer.

There are, however, significant differences among these protagonists, and it has been the task of this study to distinguish Raymond Chandler's Philip Marlowe from those of other hard-boiled writers, most specifically as seen through an ideological lens. Where Carroll John Daly's, Dashiell Hammett's, and Mickey Spillane's heroes display the self-sufficient, self-aggrandizing traits of classic rugged American individualism, Chandler, through Marlowe, critiques the individualist ethos. While other hard-boiled detectives often abuse the power they possess and isolate themselves in the process, his actions are pointed consistently at getting contentious or potentially contentious individuals to work together. Unlike other hard-boiled heroes, Marlowe is acutely critical of his own thoughts and actions; he questions his own role and the power he wields, and his actions reflect changes in attitude as he learns from others.

Significantly, he is critical towards violence in a profession predicated on its use. Before Chandler, the hard-boiled detective reflected the society's frustration with violent crime, and the private investigator answered criminal violence with violence, sometimes reluctantly, sometimes gleefully.

Conclusion

All the more striking, then, is Marlowe's comment that "Guns never settle anything," in Chandler's last complete novel, *Playback* (*Later Novels* 756). The fact that he kills only one man — Canino in his first novel, *The Big Sleep*— in the course of seven novels testifies to his preference for nonviolent solutions, especially as compared to the high body counts of Mike Hammer or the Continental Op. In a world in which the police are as guilty of egregious violence as criminals, Marlowe roundly condemns both; his toughness is measured not by resorting to such extreme measures, but by his refusal to respond violently to the threats of gangsters (Eddie Mars in *The Big Sleep*, Laird Brunette in *Farewell, My Lovely*) or the police (Christy French in *The Little Sister*, Detective Dayton in *The Long Goodbye*). When he quietly prevents Lanny, a minor hoodlum, from robbing Vivian Regan in *The Big Sleep*, he is careful to leave the man with his self-respect intact and proves that he is more likely to disarm a criminal than to shoot one.

In *The Long Goodbye* he comes to the rescue of Roger Wade, the only patient at Dr. Verringer's dubious sanitarium, and confronts Earl, the doctor's dangerous and mentally unstable assistant. In a situation in which Mike Hammer would first humiliate, then destroy his adversary, Marlowe shows Earl that he's armed, but, since the unbalanced assistant still attacks him, he fires his automatic through an open window. The noise of the shot proves to be enough to rouse Earl out of his frenzy and Marlowe is able to disarm him by simply speaking to him rationally.

Marlowe is even capable of denigrating the importance and efficacy of violence, especially the kind represented by firearms, and often achieves this in a humorous, self-deprecating fashion. While escaping yet another dubious clinic — Dr. Sonderborg's Bay City establishment in *Farewell, My Lovely*—he orders Sonderborg at gunpoint to open his wall safe. When he refuses, Marlowe comments, "Damn it.... When you have a gun in your hand, people are supposed to do anything you tell them to. It doesn't work, does it?" (*Stories* 901). When, in *The Big Sleep*, Joe Brody threatens him with a gun, Marlowe deflates the grifter's intentions when he responds, "Tsk, tsk.... Such a lot of guns around town and so few brains. You're the second guy I've met within hours who seems to think a gat in the hand means a world by the tail" (*Stories* 647). Although never in doubt as to

Conclusion

the danger posed by weapons, Marlowe knows that no significant change can be effected by using them; supported by the stylistic flourishes Chandler provides him, his weapon is primarily verbal. Indeed, in certain moments the novels lose the kind of dynamic thrust Hammett excelled in creating because Chandler prefers to have Marlowe consider carefully what course of action to take or to negotiate extensively among "combatants." He discusses problems of law enforcement with police and defuses deadly confrontations among criminals. Although the compromises he achieves are far from perfect, comparison with other hard-boiled fiction underscores Marlowe's success, such as when the corrupt Bay City police department is reformed in *Farewell, My Lovely*.

This study has also sought to recover Raymond Chandler from the critical underappreciation that is often the result of analyzing works of popular culture superficially. Critics such as John G. Cawelti place the heroes of popular culture in the context of traditions that reach back to the beginnings of recorded history and view the hard-boiled heroes in much the same way as they view the Western hero; the hero is an outsider, often possessing powers of mind or muscle beyond that of ordinary mortals, who can never become a part of the community he serves. In *Adventure, Mystery, and Romance* Cawelti suggests that the hard-boiled detective is, by definition, an autonomous, even desperate, individual whose heightened sense of morality and justice exclude him from the ranks of the corrupt, powerful elite. In delineating what he calls the "typical hard-boiled pattern of action," he posits that the private eye's investigation invariably "comes up against a web of conspiracy that reflects the presence of a hidden criminal organization" (148). Cawelti views the detective as primarily defending himself against such dangerous forces: "the detective's role changes from classical ratiocination to self-protection against the various threats, temptations, and betrayals posed by the criminal" (148). Backed into an urban corner, as it were, with the closing of the frontier, the detective is on the defensive; he can expect only to save himself, the last uncorrupted individual. Cawelti's rendering, however, conflicts with evidence found in detective fiction. While his concept of conspiracy is tenable for those most ruggedly individualistic protagonists, such as Carroll John Daly's Race Williams and Mickey Spillane's Mike Hammer, he gives too little credit

Conclusion

to the more socially responsible private eyes. By defining the detective's antagonists in terms of an amorphous "web of conspiracy," Cawelti oversimplifies; in Hammett's *Red Harvest* the Continental Op understands almost immediately who belongs to which of the warring Poisonville factions and focuses on eliminating them. If we can speak of Gutman, Cairo, and O'Shaughnessy in *The Maltese Falcon* as conspirators at all, it is as highly divisive, only temporarily hidden ones. Chandler's novels downplay the existence of conspiracy (so beloved by Mickey Spillane) even more, and his hero contrasts markedly with those of Hammett in his focus on active participation in remedying social injustices.

Revisionist critics have questioned any kind of community "service" on the part of the detective. Marlowe's loner status is seen as antisocial behavior, and his dissociation from his community negates any temporary success he might achieve. Speaking of the genre as a whole, Dennis Porter overlooks the distinction between private eye and the police and views both as instruments of a "repressive state apparatus" (121). Stephen Knight underscores the anomic persona of Chandler's hero when he states that Marlowe's values are "defined by his rejection of a social world viewed as a hostile and corrupt unit" (138). Echoing both Knight and Porter, Cynthia S. Hamilton insists that, in keeping with the genre, "Chandler's misanthropy demands an absolute separation between Marlowe and the moral squalor of his society" (161). In her view Marlowe is antisocial, an "alienated outsider who vindicates that stance by his demonstrable superiority in a society unworthy of his services" (155). Such criticism does not begin to explain, however, the incongruity of the private eye taking incredible external risks at low pay merely in order to feel internally superior to those around him. Marlowe is introspective, but his introspection is aimed at solving social problems, not existential crises of the self, and the risks he takes are in the service of his fellow citizens.

Although he clings to the notion of Chandler as a disillusioned romantic whose hero struggles against corruption in the name of an intensely personal moral code, Jerry Speir hints at ways of viewing the detective as something between the mythological hero, an otherworldly superhero, and the figure seen as a social defeatist by Dennis Porter and Stephen Knight. For Speir, Marlowe, in *The Long Goodbye*, is driven by

Conclusion

his chivalrous code to help the hopelessly inebriated Terry Lennox, and although he knows that a drunk is hardly likely to appreciate the "magnanimous gesture," the detective "makes the effort nonetheless" (67). That which Speir insists on labeling "knight errantry" (67), however — implying a hierarchical distance between the socially privileged detective and Lennox — can be more fruitfully viewed as a communitarian urge, one very much in keeping with Marlowe's job, which, after all, is to help people. He achieves this while maintaining a status of equals; while he often feels that he has the insight and experience to argue persuasively for his personal ethics, this does not give him a sense of superiority, and he remains open to the arguments and desires of others.[1]

Along with most of the hard-boiled American writers, Chandler reduced the emphasis on problem solving in detective fiction characteristic of the British school in order to present an accurate picture of social ills. Marlowe typically begins a narrative by accepting the task of finding a missing person or object, but he soon transforms his goal into one of clearing an innocent person of false accusations or protecting that person from harm. Chandler learned from Hammett that in a world shot through with corruption the hard-boiled detective must be skeptical of all he comes in contact with, including those who pay for his services; these employers are often skillful manipulators attempting to deflect suspicion from their own inadequacies or crimes. In *The High Window* he resists Elizabeth Bright Murdock's assumption that Linda Conquest, an innocent woman, has stolen a valuable coin, and clears the latter of suspicion. He also frees Merle Davis from the psychological tyranny of the same client. Hired to track the movements of Betty Mayfield in *Playback*, the detective questions the motives of his client, lawyer Clyde Umney, and, convinced of her innocence, Marlowe soon reveals his identity and his assignment to Mayfield. The heretofore spied-upon woman is understandably suspicious, but Marlowe's persistence finally convinces her that he can and will work in her best interests. Not only does his emphasis shift from ratiocination to interpersonal conflict; Chandler is more truly skeptical in its denotative sense than the merely cynical Spade. He suspends judgment in the interest of fairness.

In a genre predicated on verbal as well as physical violence, Marlowe's

Conclusion

soft-spoken approach also contrasts vividly with Sam Spade: whereas Marlowe typically speaks civilly to district attorneys, arguing with them coolly over the ethics of law enforcement, Sam Spade reacts in near-paranoid fashion. In *The Maltese Falcon*, for example, he remonstrates heatedly to District Attorney Bryan's theory about Floyd Thursby's murder. When Bryan posits that Thursby was murdered because he was the bodyguard for a gambler who "welshed" on $200,000 worth of bets, Spade feels that Bryan is making him complicit, insinuating that he was even hired by the disgruntled gamblers to locate or murder Thursby, much to the surprise of the D.A. While it is true that Bryan does pressure Spade by suggesting that the detective is holding back information so as not to incriminate himself, Spade's red-faced reply — "I've got nothing to tell you or the police and I'm God-damned tired of being called things by every crackpot on the city payroll" (394) — goes far beyond the bounds of self-defense. Hammett's heroes tend to think of themselves as backed into a corner and must lash out at any perceived threat or accusation. While some threats are real, Spade here demonstrates the desperate quality of the autonomous individual, keen to come out ahead in the survival of the fittest.

Jopi Nyman sees this kind of social Darwinism as a force that diminishes, rather than enhances, the status of the individual, for in the hard-boiled world "man is no more than an animal who is not entitled to rights." He finds a "reduction of the specific status of humans, and, consequently, the basis of human rights" (237), but by making these claims for the entire genre, he casts his net too wide: since he focuses on James M. Cain's *The Postman Always Rings Twice* and Horace McCoy's *They Shoot Horses, Don't They?*, it comes as no surprise that he views the genre as reflecting "a cynical and pessimistic view of the human race" (237). By ignoring Chandler, however, he overlooks instances of social engagement aimed at restoring a sense of humanity to those whose rights are threatened. In this respect Chandler paved the way for hard-boiled writers such as Ross Macdonald, whose heroes are presented as socially or even psychologically healing agents.

Conscious of a sense of his role within a larger civic context, Marlowe is convinced that he has a responsibility to his fellow man and that his efforts can make a difference. When he first encounters Terry Lennox in *The Long Goodbye*, he helps the stranger home after the extremely drunk Lennox has been abandoned by his wife in the parking lot of a swank nightclub. Marlowe's concern seems exaggerated to the parking lot attendant, who is quick to volunteer his own selfish philosophy: "I'd just drop him in the gutter and keep going. Them booze hounds just make a man a lot of trouble for no fun.... The way the competition is nowadays a guy has to save his strength and protect hisself in the clinches." Marlowe's narration acknowledges such "trouble," but he also claims that "after all that's my line of work" (*Later Novels* 421). Marlowe performs such tasks not only without remuneration, but often without the reciprocation of respect.

On a second occasion, Marlowe rescues Lennox from two policemen ready to take the publicly intoxicated man to the drunk tank. Marlowe helps Lennox to a taxicab, whose driver is at first reluctant to accept a man who "could get sick somewheres else," before a promise of $5 proves more than he can resist. Marlowe also convinces a skeptical police officer that Lennox is in good hands. The taxi fare is low, since they only drive a short distance to Marlowe's own car, but when he offers the driver the promised $5, the cabbie demurs: "Just what's on the meter, Jack, or an even buck if you feel like it. I been down and out myself. In Frisco. Nobody picked me up in no taxi either" (*Later Novels* 425). The detective has not only spared Lennox the discomfort and humiliation of arrest, but, in his own small way, has succeeded in influencing fellow citizen to an act of mercy. By setting this encounter during the Christmas shopping rush, Chandler deftly contrasts the commercial, corrupted values of the holiday with Marlowe's "Good Samaritan" deed. Marlowe also criticizes Sylvia Lennox for abandoning her (now ex-) husband: "The guy was down and out, starving, dirty, without a bean. You could have found him if it had been worth your time" (*Later Novels* 429). These opportunities, together with Marlowe's far riskier act of helping Lennox escape to Mexico, establish Lennox as a kind of litmus test of Marlowe's willingness to help others.

While Lennox ultimately proves undeserving of Marlowe's friendship, the detective shows no regret for his actions nor does he judge his former friend, and there is no indication that he will abandon his social commit-

Conclusion

ment in the future. Indeed, his last meeting with Lennox provides him the opportunity to establish, if quite briefly, his allegiance to social norms. For Marlowe, what's wrong with Lennox is that his standards were "personal. They had no relation to any kind of ethics or scruples" (*Later Novels* 733). Marlowe is not arguing for strict adherence to the mores of the status quo, but against the ruggedly individualistic arrogance of any individual thinking he can sever social ties and live only by his own rules. Terry's cowardice in running away as he has from his responsibility in his wife's death, has repercussions far beyond his desire for self-preservation. His flight and his faked suicide influence Eileen Wade to kill her husband and herself; Marlowe acknowledges that Lennox had no intention of acting antisocially, but he has reneged on a kind of social contract, and his rash and selfserving behavior has played a role in death and suffering.

Mike Hammer's approach to those who might help him in *My Gun Is Quick* provides a stark contrast. After a woman he has befriended dies under suspicious circumstances, Hammer returns to the all-night diner where he last saw her. His very appearance in the diner upsets Shorty, the counterman, who goes "a little white around the nostrils" and "is suffering badly from the shakes." These visual signs are enough to convince Hammer that Shorty has something to hide, and are all the excuse he needs to threaten him, revealing his sadistic impulses as he does so: "Shorty, maybe just for the hell of it I'll take you apart. You may be a rough apple, but I can make your face look like it's been run through a grinder, and the more I think of the idea the more I like it." Guessing that the counterman is an ex-convict and likely to have returned to crime (although there is no proof of either contention), Hammer changes his approach and threatens the man with a police raid (I:169–170). Every reaction is an overreaction, his bullying nature a function of his exaggerated sense of self. His nastiness toward those he considers socially inferior is rarely held in check. Following a lead as to the whereabouts of a supposed witness, he pays three "punks" who have been making "dirty cracks at the girls passing by" $5 in beer money for information, and walks away, "hoping they'd choke on it" (I:171).

Far removed from the cruelly aloof, self-isolating attitude of Hammer is the constant social engagement of Marlowe, and Chandler has many

Conclusion

means with which he expresses it. For instance, he returns again and again to the metaphor of social groups as circles in *The Big Sleep*. Eddie Mars speaks of his "circle" by way of explaining to Marlowe that far too many people in his illicit business come to him with propositions (*Stories* 689). Chandler draws a comparison to the detective himself by means of this image. While haggling with Harry Jones for information as to the whereabouts of Rusty Regan, Marlowe insists that $200 is too high a price to pay: "Two C notes buys a lot of information in my circle" (*Stories* 713). The image is that of strictly defined social enclaves with borders that can be crossed only with the greatest effort, an effort that it is Marlowe's job to make.

In certain moments the significance of these circles is made more explicit. After Arthur Gwynn Geiger (who has been blackmailing Marlowe's client, General Sternwood) has been murdered, Owen Taylor, the Sternwood's chauffeur, also turns up dead. His death elicits sympathy from the patrician Vivian Regan, because Taylor was in love with Regan's younger sister, Carmen, had run away with her, and wanted to marry her: "Perhaps it wouldn't have been a bad idea," she ventures, "He was in love with her. We don't find much of that in our circle" (*Stories* 630). The comment helps humanize an otherwise egotistical and calculating character, but the willed isolation of this upper-class circle, symbolized by the very closeness of the atmosphere in General Sternwood's greenhouse, is extremely difficult to penetrate. Taylor hadn't succeeded; the Sternwood's brought the wayward lovers back and, at first, had Taylor thrown in jail.

Chandler found the metaphor valuable enough to use in other novels, and made sure to indicate that Marlowe is not immune to such categorization. In *The Little Sister* Hollywood starlet Mavis Weld tells Marlowe that he himself is caught within the circumscription of his own world. At this, their first meeting, fearing blackmail, she assumes the worst of the private eye, insisting that not only can he be bought, but that the price is pitifully low: "You're cheap. It's a cheap little bastard, isn't it? A hundred bucks says. Is a hundred bucks money in your circle, darling?" (*Later Novels* 264). The impermeability of the social circle is emphasized by Weld's reference to Marlowe as a thing, so far removed from Weld

Conclusion

(and her Hollywood circle) as to be inanimate, and thus inscrutably foreign.

Weld, however, is proceeding in knee-jerk fashion, aggressively protecting herself from notoriety that could ruin her career. The fact is that Marlowe is not for sale, and he does not belong to the circle of private eyes that thrives on blackmail by sifting through people's dirty laundry. He is, indeed, in the process of switching his loyalty from the untrustworthy Orfamay to her half sister Mavis, who, for all her faults, is loyal to her family and true to herself. He has not allowed the carefully guarded boundaries of the circles to keep him from working within and across them, and eventually convinces Weld of his protective, not punitive, intentions.

We find a more highly developed sense of "circles" and the difficulty the detective has in penetrating them in *The Long Goodbye*. After Marlowe twice rescues Terry Lennox, the two men meet for social drinking on an irregular basis; on one occasion Lennox explains to the detective that he doesn't "have any home life," that his wife is "happy enough, though not necessarily with me. In our circle that's not too important" (*Later Novels* 433–4), echoing Vivian Regan in *The Big Sleep*. As Lennox's sarcasm vis-à-vis his circle grows, he complains that the now-quiet bar will soon fill up with loud, obnoxious, even smelly, people. Chandler thus makes it clear to the reader that such social constriction ultimately leads to social isolation, as Lennox misanthropically cuts off any potentially new circle as well.

Chandler's wealthiest, most grandiose and ruthless character, Harlan Potter, is found in *The Long Goodbye*; he is a William Randolph Hearst-type newspaper tycoon, and the father of the murdered Sylvia Lennox. Where General Sternwood only suggested the rapaciously individualistic robber baron of a bygone era, Potter is its full-blown representative. Yet despite the many ways in which he could have expressed Potter's corruption and power, Chandler focuses on the magnate's insularity, the cost and effort expended to shield the "great man" from the world. As Marlowe informs the reader:

> Guys with a hundred million dollars live a peculiar life, behind a screen of servants, bodyguards, secretaries, lawyers, and tame executives.... Everything you read or hear about them has been processed by a public relations gang of guys

Conclusion

who are paid big money to create and maintain a usable personality, something simple and clean and sharp, like a sterilized needle [*Later Novels* 484].

Potter displays qualities of rugged individualism similar to the deterministic heroes in Hammett. His egotism is so extreme that his only concern after his daughter dies is that it will bring him notoriety. Since man "has always been a venal animal" is Potter's simplistic code, and since he can trust no one to act in anything resembling a cooperative manner, Marlowe replies, "You don't like the way the world is going so you use what power you have to close off a private corner to live in" (*Later Novels* 613). Chandler here places the rugged individualist in an isolated "corner" of his own making, but this is by no means the end of his inquiry into and critique of American individualism. Characters like Potter and Lennox are carefully constructed as foils to his more open protagonist, whose quality as a social being has yet to be fully appreciated.

One of the critics most sensitive to this issue is Fredric Jameson, for whom Chandler's fiction, especially in its careful attention to detail, attempts to make sense of the anomic nature of modern American city life, where even close neighbors are strangers; Chandler's "fragmentary pictures of setting and place" give purpose to the "shabby anonymity" of small, ultimately insignificant actions (124–25). For Jameson, the hard-boiled detective—and Marlowe in particular—is in a unique position to join the fragments together; he allows us "to see, to know, the society as a whole," since "Marlowe visits either those places you don't look at or those you can't look at: the anonymous or the wealthy and secretive" (128). We can learn through him who these people are and what it is that links them.

Jameson emphasizes, however, the passive nature of Marlowe's social interaction. He is an "involuntary explorer" (128), collecting data with no clear idea of its purpose or of his own influence on it. Jameson views, for example, the "honesty of the detective" as an "organ of perception, a membrane which, irritated, serves to indicate in its sensitivity the nature of the world around it" (131). Thus disembodied, the detective is just as fragmented as the society at large. The conclusion that this critic ultimately draws is that acts of violence in Chandler's fiction are unpremeditated; that murder, far from a puzzle or even an injustice to be solved, is mean-

Conclusion

ingless, and that Chandler succeeds best at confronting the reader with the awesome metaphysical power of death itself, at constructing a vivid momento mori. For Jameson there is no sense of Chandler creating vital human links or critiquing social norms.

In contrast to Jameson's pessimistic outlook, we may turn to the fundamentally more optimistic interpretation of similar data in the social theory of John Dewey. Dewey also takes careful note of the details of daily life and the often tentative or nonexistent connections among people, and he also sees the urgent need to address social problems locally, often characterizing such interaction as "face-to-face" encounters. He does not succumb, however, as does Jameson, to the temptation of removing the individual from the social context.

Dewey, contemplating a far broader landscape of human interaction, finds it essential to first rigorously analyze the concept of individualism itself. In *The Public and Its Problems* he historicizes specifically American concepts of individualism and recognizes that 18th-century theories of natural rights of the individual (the most politically progressive doctrine of the period) were needed to fight oppression in the American and French revolutions. However, a high social price was later paid for the privilege, inasmuch as this led to a kind of sanctification of the individual and the "antithesis of the Individual and the Social," a hallmark of the older (for Dewey, socially debilitating) theory of the democratic individual. Instead he insists that the individual does not exist in a vacuum, "in *isolation* from any associations, except those which they deliberately formed for their own ends" (*Later Works* II:289–90, my emphasis). Dewey insists again and again in his sociopolitical writings that the individual can only be defined in terms of *association* with others, in terms of his or her function within society. In *Outlines of a Critical Theory of Ethics*, he specifies that "this function consist[s] in an activity which realizes wants and powers with reference to their particular surroundings" (*Early Works* III:304). Exercising this function binds individual and community together, enhancing both, for "[i]ndividuality cannot be opposed to association. It is through association that man has acquired his individuality and it is through association that he exercises it" (qtd. in Westbrook 44).

It was part of Dewey's plan to harness the power of human discourse

Conclusion

towards the goal of participatory democracy, and in this plan he opposed what he considered the "false" liberal concept of negative freedom (so important for Locke and Jefferson), defined, in the words of Robert B. Westbrook, as the "absence of coercion or external constraints imposed on an individual by others" (46).[2] For the Dewey of *The Public and Its Problems,* the most important factor needed to realize true democracy is dialogue, which prevents ideas from stagnating, from being hoarded just as material wealth proves unproductive if not used (*Later Works* II:371). Here we have the primary difference between representations of rugged individualism in the hard-boiled novel — the self-sufficient Mike Hammer and the self-contained Continental Op and Sam Spade — and the new individualism Dewey espouses. Marlowe is generous with his words and dedicates them to breaking down the barriers between individuals and circles.

Jameson thus misreads Chandler when he interprets Marlowe as passive, as "involuntary." Rather, Marlowe exploits every possible opportunity to engage in dialogue. This study has sought to develop the concept of Marlowe as a communicator by highlighting his ability as a teacher and his willingness to learn, factors very much in the spirit of Dewey's radical democracy. Such engagement needs to take into account all forms of social interaction, including those of rugged individualists, and here as well Chandler is anticipated by Dewey's pragmatic assessment of power:

> [S]ince the public forms a state only by and through officials and their acts, and since holding official position does not work a miracle of transubstantiation, there is nothing perplexing nor even discouraging in the spectacle of the stupidities and errors of public behavior [*Later Works* II:277].

Dewey's humorous plea for a hard-headed understanding of public officials is echoed in every Chandler novel by Marlowe's discussions with law enforcement officials. Marlowe does not shirk his responsibilities when dealing with the utterly incompetent Lieutenant Nulty in *Farewell, My Lovely,* cooperating with the police detective in solving the Montgomery murder. Because of his social engagement, he is in a far better position to work with the vastly more competent and ethical Lieutenant Randall in the same novel.

Indeed, in the context of Dewey's theories and given the evidence at

Conclusion

hand, it is necessary to view Marlowe, not as an "outsider," an assumption virtually all Chandler critics heretofore have made, but as an "insider," participating actively in his local society. He operates within a Deweyan sense of social engagement and elicits like responses from his interlocutors. Chandler transformed the art of hard-boiled detective fiction by highlighting acts of communal cooperation on the part of his hero and by shifting the focus from the eye-for-an-eye ethos of violent retaliation to the verbal, diplomatic skills needed to achieve accommodation.

Given the great untapped potential for research along these lines in popular fiction (or indeed in fiction of any kind), this study has sought to open only one of many possible doors into a room of enormous proportions. Due to its self-imposed limitations, many critical considerations have had to be severely constricted or even ignored. Attention has been paid to the historical/intellectual underpinnings of Chandler's ideology, but in a larger context a more detailed historical overview must be undertaken to thoroughly place Chandler in the context of American liberalism. For example, Richard H. Pells, in *The Liberal Mind in a Conservative Age*, examines the precarious post–World War II position of the liberal-to-left American intelligentsia, the period in which Chandler wrote *The Little Sister, The Long Goodbye*, and *Playback*. Pells notes that disillusionment with Stalin's Soviet Union and the pressure applied by domestic red-baiters were potent catalysts in turning the faith of 1930s leftists in collective action into grave suspicion of faith in the powers of a strong state to create a public good:

> they neither proposed nor trusted any sweeping solutions to the difficulties of their time. At most, they urged their contemporaries to resist wherever possible the seductive blandishments of the state, the bureaucracies, the media, and the organizations for which almost everyone now labored. In this way, they hoped the citizen might assert his individuality and protect his freedom within the constraints of the existing social order [ix].

These are suspicions and doubts we also find in Chandler's later work, but if "the intellectuals' emphasis on private maladies rather than institutional shortcomings reflected their own sense of helplessness in the face of remote and omnipotent governmental structures" (Pells 190), we also find in Chandler a strong resistance to the siren song of psychoanalysis, white flight,

Conclusion

or other avenues of escape for individuals of a more prosperous, yet also politically more repressive period.

Full historical/ideological analysis notwithstanding, Chandler took on the daunting challenge of using the highly individualistic figure of the private eye to explain how and why American rugged individualism has failed. In transforming the figure of the hard-boiled detective, he created a new paradigm, not only for a new detective, but for a new individual as well.

Chapter Notes

Introduction

1. Mandel's chronology is not quite accurate: while Hammett and several other authors of the *Black Mask* school published in the 1920s, Chandler did not begin writing detective fiction until 1932.

2. Chandler's fabled reply when asked by film director Howard Hawks and screenwriter William Faulkner exactly who killed Owen Taylor in *The Big Sleep* was that he didn't know. What is normally accepted as an example of Chandler's disinterest in careful plotting can just as easily be viewed as an intentional reminder of the impossibility, even for a crack private eye, of knowing everything at all times. Chandler's fiction displays a conscious critique of omniscience and an assertion of negotiated and pragmatic reality.

3. According to Gottlieb and Wolt, Buron Fitts "had financial support from the underworld" in his successful 1936 campaign for attorney general. For Michael Woodiwiss, John Dockweiler (Fitts' "reform" successor in 1938) "made no genuine attempt to combat vice in Los Angeles County" (87).

4. Toward the end of his life Chandler interviewed Mafia don Lucky Luciano and lamented the hypocrisy of American morality: the mob provided services Americans desired and its members thus became convenient scapegoats "in order to create the illusion that our laws are being rigidly enforced" (qtd. in Hiney 263).

5. Ernest Mandel denigrates the significance of the local, criticizing Chandler's ideology since "[i]t is only the *local*, never the national, power structure that is denounced in Chandler's works" (36), but he again underestimates the ability of Chandler's concrete urban encounters to critique the national culture as a whole.

6. Criminals in these stories are, for Knight, "middle-class renegades," "respectable people gone wrong" who "should have respected the values" of their bourgeois environment (90).

Chapter Four

1. As Giles Gunn succinctly puts it, "Dewey held that individualism must be restructured around the principle that the moral development of each separate self in a democracy is in a profound and specifiable sense dependent upon the collective contribution of all other selves" (75).

2. Van Dine apparently learned much from Dorothy L. Sayers' Lord Peter Wimsey series. Vance's stilted dialogue mirrors that of Wimsey (with less credibility), and the Vance-Markham relationship closely resembles Wimsey's dealings with his friend Detective Inspector Charles Parker, who, although quite intelligent and capable, clearly assists the amateur detective and not vice versa.

3. In this context it is odd that Stephen Knight would prefer Hammett's "existential world ... which had evaluative underpinning in a radical and proto-Marxist view of society" to Chandler's "dismissing and scorning the 'supposedly average man'" (148).

Chapter Notes

Chapter Five

1. In *Kiss Me, Deadly*, for example, Hammer attacks two hit men hired to kill him in a crowded bar, endangering innocent people, and is held in check from retributive violence only by the sudden intervention of FBI agents (97–98).

2. In her review of the *Library of America* two-volume Chandler collection, Oates condemns the novels as "clogged with unwieldy incidents, unassimilated emotions, puppetry in place of characterization," and, more specifically, reminds the reader that "crudely caricatured females will appear" in Chandler's noir landscape (37–38).

3. Mike Hammer's sympathies, when present at all, slip quickly into condescension. He refers to Bobo Hopper, the simpleminded numbers runner in *I, the Jury*, as "only half human" (53) and he deliberately confuses the beekeeping Bobo by telling him to buy a king bee for his queen (57).

4. Joyce Carol Oates sees Marlowe as a "sardonic adolescent among disapproving adults" (34). Woody Haut has a similar reaction to the same passage: "Marlowe, caught in situations over which he has no control, reverts to humour and childlike petulance" (74).

Chapter Six

1. This doctor is, albeit, a psychiatrist: the origins of crime and victimhood are overwhelmingly psychological and Macdonald's novels teem with psychologists and counselors.

2. In *The Galton Case* Archer initially works for Maria Galton, rich and in her 70s, whose self-pity is expressed as impatience with those around her who cater to her needs. Mrs. Charles A. Singleton is a quite similar figure in *The Ivory Grin* who, as Archer attempts to sell her his services, replies "breathlessly in the ebb of her self-pity: 'I'm not unwilling to pay for helpful information, but if a large agency has failed to restore my son to me ... I see no reason to suppose that one man alone might succeed'" (85).

3. The creators of the film *Murder, My Sweet*, an adaptation of Chandler's *Farewell, My Lovely*, may have had something similar in mind when they transformed the role of Anne Riordan into Ann Grayle, daughter of the rich Lewin Lockridge Grayle and stepdaughter to the murderous Helen Grayle (aka Velma Valento), thus shifting attention to tensions within one family. We may also speculate that Macdonald was familiar with the film and that it influenced him.

4. Sims does Raymond an injustice by characterizing him as "something of a Watson" (xvii). While he functions as the narrator, Raymond does far more detective work in the novel than Gryce and is closer in spirit to Earl Stanley Gardner's Perry Mason.

Conclusion

1. Marlowe's stance is very much in the spirit of the concept of equality as found in Dewey's *The Public and Its Problems*: "Equality does not signify that kind of mathematical or physical equivalence in virtue of which any one element may be substituted for another. It denotes effective regard for whatever is distinctive and unique in each, irrespective of physical and psychological inequalities" (*Later Works* II:329–30).

2. In yet another context, *Freedom and Culture*, Dewey reiterates his concept of positive freedom: "[c]ooperation — called fraternity in the classic French formula — is as much a part of the democratic ideal as is personal initiative" (*Later Works* XIII:78).

Works Cited

Arieli, Yehoshua. *Individualism and Nationalism in American Ideology*. Baltimore: Penguin, 1964.
Baker, Jeffrey S. "Somewhere under Pynchon's Rainbow: Pragmatism, Protest, and Radical Democracy in *Gravity's Rainbow*." PhD diss., Purdue University, 1995.
Beekman, E. M. "Raymond Chandler and an American Genre." *Massachusetts Review* 14, no. 1 (Winter 1973): 149–173.
Bentley, Christopher. "Radical Anger: Dashiell Hammett's *Red Harvest*." In *American Crime Fiction: Studies in the Genre*, edited by Brian Docherty, 54–70. New York: St. Martin's, 1988.
The Big Sleep. Directed by Howard Hawks. Hollywood, CA: Warner Brothers, 1946.
Bruccoli, Matthew J. *Ross Macdonald*. San Diego: Harcourt Brace Jovanovich, 1984.
Cawelti, John G. *Adventure, Mystery, and Romance: Formula Stories as Art and Popular Culture*. Chicago: University of Chicago Press, 1976.
Chandler, Raymond. Introduction to *The Smell of Fear*. London: Hamish Hamilton, 1965.
———. *Later Novels and Other Writings*. Library of America. New York: Literary Classics of the United States, 1995.
———. *Selected Letters of Raymond Chandler*. Edited by Frank MacShane. New York: Dell, 1987.
———. *Stories and Early Novels*. Library of America. New York: Literary Classics of the United States, 1995.
Christie, Agatha. *Evil under the Sun*. New York: Black Dog & Leventhal, 1940.
———. *Five Complete Hercule Poirot Novels*. New York: Avenel, 1980.
Clark, Al. *Raymond Chandler in Hollywood*. Los Angeles: Silman-James, 1996.
Conan Doyle, Arthur. *The Original Illustrated Sherlock Holmes*. Reprint of *The Adventures of Sherlock Holmes*. 1982. Secaucus, NJ: Castle, 1979.
Daly, Carroll John. *Emperor of Evil*. London: Hutchinson, 1936; New York: Stokes, 1937.
———. *The Hidden Hand*. 1928. New York: HarperPerennial, 1992.
———. *The Snarl of the Beast*. 1927. New York: HarperPerennial, 1992.
Dewey, John. *The Early Works, 1882–1898*. 5 vols. Carbondale: Southern Illinois University Press, 1969.
———. *The Later Works, 1925–1953*. Edited by Jo Ann Boydston. 17 vols. Carbondale: Southern Illinois University Press, 1981–1990.
Driberg, Tom. *The Mystery of Moral Re-Armament*. New York: Knopf, 1965.
Durham, Philip. *Down These Mean Streets a Man Must Go: Raymond Chandler's Knight*. Chapel Hill: University of North Carolina Press, 1963.
Edenbaum, Robert I. "The Poetics of the Private Eye: The Novels of Dashiell Ham-

Works Cited

mett." In *The Mystery Writer's Art*, edited by Francis M. Nevins, Jr., 98–121. Bowling Green: Bowling Green University Popular Press, 1970.

Emerson, Ralph Waldo. "Self-Reliance." In *Essays and Lectures*. Library of America. New York: Literary Classics of the United States, 1983.

Gottlieb, Robert, and Irene Wolt. *Thinking Big: The Story of the Los Angeles Times, Its Publishers and Their Influence on Southern California*. New York: Putnam, 1977.

Green, Anna Katherine. *The Leavenworth Case*. Introduction Michael Sims. New York: Penguin, 2010.

Gregory, Sinda. *Private Investigations: The Novels of Dashiell Hammett*. Carbondale: Southern Illinois University Press, 1985.

Grella, George. "Murder and the Mean Streets: The Hard-Boiled Detective Novel." In *Detective Fiction: Crime and Compromise*, edited by Dick Allen and David Chacko. New York: Harcourt Brace Jovanovich, 1974.

Grossvogel, David I. "Death Deferred: The Long Life, Splendid Afterlife and Mysterious Workings of Agatha Christie." In *Art in Crime Writing: Essays on Detective Fiction*, edited by Bernard Benstock, 1–17. New York: St. Martin's, 1983.

Gunn, Giles. *Thinking across the American Grain: Ideology, Intellect, and the New Pragmatism*. Chicago: University of Chicago Press, 1992.

Hamilton, Cynthia S. *Western and Hard-Boiled Detective Fiction in America: From High Noon to Midnight*. Iowa City: University of Iowa Press, 1987.

Hammett, Dashiell. *The Novels of Dashiell Hammett*. New York: Knopf, 1965.

Hartman, Geoffrey H. "Literature High and Low: The Case of the Mystery Story." In *The Poetics of Murder: Detection Fiction and Literary Theory*, edited by Glenn W. Most and William W. Stowe, 210–229. San Diego: Harcourt Brace Jovanovich, 1983.

Haut, Woody. *Pulp Culture: Hardboiled Fiction and the Cold War*. London: Serpent's Tail, 1995.

Heise, Thomas. "'Going Blood-Simple Like the Natives': Contagious Urban Spaces and Modern Power in Dashiell Hammett's *Red Harvest*." *Modern Fiction Studies* 51, no. 3 (2005): 485–512.

Hicks, Granville. *The Great Tradition: An Interpretation of American Literature since the Civil War*. New York: Macmillan, 1935.

Hilfer, Tony. *The Crime Novel: A Deviant Genre*. Austin: University of Texas Press, 1990.

Hiney, Tom. *Raymond Chandler: A Biography*. New York: Atlantic Monthly Press, 1997.

Hoover, Herbert. *American Individualism*. Garden City, NY: Doubleday, Page and Co., 1922.

Hopkins, Ernest Jerome. *Our Lawless Police: A Study of the Unlawful Enforcement of the Law*. New York: Viking, 1931.

Jameson, Fredric. "On Raymond Chandler." In *The Poetics of Murder: Detection Fiction and Literary Theory*, edited by Glenn W. Most and William W. Stowe, 122–148. San Diego: Harcourt Brace Jovanovich, 1983.

Kloppenberg, James T. *Uncertain Victory: Social Democracy and Progressivism in European and American Thought, 1870–1920*. New York: Oxford University Press, 1986.

Knight, Stephen. *Form and Ideology in Crime Fiction*. Bloomington: Indiana University Press, 1980.

Lady in the Lake. Directed by Robert Montgomery. Culver City, CA: Metro-Goldwyn-Mayer, 1947.

Lasch, Christopher. *The Culture of Narcissism: American Life in an Age of Diminishing Expectations*. New York: Norton, 1979.

Works Cited

Librach, Ronald S. "Adaptation and Ontology: The Impulse towards Closure in Howard Hawks's Version of *The Big Sleep.*" *Literature/Film Quarterly* 19 (1991): 164–175.
Luhr, William. *Raymond Chandler and Film.* New York: Ungar, 1982.
Macdonald, Ross. *The Barbarous Coast.* New York: Bantam, 1956.
———. *The Chill.* New York: Bantam, 1964.
———. *The Doomsters.* New York: Vintage, 1958.
———. *The Drowning Pool.* New York: Bantam, 1950.
———. *The Galton Case.* New York: Bantam, 1959.
———. *The Instant Enemy.* New York: Warner, 1968.
———. *The Ivory Grin.* New York: Vintage, 1952.
———. *The Underground Man.* New York: Bantam, 1971.
———. *The Way Some People Die.* New York: Vintage, 1951.
———. "The Writer as Detective Hero." In *The Mystery Writer's Art*, edited by Francis M. Nevins, Jr. Bowling Green: Bowling Green University Popular Press, 1970.
Mandel, Ernest. *Delightful Murder: A Social History of the Crime Story.* Minneapolis: University of Minnesota Press, 1984.
Marlowe. Directed by Paul Bogart. Culver City, CA: Metro-Goldwyn-Mayer, 1969.
McCann, Sean. "Constructing Race Williams: The Klan and the Making of Hard-Boiled Crime Fiction." *American Quarterly* 49, no. 4 (1997): 677–716.
———. *Gumshoe America: Hard-Boiled Crime Fiction and the Rise and Fall of New Deal Liberalism.* Durham: Duke University Press, 2000.
Metress, Christopher. "Dashiell Hammett and the Challenge of New Individualism: Rereading *Red Harvest* and *The Maltese Falcon.*" *Essays in Literature* 42 (1990): 242–260.
Miller, D. A. *The Novel and the Police.* Berkeley: University of California Press, 1988.
Moquin, Wayne, and Charles Van Doren, eds. *The American Way of Crime: A Documentary History.* New York: Praeger, 1976.
Moss, Robert F. "Ross Macdonald." In *Mystery and Suspense Writers: The Literature of Crime, Detection, and Espionage*, edited by Robin W. Winks and Maureen Corrigan, vol. 2, 633–50. New York: Scribners, 1998.
Murder, My Sweet. Directed by Edward Dmytryk. Los Angeles: RKO, 1944.
Nevins, Francis M., Jr., ed. *The Mystery Writer's Art.* Bowling Green: Bowling Green University Popular Press, 1970.
Nyman, Jopi. *Men Alone: Masculinity, Individualism, and Hard-Boiled Fiction.* Amsterdam, Atlanta: Rodopi, 1997.
Oates, Joyce Carol. "The Simple Art of Murder." Review of *Stories and Early Novels* and *Later Novels and Other Writings*, by Raymond Chandler. *New York Review of Books* 42, no. 20 (December 21, 1995): 32–40.
Ogden, Bethany. "Hard-Boiled Ideology." *Critical Quarterly* 34, no. 1 (1992): 71–87.
Panek, LeRoy Lad. *Reading Early Hammett: A Critical Study of the Fiction prior to* The Maltese Falcon. Jefferson, NC: McFarland, 2004.
Pells, Richard H. *The Liberal Mind in a Conservative Age: American Intellectuals in the 1940s and 1950s.* New York: Harper, 1985.
Porter, Dennis. *The Pursuit of Crime: Art and Ideology in Detective Fiction.* New Haven: Yale University Press, 1981.
Raczkowski, Christopher T. "From Modernity's Detection to Modernist Detectives: Narrative Vision in the Work of Allan Pinkerton and Dashiell Hammett." *Modern Fiction Studies* 49, no. 4 (2003): 629–659.

Works Cited

Radzinowicz, Leon. *Ideology and Crime*. New York: Columbia University Press, 1966.
Ruehlmann, William. *Saint with a Gun: The Unlawful American Private Eye*. New York: New York University Press, 1984.
Schaller, Barry R. *A Vision of American Law: Judging Laws, Literature, and the Stories We Tell*. Westport, CT: Praeger, 1997.
Schumach, Murray. *The Face on the Cutting Room Floor: The Story of Movie and Television Censorship*. New York: William Morrow, 1964.
Sharp, Michael D. "Plotting Chandler's Demise: Ross Macdonald and the Neo-Aristotelian Detective Novel." *Studies in the Novel* 35, no. 3 (2003): 405–26.
Silet, Charles L. P. "The First Angry White Male: Mickey Spillane's Mike Hammer." *The Armchair Detective*, Spring 1996, 195–199.
Sims, Michael. Introduction to *The Leavenworth Case*, by Anna Katherine Green. 1878. New York: Penguin, 2010.
Skenazy, Paul. Introduction to *Raymond Chandler Speaking*, edited by Dorothy Gardiner and Katherine Sorley Walker. Berkeley: University of California Press, 1997.
Slotkin, Richard. *Gunfighter Nation: The Myth of the Frontier in Twentieth-Century America*. Norman: University of Oklahoma Press, 1998.
———. "The Hard-Boiled Detective Story: From the Open Range to the Mean Streets." In *The Sleuth and the Scholar: Origins, Evolution, and Current Trends in Detective Fiction*, edited by Barbara A. Rader and Howard G. Zettler, 91–100. New York: Greenwood Press, 1988.
Speir, Jerry. *Raymond Chandler*. New York: Ungar, 1981.
Spillane, Mickey. *The Mike Hammer Collection*. 3 vols. New York: New American Library, 2001–2010.
Spindler, Michael. *American Literature and Social Change: William Dean Howells to Arthur Miller*. Bloomington: Indiana University Press, 1983.
Stuhr, John J. "Dewey's Social and Political Philosophy." In *Reading Dewey: Interpretations for a Postmodern Generation*, edited Larry A. Hickman, 82–99. Bloomington: Indiana University Press, 1998.
Symons, Julian. *Mortal Consequences: A History from the Detective Story to the Crime Novel*. New York: Harper, 1972.
Tocqueville, Alexis de. *Democracy in America*. Edited by J. P. Mayer. Translated by George Lawrence. Garden City, NY: Anchor, 1966.
Van Dine, S. S. *The Casino Murder Case*. New York: Scribner's, 1934.
———. *The Dragon Murder Case*. New York: Scribner's, 1933.
———. *The Greene Murder Case*. New York: Scribner's, 1927.
———. *The Kidnap Murder Case*. 1936. New York: Otto Penzler Books, 1994.
———. *The Mystery of the Smoking Gun*. New York: Frederick A. Stokes Co., 1936.
———. *The Scarab Murder Case*. New York: Scribner's, 1930.
West, Cornel. *The American Evasion of Philosophy: A Genealogy of Pragmatism*. Madison: University of Wisconsin Press, 1989.
Westbrook, Robert B. *John Dewey and American Democracy*. Ithaca: Cornell University Press, 1991.
Westlake, Donald E. "The Hardboiled Dicks." *Armchair Detective* 17 (1984): 4–13.
Woodiwiss, Michael. *Crime, Crusades, and Corruption: Prohibitions in the United States, 1900–1987*. Totowa, NJ: Barnes and Noble, 1988.
Zumoff, J. A. "The Politics of Dashiell Hammett's *Red Harvest*." *Mosaic* 40, no. 4 (2007): 119–130.

Index

The Barbarous Coast 151
The Big Kill 43, 46
The Big Sleep 1, 6, 10, 18, 76, 82, 91–92, 96, 101, 103, 115, 122, 124–125, 128, 130–131, 143, 161, 164, 168, 169, 172, 179, 186, 187, 193

The Casino Murder Case 99–100
Cawelti, John G. 3, 25, 71–72, 78–79, 180–181
Chandler, Raymond: *The Big Sleep* 1, 6, 10, 18, 76, 82, 91–92, 96, 101, 103, 115, 122, 124–125, 128, 130–131, 143, 161, 164, 168, 169, 172, 179, 186, 187, 193; biography 12–14, 117, 120, 138, 146–147, 193; critics view 3–4, 16–17, 20, 22, 71–72, 79–80, 86, 106, 124, 126, 134–137, 139–140, 180–183, 188, 190, 194; *Farewell, My Lovely* 6, 14, 18, 51, 62, 82, 89, 91–92, 103, 107, 117, 123, 126, 129, 147, 157, 158, 164, 166–168, 173, 179–180, 190, 194; filmed novels 161–177, 193–194; *The High Window* 10, 18, 87, 117, 119, 139, 182; ideology 9–16, 23, 87, 89–93, 107, 109, 112, 115–116, 119–120, 125, 135, 159, 162–163, 177–178, 188, 190–193; *The Lady in the Lake* 8, 10, 20, 92, 161, 172; *Letters* 80, 111, 115, 120; *The Little Sister* 19, 82, 102, 107, 118–119, 141, 179, 186, 191; *The Long Goodbye* 10, 18, 73, 87, 102, 116, 121, 132–133, 179, 181, 184, 187, 191; *Playback* 116, 137, 179, 182, 191; "The Simple Art of Murder" 13, 16, 54, 80, 93, 116, 120, 125, 133, 138–139, 172; style 10–11, 15, 18, 20–23, 29, 51, 53, 62, 70, 74, 76, 80, 82, 85–87, 89, 92–96, 98, 100, 102–105, 107–110, 114, 117, 119–125, 128, 130–132, 138–142, 155, 159, 163, 179–182, 184–189.
The Chill 143, 145, 151, 155
Christie, Agatha 11–12, 19, 36, 51, 68, 80, 98, 147–148
Conan Doyle, Arthur 11, 19, 35–36, 98
cooperation 9–10, 40, 48, 52–54, 57, 62, 64–67, 69, 77, 88, 90, 93, 96, 106–107, 111, 152, 156–158, 175

The Dain Curse 15, 61–62, 64
Daly, Carroll John 10, 23, 28–29, 32, 34–35, 37–40, 44, 53–54, 57–58, 60, 63, 73, 76, 178, 180; *The Hidden Hand* 10, 28, 32, 34, 76; *The Snarl of the Beast* 28, 33, 34, 37, 49, 60
detective fiction 1, 3–6, 11, 22, 37, 41, 51, 70, 72, 79, 89, 91, 147, 180, 182, 191, 193
Dewey, John 5, 7, 9, 17, 22, 74–77, 85, 89–93, 112–113, 133, 136, 177, 189–191, 193–194
The Doomsters 145
The Dragon Murder Case 81
The Drowning Pool 141, 149, 151, 156

Emerson, Ralph Waldo 7, 30–31, 41, 74–75, 77

Farewell, My Lovely 6, 14, 18, 51, 62, 82, 89, 91–92, 103, 107, 117, 123, 126, 129, 147, 157, 158, 164, 166–168, 173, 179–180, 190, 194

The Galton Case 152, 194
The Girl Hunters 48, 50
The Greene Murder Case 37
Gunn, Giles 5–7, 114, 135, 193

Hammett, Dashiell 1, 3, 10–11, 15, 20, 23, 28–29, 54–61, 63–71, 73, 81, 87, 93–94, 101, 105, 111–113, 118, 121–122, 129, 131, 134, 136, 138, 159, 178, 180–183, 188, 193; *The Dain Curse* 15, 61–62, 64; *The Maltese Falcon* 15, 20, 63–64, 66, 69, 101, 109, 129, 136, 181, 183; *Red Harvest* 10, 15, 54, 56–61, 68, 110, 112, 118, 136, 181; *The Thin Man* 54, 64–68
hard-boiled genre 3–11, 15–23, 27–28, 33–37, 51, 54, 57, 66, 69, 70–79, 84, 86–87, 89–91, 93, 98, 107–110, 116–119, 128, 137–

199

Index

140, 147, 152, 161–164, 168, 170, 172, 178, 180–183, 190–192
The Hidden Hand 10, 28, 32, 34, 76
The High Window 10, 18, 87, 117, 119, 139, 182

I, The Jury 40, 42, 44–46, 131, 194
ideology 1–6, 9–16, 19, 23, 30–32, 35–36, 47, 51, 53, 74–75, 87, 89–93, 107, 109, 112, 115–116, 119–120, 124–125, 133–135, 162, 159, 162–163, 177–178, 188, 190–193
individualism 79, 21–35, 37–43, 56, 61, 70, 71, 74–77, 82–85, 90, 111, 121, 133, 137, 161–163, 167, 177, 178, 188–193
The Instant Enemy 141, 144, 146
The Ivory Grin 142, 157, 194

Jameson, Fredric 16–17, 188–190

The Kidnap Murder Case 100
Kiss Me, Deadly 42, 111, 194
Knight, Stephen 4–5, 14–15, 20, 22, 36, 71, 80, 83, 85, 89, 103, 106, 121, 181, 193

The Lady in the Lake 8, 10, 20, 92, 161, 172
Letters 80, 111, 115, 120
The Little Sister 19, 82, 102, 107, 118–119, 141, 179, 186, 191
The Long Goodbye 10, 18, 73, 87, 102, 116, 121, 132–133, 179, 181, 184, 187, 191

Macdonald, Ross 23, 36, 57, 63, 73, 114, 134–135, 138–153, 155–160, 183, 194; *The Barbarous Coast* 151; *The Chill* 143, 145, 151, 155; *The Doomsters* 145; *The Drowning Pool* 141, 149, 151, 156; *The Galton Case* 152, 194; *The Instant Enemy* 141, 144, 146; *The Ivory Grin* 142, 157, 194; *Underground Man* 142; *The Way Some People Die* 142, 144
The Maltese Falcon 15, 20, 63–64, 66, 69, 101, 109, 129, 136, 181, 183
Marlowe 174
Marlowe, Philip 3–23, 29, 65, 69–98, 101–110, 112–138, 140–147, 151, 157–161, 164–188, 190, 191, 194
Murder, My Sweet 161, 164–169, 172, 173, 194
My Gun Is Quick 41–43, 49, 185

One Lonely Night 47, 111, 194

Playback 116, 137, 179, 182, 191
Pragmatism 5, 6, 114, 135

Red Harvest 10, 15, 54, 56–61, 68, 110, 112, 118, 136, 181

The Scarab Murder Case 99
"The Simple Art of Murder" 13, 16, 54, 80, 93, 116, 120, 125, 133, 138–139, 172
Slotkin, Richard 25–28, 58, 64, 71, 79
The Snake 50–51
The Snarl of the Beast 28, 33, 34, 37, 49, 60
Spillane, Mickey 3, 8, 10–11, 18–19, 23, 28–29, 39–47, 49–54, 57, 61, 71–73, 75, 79, 85–86, 101, 111–115, 131, 134, 178, 180–181; *The Big Kill* 43, 46; *The Girl Hunters* 48, 50; *I, the Jury* 40, 42, 44–46, 131, 194; *Kiss Me, Deadly* 42, 111, 194; *My Gun Is Quick* 41–43, 49, 185; *One Lonely Night* 47, 111, 194; *The Snake* 50–51; *The Twisted Thing* 51, 53; *Vengeance Is Mine* 45
style 10–11, 15, 18, 20–23, 29, 51, 53, 62, 70, 74, 76, 80, 82, 85–87, 89, 92–96, 98, 100, 102–105, 107–110, 114, 117, 119–125, 128, 130–132, 138–142, 155, 159, 163, 179–182, 184–189

The Thin Man 54, 64–68
Tocqueville, Alexis de 29–30
The Twisted Thing 51, 53

Underground Man 142

Van Dine, S.S. 37–38, 51, 81, 98, 193; *The Casino Murder Case* 99–100; *The Dragon Murder Case* 81; *The Greene Murder Case* 37; *The Kidnap Murder Case* 100; *The Scarab Murder Case* 99
Vengeance Is Mine 45
vigilantes 19, 28, 34–39, 42, 44, 58, 60–61, 76, 79, 82, 115
violence 3, 10, 26, 28, 33–34, 37–38, 40–42, 44, 51, 58, 60, 73, 78, 82–83, 110–113, 123, 136, 147, 153, 171, 176–179, 182, 188, 194

The Way Some People Die 142, 144

www.ingramcontent.com/pod-product-compliance
Lightning Source LLC
Chambersburg PA
CBHW032059300426
44116CB00007B/820